THE ILLUSTRATED ENCYCLOPEDIA OF CAT BREEDS

THE ILLUSTRATED ENCYCLOPEDIA OF CAT BREEDS

Angela Rixon

BLANDFORD

A QUARTO BOOK

First published in the UK
1995 by Blandford
A Cassell imprint
Wellington House
125 The Strand
London WC2R 0BB

British Library Cataloguing-in-Publication Data
A catalogue record for this book is available from the
British Library
ISBN 0–7137–2576–1

This book was designed and produced by
Quarto Publishing Plc
The Old Brewery
6 Blundell Street
London N7 9BH

Art Director: Moira Clinch
Senior Art Editor: Penny Cobb
Designer: Karin Skånberg
Senior Editor: Sian Parkhouse
Copy Editor: Sandy Ransford
Editorial Director: Mark Dartford
Photographer: Paul Forrester
Picture Researcher: Jo Carlill
Picture Manager: Giulia Hetherington

Typeset in Great Britain by Genesis Typesetters, Rochester
Manufactured in Singapore by Eray Scan Pte Ltd
Printed in Singapore by Star Standard Industries (Pte) Ltd

INTRODUCTION

8
The Cat

11
Origins

16
Body shape

26
Behaviour

32
Sexual behaviour

35
Maternity

38
Breeding pedigree cats

42
Showing

46
Cat care

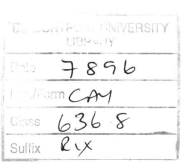

CONTENTS

LONGHAIRED BREEDS

58
Longhair
60 White
61 Black
62 Red
63 Cream
64 Blue
65 Blue-cream
66 Smoke
69 Cameo
70 Bi-colour
72 Tabby
75 Tortoiseshell
76 Silver and Golden

78
Colourpoint
80 Solid points
82 Tabby points
84 Chocolate and lilac

SHORTHAIRED BREEDS

120
British Shorthair
122 Solid varieties
125 Bi-colour varieties
126 Tortoiseshell varieties
128 Tabby varieties
132 Other varieties

134
Chartreux

136
Manx
138 Manx varieties
139 Cymric

140
Scottish Fold

142
European Shorthair
144 European Shorthair varieties

146
American Shorthair
148 American Shorthair varieties
149 Tabby varieties

154
American Wirehair

156
Exotic Shorthair
158 Solid varieties
159 Tabby and Bi-colour varieties
160 Other varieties

SEMI LONGHAIRED BREEDS

88
Birman
90 Solid points
92 Tortoiseshell and tabby points

94
Maine Coon
96 Solid varieties
96 Tortoiseshell and Parti-colour varieties
97 Smoke and shaded varieties
98 Tabby varieties

100
Ragdoll
102 Mitted
103 Bi-colour
104 Colourpoint

105
Snowshoe

106
Norwegian Forest Cat
108 Solid varieties
109 Tabby varieties
110 Parti-colour varieties
111 Smoke and cameo varieties

112
Angora
114 Angora varieties

116
Turkish

FOREIGN SHORTHAIRED BREEDS

164
Abyssinian
166 Abyssinian varieties

168
Somali
170 Somali varieties

174
Russian Blue

176
Korat

178
Havana Brown

180
Egyptian Mau

182
Ocicat

184
Bengal
186 Bengal varieties

188
Cornish Rex
190 Cornish Rex varieties

192
Devon Rex
194 Devon Rex varieties

196
Sphynx

198
Japanese Bobtail

200
Burmese
202 Solid varieties
205 Tortoiseshell varieties

206
Tiffanie

207
Singapura

208
Tonkinese
210 Mink varieties
212 New varieties

214
Bombay

216
Burmilla
218 Burmilla varieties
221 Asian

ORIENTAL BREEDS

224
Siamese
226 Siamese varieties

230
Colorpoint Shorthair
232 Colorpoint varieties

234
Balinese
236 Balinese varieties

238
Oriental
240 Solid varieties
243 Tortoiseshell varieties
244 Tabby varieties
246 Smoked, shaded and tipped varieties

249
Seychellois

250
Javanese

252
Index

256
Acknowledgements

INTRODUCTION

The domestic cat enjoys a special niche in human society. There are anthologies of poems and prose, encyclopedias of breeds, manuals on care, breeding and showing; cats appear on greetings cards, stationery and fabrics; glass and china ornaments abound – whether in natural or cartoon form the cat is the most enduringly popular animal portrayed throughout the world.

CATS HAVE BEEN valued and protected and their history recorded since the days of the Ancient Egyptians, and although their fortunes have fluctuated from time to time, they have managed to remain virtually unchanged in overall size and basic character. Today's domestic cat tolerates its relationship with humans and takes advantage of the comforts of a good home environment while retaining its independent

nature. The innate behaviour patterns of the cat's wild ancestors still exist, even in a highly-bred pedigree cat whose coat and conformation bear little resemblance to them. Even the most pampered of today's pet cats reacts to the thrill of hunting, retains all the physical skills and abilities of its forebears.

Having a pet cat in the home can be therapeutic, as well as rewarding. No other pet is as clean and fastidious in its habits, or as easy to care for. Every cat is beautiful in its own way, but the very wide range of breeds, colours and varieties of pedigree cats existing today means every cat lover can indulge his or her particular preference.

The cat is probably the most common domestic animal in most parts of the world. Wherever there are concentrated populations of people there are groups of cats, either living as free-ranging feral animals or kept as pets to keep down rodents, insects or snakes. Yet despite its familiarity with humans, the domestic cat manages to retain its air of mysterious independence.

A paradoxical animal, the cat can be both loving and bold. It combines caution with courage, and alternates periods of total relaxation with those of remarkable agility. It is often easy to imagine, in watching one's pet cat, its successful little mammalian ancestor *miacis*, which first evolved during the age of the dinosaurs. Small in build, the cat has always had to rely on skill and speed to escape from predators and to catch its own prey. Its specialized dentition and retractile claws helped to ensure its survival as a

A resting ginger adorns the lid of a small tin (top left), a nursery rhyme feline family make a simple jigsaw puzzle (top), while a trio of stylized nesting cats make an unusual keepsake (left).

Even the most sophisticated of today's pedigree cats, like this Abyssinian (right), retains all of its natural hunting instincts.

THE EVOLUTION OF THE CAT

Dinictis About 50 million years ago, this carnivorous cat-like mammal, ancestor of the cats, inhabited the earth.

Pseudaelurus Until about 25 million years ago, this relatively long-legged mammal had evolved with more cat-like features.

Felis lunensis Among several species of wild cat that evolved, and lived until about 12 million years ago was Martelli's wildcat.

Felidae Today's cats, large and small. Highly developed and efficient carnivores, designed for hunting and killing.

SELECTIVE BREEDING
Over the years cats have been selectively bred to conform to standards of points laid down by the various cat associations. Here we see the extremes in type between the svelte, long headed Oriental (left) and the heavy, round headed Persian (below).

carnivore during its evolution, and these qualities stand the cat in good stead.

Today, the genetic make-up of the domestic cat has been so manipulated by selective breeding that some felines bear very little resemblance to those of ancient Egypt's homes and granaries. The noses of Persian cats have been reduced in size, those of the Orientals have been lengthened. Breeders have selected for heavy bone in some breeds, for light bone in others. Despite all the efforts to thwart nature, however, the basic structure of the domestic cat has been undefiled by human intervention, and the biology of the animal is the same whether it is a champion Chinchilla or a stray tabby. The great cat goddess Bast continues to watch over *Felis domesticus* ensuring that all cats remain virtually the same in size and character; affectionate, fastidious felines who are willing companions, but who will never be subordinate or subservient to humans.

The aim of this book is to show the diverse and interesting range of domestic felines throughout the world, exploring conformation, coat types and patterns. It also examines the breeds' varying care requirements, their special characteristics, and acts as an introduction to the world of showing.

ORIGINS

A weasel-like creature called Miacis lived on Earth in the Eocene period of 50 million years ago. From this fierce, successful creature evolved countless generations of carnivores. We can recognize in those early creatures the forebears of our domestic cats, and identify the same survival skills.

ANCIENT EGYPT
The cat was deified in Ancient Egypt, and also used for the protection of the granaries and for wildfowling.

AS ANY PAIR of domestic cats, from anywhere in the world, will readily interbreed, it means that they are of a single species, descended from a common ancestor.

Domestication of the cat probably first took place in the Middle East, and the cats encouraged to approach people were almost certainly *Felis lybica*, the African wild cat. This is a lithe animal, very similar to a domestic tabby in colour. Many of the skulls from Ancient Egyptian cat cemeteries resemble *Felis lybica*, while a small proportion are of cats resembling the jungle cat, *Felis chaus*. It would appear that the Ancient Egyptians tamed both types, but the African wild cat was easily the more popular, and probably more amenable to domestication.

Egypt was the greatest corn-growing area of the ancient world, and huge granaries were constructed to store the grain from good harvests for use in leaner years. As rodent controllers, cats must have been vital to the economy of those times. The Ancient Egyptians also appreciated the natural link between the cat and the lion, and worshipped the goddess Bast, also called Pasht or Oubasted, who first appeared with the head of a lion, and later with the head of a cat. Bast was seen as a goddess of love, and of the moon. The cat was connected with her as love-goddess because of the animal's natural fecundity, and as moon-goddess because of the varying shape of the pupils of the cat's eyes, which were thought to enlarge and contract with

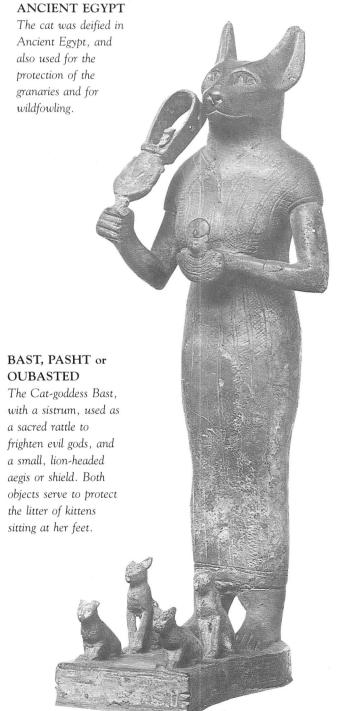

BAST, PASHT or OUBASTED
The Cat-goddess Bast, with a sistrum, used as a sacred rattle to frighten evil gods, and a small, lion-headed aegis or shield. Both objects serve to protect the litter of kittens sitting at her feet.

DESCENT OF THE MODERN CAT

All cats, including our domestics, trace their ancestry to the small weasel-like *Miacis* of some 40 million years ago. They shared this common ancestor with other carnivores, including bears, civets and dogs.

SMALL CATS
Felis

CARNIVORES
Carnivora

CATS
Felidae

MAMMALS

HERBIVORES
Herbivora

CHEETAH *Acionomyx*

ROARING CATS
Panthera

LION *P. leo*

TIGER *P. tigris*

LEOPARD *P. pardus*

CLOUDED LEOPARD
*P. nebulosa**

JAGUAR *P. onca*

SNOW LEOPARD
P. uncia

DOMESTIC CATS *F. Catus*
AFRICAN GOLDEN CAT *F. aurata*
ASIATIC GOLDEN CAT *F. temmincki*
BAY CAT *F. badia*
BLACK-FOOTED CAT *F. negripes*
BOBCAT *F. rufus*
CARACAL *F. caracal*
CHINESE DESERT CAT *F. bieti*
FISHING CAT *F. viverrina*
FLAT-HEADED CAT *F. planiceps*
GEOFFROY'S CAT *F. geoffroyi*
JAGUARUNDI *F. yagouaroundi*
IRIOMOTE CAT *F. iriomotensis*
JUNGLE CAT *F. chaus*
KODKOD *F. guigna*
LEOPARD CAT *F. bengalensis*
LYNX *F. lynx (F. pardina)*
MARBLED CAT *F. marmorata*
MARGAY *F. wiedi*
MOUNTAIN CAT *F. jacobita*
OCELOT *F. pardalis*
PALLAS'S CAT *F. manul*
PAMPAS CAT *F. colocolo*
PUMA *F. concolor*
RUSTY-SPOTTED CAT *F. rubiginosus*
SAND CAT *F. margarita*
SERVAL *F. serval*
TIGER CAT *F. tigrinus*
WILD CAT *F. silvestris*

*sometimes classed as a separate genera

A Roman mosaic found in the ruins of Pompeii, and dating from the first century BC, depicts a bright-eyed cat pouncing on its prey.

the waxing and waning of the moon. Egyptian statues of Bast show her connection with fertility and pleasure. In several statues she stands upright, an alert cat's head surmounting a figure holding a sistrum in one hand and a rattle in the other. The rattle symbolized both phallus and womb, and the symbolic fertility of the goddess was further reinforced by several kittens, normally five, sitting at her feet. Women of the period often wore fertility amulets depicting Bast and her feline family.

The original Egyptian name of the cat was *mau*, perhaps from its call of "miaow", which also meant "to see". The Egyptians considered the cat's unblinking gaze gave it powers to seek out truth and to see into the afterlife. Bast was sometimes called the Lady of Truth, and was used in mummification ceremonies to ensure life after death.

Cats played such a complex and important part in the lives of the Ancient Egyptians that the living animals were pampered and in some cases worshipped. After the death of a cat, whole families would go into mourning, and the cat's body was embalmed and placed in a sacred vault. Thousands of mummified cats have been discovered in Egypt, some so well preserved that they have added to our store of knowledge of the earliest domesticated cats.

The custom of keeping cats spread slowly throughout the Middle Eastern countries. A Sanskrit document of 1000 BC mentions a pet cat, and the Indian epics *Ramayana* and *Mahabharata*, of about 500 BC, both contain stories about cats. The Indians at that time worshipped a feline goddess of maternity called Sasti, and for decades Hindus were obliged to take responsibility for feeding at least one cat. Cats reached China around AD 400, and in AD 595 an empress was recorded as having been bewitched by a cat spirit. By the twelfth century AD rich Chinese families kept yellow and white cats known as "lion-cats", which

were highly valued as pets. Vermin control was undertaken by longhaired cats, and cats were traded in street markets. Pet cats were introduced into Japan from China in the reign of Emperor Ichi-Jo who lived from AD 986 to 1011. It is recorded that on the tenth day of the fifth moon the emperor's white cat gave birth to five white kittens, and a nurse was appointed to see that they were brought up as carefully as royal princes. Many legends and stories of cats survive in Japanese literature, the most enduring image being that of the *Maneki-neko*, the listening or beckoning cat, which is still to be found in ornaments and amulets today.

The beckoning cat provides an example of the dual role of charms and amulets to attract good fortune and to ward off evil.

Throughout the world, prior to the witch-hunts of the Middle Ages, cats were treated with affection and respect. Their greatest attribute was their efficiency in controlling vermin.

Gods of one religion may become the demons of its successor, and in the case of the cat, its nocturnal habits, independence, sense of self-preservation and often erotic behaviour accelerated the process during the sixteenth and seventeenth centuries. Witch-hunting then reached its climax, and cats figured prominently in most witch trials throughout Europe. Even as late as the nineteenth century Basque farmers claimed that witches appeared as black cats and were greatly feared.

Eventually the cat's fortunes turned once more. They became prized possessions, and those with unusual colours and markings were favoured as pets. They were carried between the world's continents as precious gifts, and gave rise to the many breeds and varieties that we know today.

In the middle-ages, the art of witchcraft was rife. A witch would often have as her "familiar" a black cat. The witch was said to be able to transform herself into her familiar's form.

North America

The fact that domestic cats have been systematically bred for only about one hundred years makes it difficult to ascertain the origins of certain key factors in their makeup. The stocky body type found in the Persians and the various Shorthairs points to the possible influence of the European wild cat in their ancestry, whereas the lightboned and slender "foreign" cats, such as the Abyssinian, have bodies similar to that exhibited by the African wild cat. In Asia, lightboned cats have been known for centuries and isolated gene pools aided the standardization of specific colours and coat patterns. Very few mutations affecting the original wild type conformation, coat length, colour and pattern have been necessary to provide the ingredients from which all of today cats have been bred.

MAPS

The country of origin of the cat is given for each breed. This is shown on the small map at the top of the entry in every case.

REX
The first Cornish Rex, its curled coat caused by the action of a mutant gene, was discovered in a litter of kittens in 1950.

MANX
The Isle of Man, midway between England and Ireland, is generally agreed to be the homeland and birthplace of the Manx.

SPREAD OF THE DOMESTIC CAT

Archangel

UK

France

Burma

Thailand

Ethiopia

RUSSIAN BLUE
*Shorthaired blue cats
are said to have been
brought from the port
of Archangel, in
Russia, and were
called Russian Blue.*

BIRMAN
*At the end of the
Second World War, a
pair of temple cats
were sent to France,
and from these the
breed was established.*

CHINCHILLA
*The Chinchilla was
man-made by crossing
cats of various colours
with Silver Tabby
Persians in England in
the late 1800s.*

ABYSSINIAN
*In the 1880s, such
cats were taken from
Ethiopia by servicemen
returning to Britain at
the end of the
Abyssinian War.*

SIAMESE
*First brought to
England from Thailand
in the 1880s, the first
Siamese are said to
have been prized by the
Thai royal family.*

BURMESE
*A cat called Wong
Mau was taken from
Burma to the United
States in 1930, and
was the foundation
queen of the breed.*

BODY SHAPE

For over a century, cat fanciers have tried, using various techniques, to manipulate the conformation, coat colours and patterns of their favourite varieties of the domestic cat. By carefully controlled selective breeding, they have endeavoured to create new varieties and even entirely new breeds.

IN GENERAL SHAPE and overall size, all breeds of domestic cats have retained the same basic structure as their ancestors, unlike dogs, which have been selectively bred to produce very wide ranges of shape and height. Cats are therefore free from many of the skeletal abnormalities that can affect dogs. Some defects are occasionally encountered: these include shortened, bent or kinked tails, cleft palates, flattened chests and polydactylism (extra toes). In the main, evolution seems to have been particularly kind in designing the cat, proceeding along such a well-ordered path of natural selection that it remains an efficient and perfect carnivore of convenient size, still well capable of hunting and killing small animals and birds. The cat's frame permits fluid, co-ordinated and graceful movements at all speeds. Its taut-muscled body and legs enable it to make impressive leaps and bounds. The retractile nature of the sharp claws allows fast sprinting over short distances, holding and gripping of prey, and fast climbing of convenient trees

when danger threatens. The cat's brain is large and well developed, enabling it to rapidly assimilate facts and react quickly. Its adaptable eyes can cope with extremes of lighting conditions, allowing perfect vision in both bright sunlight and dim twilight. The mobile ears work to catch the faintest sound, and the sensitive nose, allied to the perceptive Jacobson's organ in the mouth, can identify the faintest of scents imperceptible to humans.

Pedigree breeds of domestic cats have been developed to fit certain standards of conformation, colour and coat pattern. This has been done over many generations, with dedicated breeders working out exactly what the desired feline end-product would look like, and setting out to achieve it with careful and selective breeding. Today there are two main types of pedigree cat: those with chunky, heavyweight bodies and large round heads, and a lighter, finer type with lighter bone and a longer head.

Cats of the heavier type come in a wide range of

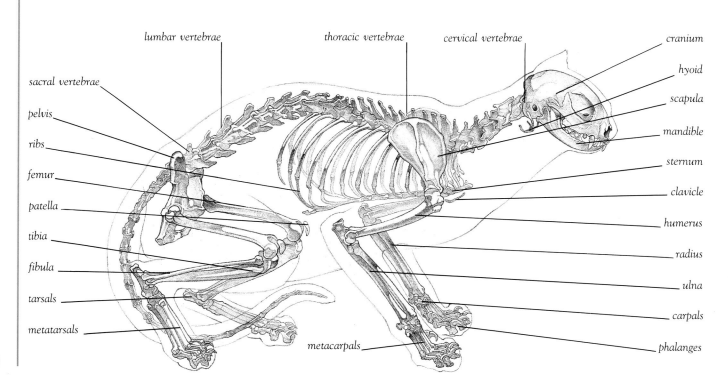

lumbar vertebrae   thoracic vertebrae   cervical vertebrae   cranium

hyoid

sacral vertebrae   scapula

pelvis   mandible

ribs   sternum

femur   clavicle

patella   humerus

tibia   radius

fibula   ulna

tarsals   carpals

metatarsals   metacarpals   phalanges

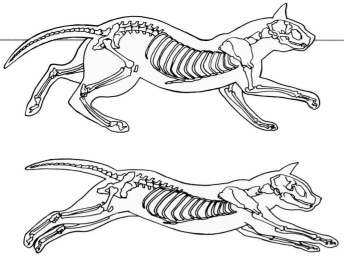

The cat is the perfect predator, and built for a combination of speed and coordination. Its skeleton consists of a highly evolved framework of efficient levers, connected by powerful muscles. Massive muscles in the hindquarters enable the cat to propel itself forward in short bursts of speed.

colours and coat patterns, and may be longhaired or shorthaired. The former include Persians and similar breeds; while the shorthairs cover cats such as the British, American, European and Exotic shorthairs. Lightweight cats are more variable in their characteristics. The Orientals, including the distinctive Siamese, are at the furthest extreme from the heavier types, with very fine bone, very long bodies, legs and tails, long wedge-shaped heads and large ears. Less extreme are the Foreign Shorthairs and Rex cats, each variety having its own very recognizable features. Some breeds have arisen from mixtures of heavy and lightweight types; these have intermediate features.

Cats keep their muscles in trim at all times. The awakening cat yawns and stretches, first the spine, tail and forelegs, then the hips and the hindlegs.

THE SELF-RIGHTING REFLEX

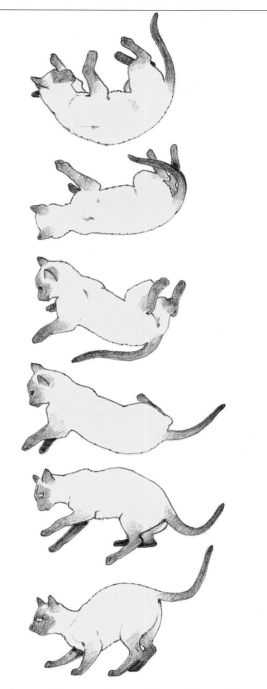

The famous feline attribute of always being able to land on its feet is not wholly accurate, but a falling cat is often able to reposition its body during falling to avoid serious injury on landing. A set of information which reaches the brain from the eyes is combined with impulses from the vestibular apparatus in the ears to transmit an orienting signal to the animal's neck muscles. The head is twisted into an upright and horizontal position and the rest of the body twists and lines itself up accordingly before landing.

SIGHT

A cat's eyes differ from ours in several ways. They observe less of the colour spectrum, having fewer cones, but more rod sensors allowing the perception of more brightness in dim light. The iris of the cat's eye opens and closes to a greater extent and the eyeball is more spherical and in relation to body size very much larger than in the human.

Although it is said that cats can see in the dark, this is not true, though the feline pupils are able to expand widely, giving excellent vision in very dim light conditions. The pupil is contracted and expanded by an intricate web of muscles set in a figure-of-eight configuration in the iris. Within the eye light is reflected off the *tapetum lucidium* which has a photomultiplying effect on the light admitted.

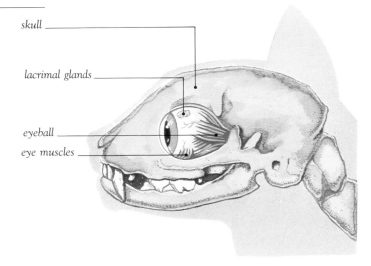

skull

lacrimal glands

eyeball

eye muscles

The cat's eye is set in a bony socket in the skull, cushioned by pads of fat and connected by muscles, enabling it to move in various directions. Lacrimal glands provide tears to wash the eye.

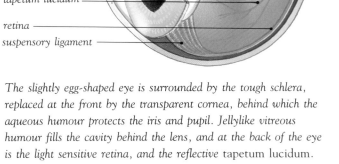

sclera

optic nerve

vitreous humour

cornea

iris

pupil

aqueous humour

lens

tapetum lucidum

retina

suspensory ligament

The slightly egg-shaped eye is surrounded by the tough schlera, replaced at the front by the transparent cornea, behind which the aqueous humour protects the iris and pupil. Jellylike vitreous humour fills the cavity behind the lens, and at the back of the eye is the light sensitive retina, and the reflective tapetum lucidum. The optic nerve transmits signals from the eye to the brain.

VISION

Humans may have better daylight vision than cats, but as dusk falls the cat scores, for although it cannot see in total darkness, its unusual pupils are able to expand to give excellent vision in very dim conditions.

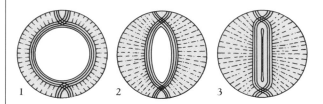

1   2   3

1 *Changes in the size and shape of the pupil generally relate to the amount of light entering the eye. In darkness the pupil dilates.*
2 *In natural diffused daylight the pupil is seen a normal vertical oval shape.*
3 *In very natural light, when the cat is relaxed, the pupil closes down to a narrow slit.*

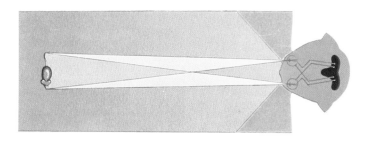

Both eyes face forward allowing the fields of vision to overlap. This produces stereoscopic sight and enables the hunting cat accurate assessment of distance and prey location.

TASTE AND SMELL

Smell is the most important of its senses to the cat. Smell is closely linked to taste since the nasal passage opens into the mouth. As well as assisting its hunting pursuits, smell is an essential part of the cat's sexual life. The vomeronasal or Jacobson's organ in the roof of its mouth enables the cat to identify minute particles of scent.

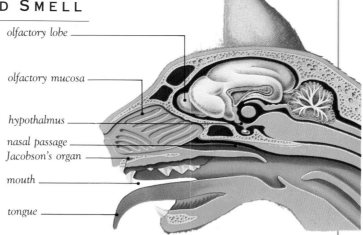

olfactory lobe

olfactory mucosa

hypothalmus

nasal passage

Jacobson's organ

mouth

tongue

The cat exhibiting the flehmen reaction stretches its neck, opens its mouth and curls back its upper lips in a snarl. It may be so affected by a smell that it also starts salivating.

Flehmen Reaction This is exhibited when the cat is confronted by chemicals in smells, either of sexual origin or from musky odours. Airborne molecules are trapped on the tongue which is flicked back to press on the opening of the Jacobson's organ. Information is relayed to the brain's hypothalamus, which dictates the cat's response.

HEARING

This sense is highly developed in the cat and registers two octaves higher than the human ear. The comparatively large and mobile ears of the ordinary domestic cat enable it to flex them sideways and backwards in order to pinpoint the source of very slight sounds – important to a natural crepuscular predator.

Even when apparently occupied, cats are alert to sounds around them.

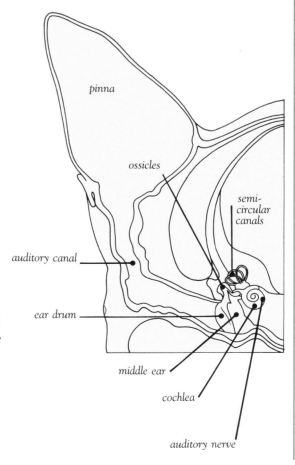

pinna

ossicles

semi-circular canals

ANATOMY OF AN EAR
Sound waves are funnelled down the external auditory canal to the ear drum. In the middle ear, weak vibrations are turned into stronger vibrations. Nerve signals are then sent along the auditory nerve to the brain.

auditory canal

ear drum

middle ear

cochlea

auditory nerve

CLAWS

The domestic cat has retractile claws which are normally sheathed, allowing the animal silent footfalls. When required for grasping prey, defensive measures or climbing, the claws are extended by muscles tightening the tendons.

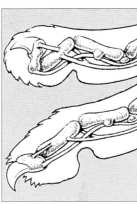

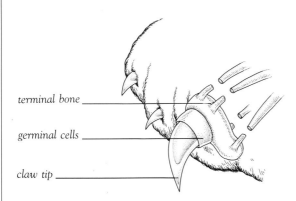

terminal bone _____

germinal cells _____

claw tip _____

DECLAWING Onychectomy is an operation involving the surgical removal of a cat's claws, normally performed only on the forepaws. Illegal in Britain and not generally advised by the US veterinary profession, the declawing process removes the claw and the germinal cells responsible for its regrowth as well as all or part of the terminal bone of the toe. Declawed cats are deprived of their prime form of defence and therefore should never be allowed out of the home.

BODY TYPES

The Longhaired or Persian body type is large boned and stocky.

The Shorthair breeds are similar in structure to Persians.

Foreign and Oriental cats are fine-boned and dainty.

HEADS AND EYES

Most cat breeds with heavy conformation, such as the Persian and the Shorthair, have large round heads, with large round eyes set wide apart above a short snub nose on a broad face. The ears are small but have a wide base, and are placed far apart on the head, complementing the rounded appearance of the skull.

Cats of light conformation, such as the Oriental and Foreign Shorthairs, have longer heads of various shapes, and the eye shape varies for each specific breed. Long-coated cats with light conformation have various head and eye shapes, according to the standards laid down by their breed associations.

The head of the Longhair or Persian is typically round, with round eyes and full cheeks. The tiny ears set wide apart.

The head of the Shorthair is similar in shape to that of the Persian when viewed from the front only.

Foreign and oriental cats have long narrow heads and large ears. Head shape varies in the individual breeds.

In profile the Persian's head is rather flat. The short snub nose shows a definite "break" at eye level.

The profile of a typical Shorthair breed is less flat than that of the Persian with a short, broad nose.

Oriental cats have long, almost Roman noses with no "break" at eye level and a flat forehead.

EYES

ROUND
Longhaired or Persian cats as well as most of the Shorthairs have large, round, lustrous eyes.

OVAL/ALMOND
Some breed standards call for oval or almond-shaped eyes often tilted at the outer edge towards the ears.

ORIENTAL
Siamese and similar related breeds have eyes of Oriental shape, set slanting towards the outer edge of the ear.

COAT TYPES

Pedigree cats have a diverse range of coat types ranging from the full and profuse pelt of the Persian to the very fine sleek and close-lying coats of the Siamese and Orientals. Between the two extremes are the long, soft and silky coats of the longhaired foreign breeds and the thick, dense coats of some of the shorthaired varieties. Some breeds should have "double" coats, with a thick woolly undercoat and a longer, sleeker top coat. The Cornish Rex has a coat devoid of guard hairs, and naturally curled awn and down hairs. The Devon Rex has modified guard, awn and down hairs which produce a waxy effect. The Sphynx or Canadian Hairless cat is at the extreme end of the coat-type range, being merely covered in some parts with a fine down.

PERSIAN
Long, soft coat with profuse down hairs nearly as long as the guard hairs, producing a typically long and full coat.

MAINE COON
Long silky coat, heavier and less uniform than that of the Persian due to less uniform and denser down hairs.

SHORTHAIR
Shorthair coats are very variable, ranging from the British and American breeds to the foreigns.

SPHYNX
Apparently hairless, the Sphynx does have a light covering of down hairs on some areas of the body.

CORNISH REX
The tightly curled coat of the Cornish Rex is caused by the absence of guard hairs and short awn hairs.

DEVON REX
Genetically modified guard and awn hairs in this breed closely resemble down hairs.

AMERICAN WIREHAIR
Quite different to the two rex coats the wirehair has crimped awn hairs and waved guard hairs.

ORIENTAL
In the Siamese and Oriental cats, the coat is short, fine and close-lying, quite different from other cats.

TYPES OF TIPPING

In the unusually coloured tipped, shaded and smoke breeds, each effect is produced by a proportion of each hair having a coloured tip while the rest of the hair is of a paler colour.

1 *Tipped cats such as the British Tipped or Chinchilla have tipping at the very ends of the hairs, producing a sparkling effect.*
2 *Tipping extending further down the hair shaft produces the more strongly coloured shaded varieties.*
3 *Variable bands of colour in different areas of the coat give rise to tabby effects.*
4 *Tipping extending almost to the white hair roots produces the smoke coat in many breeds.*
5 *In golden varieties, the white base coat of the silver varieties is replaced by a tawny yellow colour.*

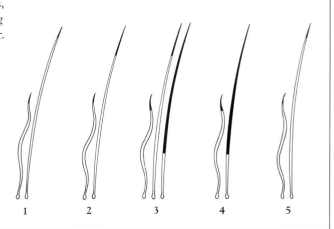

COAT COLOURS AND PATTERNS

The natural colour of the domestic cat is tabby, which may be one of four basic patterns. The wild type is ticked tabby or agouti, and the other tabby patterns are mackerel (striped), spotted, and classic (marbled or blotched). The pigment melanin produces black hairs, and most of the self-coloured coats seen in cats are produced by modification of this pigment, or by the way in which it is distributed in the individual hair fibres.

Solids
Cats of self- or solid-coloured breeds must be of a single, solid colour throughout with no pattern, shading, ticking or other variation in colour. These are the most common solid colours.

BLACK

BLUE

CHOCOLATE

LILAC

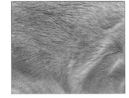
RED

CREAM

CINNAMON

WHITE

Tabby Markings
There are four varieties of tabby patterns, each of which can be found in any of the tabby colours.

TICKED

MACKEREL

SPOTTED

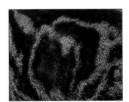
CLASSIC

Tabby Colours
Tabbies are found in a wide range of colours. Here we show a selection.

BROWN

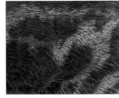
BLUE

CHOCOLATE

BROWN PATCHED

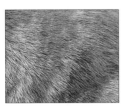
BLUE PATCHED

RED

SILVER

Abyssinian
Abyssinian cats have coats which are gently shaded, because each hair is lighter at the root and darker at the tip.

USUAL   BLUE   SORREL   FAWN

Coloured Tips
Coats of this sort, with the hairs darkening in varying degrees towards the roots, are found in a number of colours, some of which are shown here.

BLACK SMOKE   BLUE SMOKE   CHOCOLATE SMOKE   LILAC SMOKE

   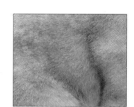

CHINCHILLA SILVER   CHINCHILLA GOLDEN   BLACK TIPPED SILVER   BLUE TIPPED SILVER

Himalayan
Cats with the Himalayan coat pattern, such as the Siamese, have pale coats with the main colour restricted to the head and extremeties.

SEAL POINT   BLUE POINT   RED POINT

CREAM POINT   LILAC POINT

CHOCOLATE POINT   SEAL TABBY   RED TABBY POINT

Tonkinese

Tonkinese cats, which are light-phase Burmese cats, show a modified "pointed" effect. The coats are darker than those of cats with true Himalayan colouring, so the "points" are not so dramatic.

BROWN

LILAC

CHOCOLATE

RED

CREAM

LILAC TORTIE

BLUE TORTIE

TABBY

Multiple Colours

As every cat lover knows, cats come in coats of many colours apart from those already described, most of which are recognized for show purposes in one breed or another. The tortoiseshells are the most common, but there are endless varieties, including the unusual Mi-ke pattern of the Japanese Bobtail.

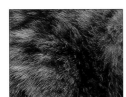

TORTOISESHELL

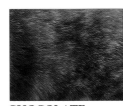

CHOCOLATE
TORTOISESHELL

LILAC
TORTOISESHELL

BLUE
TORTOISESHELL

TORTOISESHELL
AND WHITE

BLUE
TORTOISESHELL
AND WHITE

MI-KE

BEHAVIOUR

An insight into feline behaviour can enhance the cat owner's enjoyment of the pet cat, and a basic understanding of the animal's complex psychology assists in simple training and in providing the very best of care. Cats are intuitive and highly sensitive creatures who respond and react to the sort of treatment they receive from humans.

CATS ARE OFTEN considered to be less intelligent than dogs, possibly because they do not respond to training to sit on command, and will rarely perform tricks. It is questionable whether the performance of unnatural actions necessarily equates with a high intelligence quotient. It may be that the cat is better equipped to channel its brain power into different behaviour, such as survival techniques, and adapting to environmental change. And perhaps cats could be considered more intelligent than dogs for questioning the reason behind performing tricks, or being obedient to commands?

Young kittens begin to exhibit predatory behaviour at about six weeks old. In the wild, the mother cat would bring prey to the kittens. In the domestic situation, a mother cat brings small pieces of meat to the maternity box, making a special encouraging sound to attract her kittens' attention. Mother cats often pat the meat, teaching the kittens to pounce

Though cats and dogs get along well together as family pets, it is sometimes difficult for them to understand one another's body language and play behaviour.

upon it. At this stage of their development, kittens begin to practise hunting movements, crouching down, pouncing and making mock attacks on their litter-mates.

Adult cats prefer to hunt alone within the confines of their own established territory. Some cats roam long distances from home to visit favourite hunting grounds, and very occasionally, cats from the same family learn to hunt co-operatively. Acute hearing and excellent vision in dim light enable cats to become efficient, silent hunters. A cat often lies in ambush, waiting with infinite patience for its victim to emerge from its place of refuge. The cat attacks in a swift bounding leap, grasping its prey with extended claws and killing with a lethal bite to the creature's neck. Hungry cats dispatch their prey quite quickly, but well-fed cats, highly stimulated by the excitement of stalking and capture, often play with the prey for some time before finally dispatching it. Playing with prey gives the cats the opportunity to practise their trapping techniques.

Throughout its lifetime the cat's behaviour is governed by the innate patterns inherited from its wild ancestors. Here we see a Burmilla hunting (left) a Persian playing at killing prey, and a pair of Oriental kittens play-fighting (below).

Despite centuries of domestication, most cats will hunt, given the chance. If you keep pet cats entirely indoors you should compensate for their loss of hunting opportunities by providing lots of toys, and encouraging them to play chasing, pouncing and catching games. Such stimulation and exercise keeps them fit, stops them getting too fat and may help to ensure their survival if they should ever get lost.

TERRITORIAL MARKING

Cats identify their property and places by scent marking. They employ various glands for this purpose. Scent glands on the head, called temporal glands, are situated above the eyes on either side of the forehead. The perioral glands are along the lips and both sets of glands are used for marking when the cat rubs its head against a friend or a chosen object – behaviour which appears to give the cat extreme pleasure. Some cats, usually full males, mark their territory by urine-spraying on various boundaries (below). Head rubbing (middle) is used for identifying objects rather than as boundary marking. Some stropping behaviour is used to scratch at a cat's boundary marker after spray marking (top).

Sleeping

Cats have two distinct types of sleep – light sleep and deep sleep. During light sleep the blood pressure remains normal, the body temperature drops slightly and the muscles are mildly tensed. In deep or paradoxical sleep, the blood pressure falls, the body temperature rises and the muscles relax completely. The hearing, however, remains extremely acute and any sudden sound will wake the cat instantly. Cats seem able to sleep at any time, in any temperature and in all manner of seemingly uncomfortable situations.

Newborn kittens spend most of the time in periods of deep sleep, secure in the nest area chosen by their mother.

Small kittens sleep most of the time, and this is an important part of their development process. Newborn kittens spend most of their first week of life in deep sleep, and during the next three weeks have gradually increasing periods of wakefulness.

Dreaming takes place during deep sleep, and cats often twitch their muscles, growl or purr. They may make sucking sounds and twitch the tail. It is probably during dreaming that the cat's brain sorts and sifts data for storage in its long-term memory. At least one-third of the cat's sleeping time is spent in deep sleep mode, and this seems to be essential for its well-being.

Cats like to sleep in unusual places, and enjoy curling up in confined spaces which make them feel protected and secure.

SLEEP PATTERNS

As a cat becomes drowsy and falls into a light sleep it may remain sitting or lying with its head up but relaxed, and its paws tucked into its body. It may remain in this condition for 10 to 30 minutes and at this stage it is easy to awaken with any slight noise.

In deep sleep the cat is completely relaxed and usually curled on its side. Deep sleep is characterised by rapid eye movements, and the cat may also twitch its whiskers and paws, or quiver the ears, and tail. It may even growl or emit little muttering sounds. Deep sleep normally lasts for about 6 to 10 minutes before the cat resumes a period of light sleep.

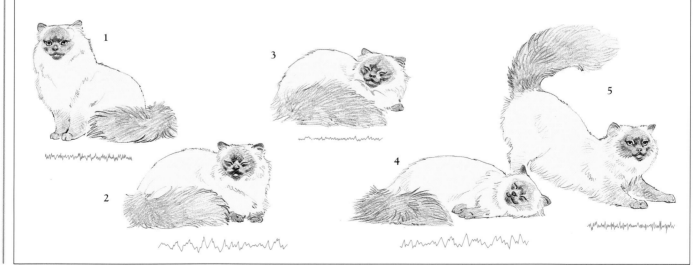

WASHING

The cat thoroughly cleans each shoulder and flank.

It washes its underside and inside each hindleg in turn.

The paws are licked and any dirt is bitten from between the paws.

Each forepaw is licked in turn and used to wash the corresponding side of the face and head.

Most cats wash themselves frequently. Family cats often indulge in mutual washing sessions, and mother cats spend a great deal of time washing their young kittens. Pet cats will often attempt to wash their humans, and many cats wash meticulously after being touched or stroked by humans, probably in an attempt to remove an unacceptable scent from their coats.

The cat uses its tongue and paws to groom itself. The tongue, covered with tiny hooked projections called papillae, acts as both brush and comb. Front paws are used to clean the places the tongue cannot reach. The cat sits up and licks a paw until it becomes damp, then passes the paw over its face, over and into the ear, across the forehead and eye and down the cheek to the chin. It repeats the procedure with the opposite paw to clean the other side of the face. It licks and grooms each shoulder and foreleg in turn, then attends to its flanks and underside, the anus, genital region and hindlegs, and finishes by washing the tail from the base to the tip. It teases out tangles and knots with its teeth, and bites out patches of dirt from between its paws.

As well as keeping its coat clean and well groomed, the cat's washing technique has another important purpose. The effect of sunlight on the coat produces its nutritional requirement of Vitamin D, which it transfers from the coat into the body by the licking and washing action.

The cat licks a paw then uses it to wash one side of its face.

Friendly cats often indulge in mutual grooming of each other's fur, which both seem to enjoy.

Communication

Cats recognize each other initially by smell. Friendly cats greet one another by touching noses or rubbing their foreheads together. They may rub their bodies together and sniff at each other's genital regions.

The alert cat has a direct gaze and points its ears and whiskers forwards. If it is also slightly nervous it will twitch its nostrils, attempting to identify by scent. When a person has been identified as a friend, the cat's expression relaxes, and its tail rises in greeting.

A cat under threat first freezes, staring at the aggressor with wide eyes. Its tail flicks slowly from side to side. If further threatened, the cat pulls in its chin, lays back its ears and gradually runs sideways on to the enemy. Simultaneously the hairs on the body and tail begin to erect, presenting the largest possible body area. The cat draws back its lips to reveal its teeth and growls an unmistakable warning. Its muscles are poised for either fight or flight, the weight of the body taken on three legs while the fourth is held ready to strike.

An agitated, nervous cat is dangerous to touch, for it may react as violently as if receiving an electric shock. Such a cat will be crouched down with tucked-in chin, wide eyes and ears held sideways. It must be talked out of this state and calmed down, or left in peace and quiet to recover its composure.

The mechanism of purring is not fully understood, but it must be one of the most endearing characteristics of the domestic cat. Some cats purr softly and only rarely, but many cats regularly purr with content-

Cats recognize each other basically by smell, and when two friendly cats meet up they generally touch noses or rub their foreheads together.

FELINE BODY-LANGUAGE

Cats are masters in the art of body-language, conveying their moods and intentions by a series of well-defined postures, clearly understood by humans, as well as fellow felines.

Cats use a variety of sounds in communicating with humans. This cat is voicing feelings of nervousness.

This Blue Smoke Persian is obviously upset and emitting an extremely loud yowl.

An unhappy lilac Burmese squats into a defensive posture with wide eyes and flattened ears.

ment and to show affection. Even tiny kittens are able to purr as they nurse, though they will not purr in response to human handling until about six weeks old. Cats may purr in response to their owner's voice or touch, and some purr when suffering the pains of labour or terminal illness.

Most cats can make a range of sounds in three basic categories. The quietest is similar to a human murmur and includes soft purring. Murmurs are made with the mouth closed. The middle category of feline sounds may be thought of as vowel sounds, each being a variation of the "miaow", and each being used to express a different need, such as asking to be let out.

The most interesting range of cat talk is that made by a mother cat teaching her kittens to eat solid food, to follow her from the nest, and to behave properly. The kittens themselves are able to purr, spit and growl, and also have a loud distress call with which they cry to their mother when they are lost or frightened.

The typical tail-up greeting of a cat indicating its pleasure and soliciting a stroke from its owner.

An American Wirehair rolls over to solicit attention.

FACIAL EXPRESSIONS

A contented cat with upright ears and relaxed whiskers.

Nervous or apprehensive, ears start to go back and whiskers tense slightly forward.

A frightened or very angry cat. Ears flat, eyes narrowed and whiskers forward, ready for defence or attack.

Alert and ready to pounce on its prey, the cat assumes an expression midway between normality and fear.

Relaxed and contented while being petted with half-closed eyes and relaxed whiskers.

SEXUAL BEHAVIOUR

Both male and female domestic cats reach sexual maturity when very young, little more than kittens in fact, and will readily reproduce unless confined or neutered. Females are able to produce two or three litters each year.

FEMALE KITTENS MAY reach sexual maturity as early as five months old, and may then come into season every three weeks during the breeding season, even though they will not be physically fully grown until they are over one year old. Male kittens may reach sexual maturity from six to eight months old, although in some pedigree breeds this may be delayed for as long as eighteen months. Domestic cats destined for life in the family home make much better pets when they are de-sexed, which removes their often unsocial sexual behaviour patterns.

Male

A mature male cat is able to mate at any time, though he will be more sexually active in the spring and summer months. He is initially attracted to the female by the special evocative odour that she emits during oestrus, and also responds to her inviting cries. The scent and cry of the female cat in oestrus is said to carry over long distances, and any mature male cats in the vicinity will respond. When the cats meet, the rolling and posturing of the female further excites the male, who will mount and mate with her as quickly as possible. In a natural environment, several males may be attracted to one female and will bicker and fight for dominance and the privilege of mating. Sometimes a subordinate male will mate with the female while his superiors are engaged in battle. During her oestrus period, the female cat will mate many times, either with the same male, or with several different males.

Entire male cats which roam freely treat their homes as bases for food and shelter only. They are totally motivated by their strong sexual drive and spend their days patrolling their territories, marking their boundaries with spurts of pungent urine to deter interlopers. They constantly search for sexually receptive females to fight over and mate with, but often need to take time off for rest and recuperation. When male cats fight, their long, sharp, canine teeth inflict deep puncture wounds in their opponents, and the raking of their hooked claws causes deep scratches, all of which take a long time to heal. A cat fight between

---

SEXUAL DIFFERENCES

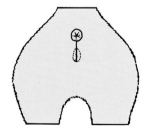

FEMALE ADULT
The vulva is a vertical slit about 1cm from the circular anal opening.

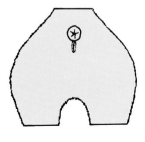

FEMALE KITTEN
The vulva is a vertical slit almost joined to the circular anal opening.

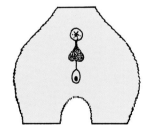

MALE KITTEN
The tiny round opening in which the penis is concealed is about 1cm below the circular anal opening, with an indication of the scrotal sacs as slightly raised areas.

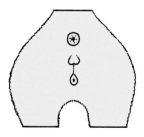

MALE ADULT
The testicles are clearly visible in the male, set between two openings at least 2.5cm apart.

CAT FIGHTS

1 Cats meeting and investigating each other by smell and observation of body posturing.
2 One cat may take the initiative and advance to investigate more thoroughly. The less confident cat cringes in a defensive posture.
3 As the dominant cat advances further, the defendant cat backs away, perhaps lifting a paw to fend off a likely attack.
4 The defendant decides not to back down, both cats growl and wave their fluffed out tails.
5 The dominant cat presses forward, turning sideways to present a bigger threat and the

defendant flattens his ears and hisses loudly.
6 The aggressive cat finally attacks in earnest and leaps onto the defending cat which turns onto its back extending its claws. Both cats are locked together in a growling mass gripping each other with jaws and forelegs and each raking at the other's body with the claws of the powerful hind legs. Eventually the less powerful cat breaks away and escapes.

two males is bitter and serious. The cats confront each other, making huffing sounds, with cheeks puffed out, sometimes salivating and emitting low, fierce growls. They hunch up their shoulders and hips to look as large and powerful as possible. They circle, stiff-legged, then each cat lunges at the other's throat, biting hard. The cats lock together in a rolling ball and rake each other with the back claws, causing lots of flying fur. When they break apart, one may run away and receive a final, deep bite at the root of the tail or the testes. On subsequent meetings with the vanquished cat, the dominant male may underline his superiority by biting the submissive male on the neck and mounting him briefly, before releasing him and walking away with stiff legs and tail. A male previously beaten into submission usually does his best to avoid any such confrontations, or will crouch down, offering the scruff of his neck to the dominant cat. Males rarely fight with females, but females will fight, particularly in defence of their kittens.

As they approach puberty kittens will often show the first signs of sexual gestures in their usual greeting and play behaviour.

Female

Oestrus, or breeding condition, in the female cat is easy to recognize and consists of four stages. In pro-oestrus, the reproductive organs undergo changes in preparation for mating and pregnancy. The cat is extra affectionate, solicits stroking and restlessly roams around the house seeking a way out. After five days of the first stage, true oestrus begins, lasting for about seven days, during which time the cat will be ready and willing to mate. When stroked she assumes the mating position (see page 34). She may become agitated and roll on the floor as if in pain. Most cats wail, and in some pedigree breeds, such as the Siamese, the wailing can be indescribably loud and prolonged. If mating does not take place, the third stage, meto-oestrus, begins and the reproductive system relaxes until the fourth stage of anoestrus is reached. During anoestrus, the female cat's behaviour is contented and calm until the next cycle begins.

When the breeding queen reaches the receptive part of oestrus, she exhibits the typical mating position known as lordosis.

MATING

When a female cat is ready to mate, she adopts a characteristic hollowed back position, crouching and presenting her hindquarters, with her tail bent to one side. The male approaches her from the side and rear, running forward and grasping her by the loose skin at the scruff of the neck. He mounts her by straddling her body with his front legs, then arches his back in order to correctly position his penis for mating. The female also manoeuvres her pelvis to help penetration. After a few pelvic thrusts the male achieves penetration and quickly ejaculates. The female immediately pulls forward, growling fiercely, and attempts to turn and attack the male, who leaps away to safety. The female rolls, sometimes still growling, then both cats sit apart from each other and lick their own genital areas clean. After a few minutes, they will probably mate again.

Mating can occur up to ten times in an hour, or until the male is exhausted. If there are several males present, the female will mate with one or more of them in succession.

1 *The male approaches from the side and rear.*
2 *He mounts by straddling the queen's body and grasping the loose skin at her scruff.*
3 *The queen assists mating by raising her pelvis and turning her tail to one side.*
4 *After mating the male leaps away and the female turns, spits and fiercely growls.*

MATERNITY

The female cat or queen makes a model mother, secreting her litter away from harm within a nest area. She feeds the kittens at regular intervals, keeps them spotlessly clean, and curls around them, purring, to rest and sleep. She will devote herself to their every need for as long as she needs to.

FELINE MOTHERS CARE for their kittens in a completely dedicated way until the kittens are well able to take care of their own needs. Male cats are not involved in the rearing of kittens, though they have been observed playing with kittens in feral cat colonies.

After mating the fertilized ova become implanted in the uterine wall of the female cat, and glands secrete hormones giving rise to certain patterns of behaviour. The cat becomes even more sensitive to danger, she grooms herself even more thoroughly than before, and her appetite gradually increases. If she is a free-roaming cat she will hunt with more dedication, and she will also nibble selected grasses and herbage. As her pregnancy advances the cat chooses secluded sleeping areas. Her self-grooming sessions increase, and she pays particular attention to her genital area and gradually enlarging breasts. As the period of gestation of about sixty three days reaches its end, the cat searches for a suitable site in which to give birth. The first stage of labour can extend for many hours. The cat is restless and will not eat, though she will drink from time to time. Eventually, when the second stage of labour commences, with typical contractions, the cat will generally go to the place she has chosen to give birth. The contractions gradually become

The mother cat constantly grooms her kittens, washing them by licking them all over with her rough tongue.

stronger and more frequent, and prior to the expulsion of the first kitten, a sac of fluid may be passed, preparing the passage for the birth.

Kittens may be born head first or tail first, both presentations being equally normal. The head or rump appears, and the cat licks at the membranes as contractions push the tiny kitten out. Sometimes, particularly with the first born, the kitten seems to be held back by its shoulders or hips, but it is normally expelled without human interference as the cat shifts her position and bears down. She licks away all the membranes encasing the newly born kitten, and chews the umbilical cord to within about two centimetres (half an inch) of the kitten's body. The stump of cord dries and drops off, leaving a neat navel within about a week. The placenta may be passed still attached to the kitten, or may be expelled later, after the kitten is clean, dry and nursing. The mother cat will normally eat the placenta, which is rich in nutrients, and which, in the wild, would sustain her until she was fit enough to hunt for food.

Kittens are born blind and deaf but have a strong sense of smell which enables them to find a nipple, and to start feeding even before they are perfectly dry.

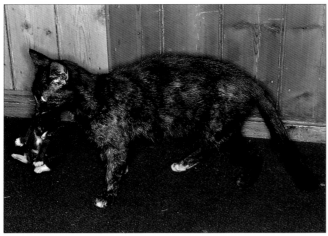

A mother cat may decide to move her litter to a new nest and carries the kittens one at a time, holding them firmly by the scruff of the neck.

and stimulating it to breathe. She also licks vigorously at the kitten's anal region, stimulating the tiny animal to pass the meconium, a dark plug which stops up its bowel until released.

When the last kitten of the litter has been born, the mother cat washes her own genital region, legs and tail. She gathers her kittens together and lying on one side, encourages them to suckle. She may not leave the nest for up to twenty-four hours for food and a drink. Young kittens urinate and defecate only when stimulated to do so by being licked in the genital and anal regions by the mother cat. She has a set routine for kitten care. After nursing the kittens, she washes and grooms them in turn, and swallows all the excreted material they produce, to ensure that the nest remains clean. This would be a safety factor in the wild, preventing scent leaving clues as to the kittens' whereabouts and thus attracting predators.

After the birth of the first kitten, the rest of the litter follow at regular or irregular intervals, and the mother cat deals with each in the same way. She licks and washes each kitten, clearing the membrane from its body, cleaning the mucus from its nose and mouth

Even after centuries of domestication, cats often revert to the innate behaviour patterns of their wild forebears. Three weeks or so after the birth of her litter, the cat may suddenly decide to move the kittens to another, often quite unsuitable, location. She grasps

DEVELOPMENT OF KITTENS

Kittens are born blind and deaf. They have a strong sense of smell however, which enables them to locate their mother's nipples, and a strong sucking reflex which ensures that they take in enough milk to satisfy their needs. At about one week to ten days after birth, the eyes open and the hearing starts to develop, and until the litter is three weeks of age the queen looks after the kittens constantly, feeding and grooming them and stimulating them to urinate and defecate by licking at their genital regions. The queen ingests the kittens' wastes at this time and spends about 70% of her time curled up with, and attending to, her family.

At two weeks the kittens can scrabble around their nest box and at three weeks start to stand up on their legs and pay attention to what is going on around them. Between three and six weeks they make great advances, learning to play, to make sounds, and show an interest in solid food. From about four weeks they will use a corner of their box for toilet purposes and by six weeks can be taught to use a litter tray. Having learned to eat a variety of foods and to spend less time with their mother, most kittens are fully independant and self-sufficient by about eight to ten weeks of age.

Newborn

One week

Two weeks

Three weeks

Six weeks

each kitten round the neck, holding in in her jaws, but not piercing the skin with her teeth, then lifts the kitten by raising her head and carries it between her straddled forelegs to its new resting place. The cat will carry each kitten in turn until she is satisfied that the litter is in a new, safe haven. When kittens are grasped around the neck, their natural response is to assume the foetal position and go completely limp. This ensures that they are rarely harmed by being carried by their mother.

Until the kittens are about three weeks old, the mother cat looks after all their needs. She leaves the litter only for short periods to eat, drink and relieve herself, and returns as quickly as possible to her babies. By ten days, the kittens have opened their eyes and gradually begin to respond to various stimulae. During their third and fourth weeks, they try to leave the nest area, and as they become stronger and more mobile, and gradually accept solid food, the mother spends less time with them.

During their early weeks of life, their mother teaches the kittens a great deal about being feline. She encourages play behaviour including mock hunting and killing moves, and she initiates the first stages in toilet training, calling them to follow her away from the nest when they want to urinate and defecate. By the time the kittens are weaned and ready to go to new homes, their mother will have ensured that each is an independent and self-assured little cat with good feline manners.

Once her kittens are fully mobile, the mother cat encourages them to explore and to broaden their play and hunting behaviours.

NEUTERING

Unless a cat is destined for breeding purposes it should be neutered in order to make a loving and carefree pet. Neutered cats may be shown in most cat associations and are easier to maintain in peak show condition than their entire male and female counterparts.

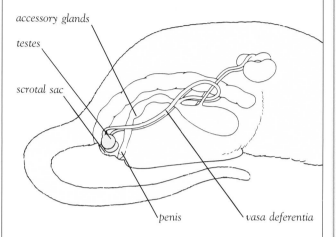

accessory glands
testes
scrotal sac
penis
vasa deferentia

Castration Castration or orchidectomy is the removal of the male sex organs. Such surgery is best carried out just before the male kitten reaches sexual maturity, and has formed his masculine character but has not shown signs of being interested in the opposite sex.

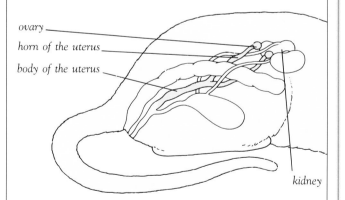

ovary
horn of the uterus
body of the uterus
kidney

Spaying Spaying or ovariohysterectomy involves the surgical removal of most of the female cat's sex organs – the ovaries, fallopian tubes and uterus. Spaying may be carried out at a very early age in the female cat, and is better performed before she has her first period of oestrus, and definitely before she has kittens.

BREEDING PEDIGREE CATS

Breeding pedigree cats is a hobby that should not be undertaken lightly. Only cats of the very best quality and with strong constitutions should be kept for breeding and they must be expertly and considerately cared for.

ALTHOUGH ORDINARY DOMESTIC cats seem to become pregnant and produce kittens without much bother, often against their owners' wishes, the production of pedigree kittens under controlled conditions can prove difficult, and cat breeding should not be undertaken lightly. Despite its many generations of domestication, a cat can resent the unnatural restrictions placed upon her during mating and pregnancy. She may prove unwilling to mate with the stud cat chosen for her; she may have a stressful gestation period or a difficult delivery. She could reject her kittens, have little or poor quality milk, or be so unsettled as to spend her time anxiously moving the kittens to new nest sites.

A successful cat breeder will be someone for whom financial gain is not important. Breeding pedigree cats is a hobby full of rewards, but none of these is financial. There is a great sense of pride and achievement in planning a special litter, seeing it born and rearing it. A true cat lover will gain a great deal from caring for the female cat, known as the brood queen, helping her through the weeks of pregnancy, attending the birth, and looking after the needs of the growing family. On the debit side is the problem of parting with the kittens when they are fully independent and ready to go to new homes at about three months old.

It may seem logical to buy a pair of cats in order to start breeding, but this is impractical. Keeping a stud male is not a job for the novice. He will not be content with a monogamous relationship with one queen, and needs special accommodation of his own so that his habit of spray-marking his territory with strong-smelling urine does not become a serious household problem.

Starting out

To start breeding it is best to buy one or two females of the breed you have chosen, seeking advice from an experienced breeder or show judge, and purchasing the very best females that you can afford. Two females will keep each other company, and if they are unrelated you will have a good foundation to lines of your own in future years. A kitten for breeding should be purchased at about three months old. She should be of sound conformation, with a good temperament and an impeccable pedigree, and should be properly registered with an acceptable cat association. She should be well grown for her age and should have received a suitable course of vaccinations for which you will be provided with certificates. Until she grows to adulthood, the kitten should lead a normal life, with good food, correct grooming and lots of play opportunities combined with tender loving care. Kittens vary as to

Oriental cats such as the Siamese often have more than the average number of kittens in a litter and need extra care in order to rear them successfully. This superb seal point has eight strong and healthy youngsters.

GESTATION CHART

The average gestation period of the domestic cat is 65 days so if the precise date of mating is known, the chart shows on which date the kittens are expected to be born. A variation of up to four days either way is not unusual, and it is important to check the pregnant cat at regular intervals in the week leading up to the expected birth.

To check the expected date of birth, refer to the date of mating in the green column. The birth date may be read from the yellow column. For example, a cat mated on 1 May will be due to have her kittens on 5 July.

JAN	MAR	FEB	APR	MAR	MAY	APR	JUN	MAY	JUL	JUN	AUG	JUL	SEP	AUG	OCT	SEP	NOV	OCT	DEC	NOV	JAN	DEC	FEB
1	7	1	7	1	5	1	5	1	5	1	5	1	4	1	5	1	5	1	5	1	5	1	4
2	8	2	8	2	6	2	6	2	6	2	6	2	5	2	6	2	6	2	6	2	6	2	5
3	9	3	9	3	7	3	7	3	7	3	7	3	6	3	7	3	7	3	7	3	7	3	6
4	10	4	10	4	8	4	8	4	8	4	8	4	7	4	8	4	8	4	8	4	8	4	7
5	11	5	11	5	9	5	9	5	9	5	9	5	8	5	9	5	9	5	9	5	9	5	8
6	12	6	12	6	10	6	10	6	10	6	10	6	9	6	10	6	10	6	10	6	10	6	9
7	13	7	13	7	11	7	11	7	11	7	11	7	10	7	11	7	11	7	11	7	11	7	10
8	14	8	14	8	12	8	12	8	12	8	12	8	11	8	12	8	12	8	12	8	12	8	11
9	15	9	15	9	13	9	13	9	13	9	13	9	12	9	13	9	13	9	13	9	13	9	12
10	16	10	16	10	14	10	14	10	14	10	14	10	13	10	14	10	14	10	14	10	14	10	13
11	17	11	17	11	15	11	15	11	15	11	15	11	14	11	15	11	15	11	15	11	15	11	14
12	18	12	18	12	16	12	16	12	16	12	16	12	15	12	16	12	16	12	16	12	16	12	15
13	19	13	19	13	17	13	17	13	17	13	17	13	16	13	17	13	17	13	17	13	17	13	16
14	20	14	20	14	18	14	18	14	18	14	18	14	17	14	18	14	18	14	18	14	18	14	17
15	21	15	21	15	19	15	19	15	19	15	19	15	18	15	19	15	19	15	19	15	19	15	18
16	22	16	22	16	20	16	20	16	20	16	20	16	19	16	20	16	20	16	20	16	20	16	19
17	23	17	23	17	21	17	21	17	21	17	21	17	20	17	21	17	21	17	21	17	21	17	20
18	24	18	24	18	22	18	22	18	22	18	22	18	21	18	22	18	22	18	22	18	22	18	21
19	25	19	25	19	23	19	23	19	23	19	23	19	22	19	23	19	23	19	23	19	23	19	22
20	26	20	26	20	24	20	24	20	24	20	24	20	23	20	24	20	24	20	24	20	24	20	23
21	27	21	27	21	25	21	25	21	25	21	25	21	24	21	25	21	25	21	25	21	25	21	24
22	28	22	28	22	26	22	26	22	26	22	26	22	25	22	26	22	26	22	26	22	26	22	25
23	29	23	29	23	27	23	27	23	27	23	27	23	26	23	27	23	27	23	27	23	27	23	26
24	30	24	30	24	28	24	28	24	28	24	28	24	27	24	28	24	28	24	28	24	28	24	27
25	31	25	1	25	29	25	29	25	29	25	29	25	28	25	29	25	29	25	29	25	29	25	28
26	1	26	2	26	30	26	30	26	30	26	30	26	29	26	30	26	30	26	30	26	30	26	1
27	2	27	3	27	31	27	1	27	31	27	31	27	30	27	31	27	1	27	31	27	31	27	2
28	3	28	4	28	1	28	2	28	1	28	1	28	1	28	1	28	2	28	1	28	1	28	3
29	4			29	2	29	3	29	2	29	2	29	2	29	2	29	3	29	2	29	2	29	4
30	5			30	3	30	4	30	3	30	3	30	3	30	3	30	4	30	3	30	3	30	5
31	6			31	4			31	4			31	4	31	4			31	4			31	6
	APR		MAY		JUN		JUL		AUG		SEP		OCT		NOV		DEC		JAN		FEB		MAR

39

when they have their first season or period of oestrus, so she must be carefully observed and not allowed to roam free. Whe her first season occurs, she should be carefully watched. At the next period of oestrus, if she is at least ten months of age, it is feasible for her to be mated if your veterinary surgeon agrees that she is sufficiently well and physically fit.

Pedigree male cats kept for breeding are called stud cats. They have usually proved their superior qualities in the show ring, attaining high show status because they conform so closely to the standard of points for their respective breeds. Because a working stud male will habitually spray his habitat with spurts of pungent urine as territorial marking behaviour he has to be confined in his own living quarters.

Matings must be strictly controlled, witnessed and recorded by the stud's owner, who will issue a breeding certificate to the queen's owner, who pays an agreed stud fee. The two cats are given some hours to become accustomed to one another, and once the stud's owner is assured that the cats are relating and not aggressive, and that the queen is really ready, she is released from the pen and the cats are allowed to mate. This procedure is repeated to ensure that a completely successful mating has taken place, usually over two or three days, then the queen is returned to her owner.

SELECTIVE BREEDING

From time to time anomalies occur in litters of kittens, in both pedigrees and domestics, and quite often, breeders fascinated by all things new or unusual may decide to try to perpetuate the unusual features and perhaps produce a new breed. It is possible, after selectively breeding one or several generations, to determine the genetic make-up of a new feline feature, and then to set out a formal and constructive breeding programme to develop a new breed. Some features which are clearly detrimental to a cat's well-being would be frowned upon by true cat lovers, and would thus prove unacceptable to most associations for registration and breeding purposes.

AMERICAN CURL
The curled ears of this breed do not appear to present any problems, and the breed is accepted by some associations in the United States of America.

SPHYNX
Those who love the apparently hairless Sphynx work tirelessly for its recognition for show and registration. Others consider that a breed which may not be viable in the wild state should not be encouraged.

SCOTTISH FOLD
Refused recognition by some associations on the premise that the tightly folded ears are impossible to keep clean and healthy, and because some skeletal anomalies were apparent in some early Fold kittens.

SYMBOLIZING GENES

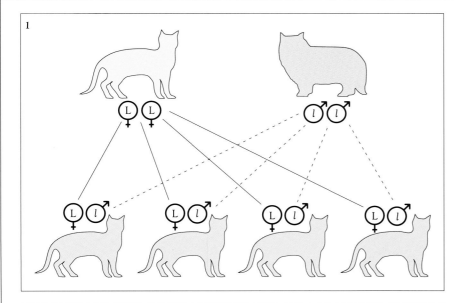

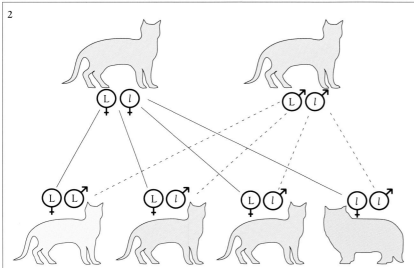

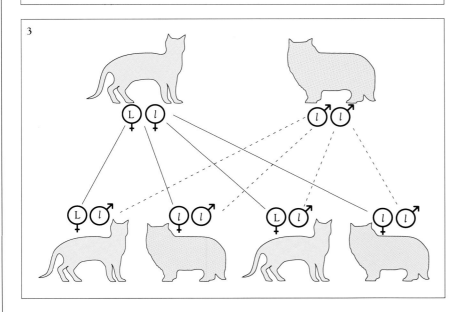

As in the human, genes in the domestic cat exist in pairs – one received from each parent – for each feature. The genes for each feature are either dominant or recessive to its opposite feature. For example the normal "wild-type" coat of the *Felis catus* is shorthaired, and is symbolized, for convenience sake, as *L*. The opposing genetic feature to short-hair (*L*) is long-hair, which is recessive to short-hair and is symbolized *l*. Dominant genes are symbolized with an upper case letter, and their corresponding recessive gene with the lower case version of the same letter.

Sperm and ova contain one of each pair of the parents' genes, so it may be seen that some features are passed on in a fairly random fashion. Once the dominance or recessivity of the genes is understood, however, it is fairly simple to deduce methods of manipulating the genes by careful selection of breeding partners in order to produce offspring with the desired traits.

A simple example is the production of long-hair in cats, as is demonstrated in these charts.

1 *A homozygous shorthaired female is mated to a homozygous longhaired male (LL × ll).*
2 *A heterozygous shorthaired female is mated to a heterozygous shorthaired male (Ll × Ll).*
3 *A heterozygous shorthaired female is mated to a homozyous longhaired male (Ll × ll).*

KEY

 gene from male

 gene from female

L   short-hair
l   long-hair

SHOWING

Throughout the world, various cat bodies and associations organise shows and exhibitions. At these functions, like-minded people are able to meet, to enter their prized pets and to compete for awards and championships.

A PERSON WHO breeds or shows cats is called a cat fancier, and usually takes up the hobby through an all-consuming love of all things feline. Cat fanciers share a common bond and interest in wanting to breed or own the perfect cat. Most cats show complete indifference to being put on public display, but owners derive great personal satisfaction in gaining top awards with their pets. There is little financial reward for the successful exhibitor as entry fees are high and prize money is often non-existent. Rosettes, ribbons and trophies are eagerly sought after, and proudly displayed at home. Exhibitors enjoy cat shows as regular social functions. All members of the family are able to attend and enjoy the proceedings, and some cats actually appear to enjoy being pampered and admired by judges and the receptive audience of the show hall.

The first cat show ever recorded was held in 1598 at St Giles Fair, Winchester, England, but the first properly benched show, with cats being placed in individual cages, took place at London's Crystal Palace in 1871. The first benched American cat show was held in Madison Square Garden, New York, in 1895. The vogue for exhibiting cats and competing for prizes spread slowly round the world, and nowadays hundreds

Though there is no monetary gain in showing cats, the winning of first place awards is the aim of most exhibitors. Here a lovely Chinchilla neuter and a kitten pose with their awards.

HOW TO USE THIS BOOK

All cat associations judge each individual cat breed using a system of points. The total is always one hundred, but the breakdown of points allocated to particular features varies from breed to breed, and from association to association. In the Breed Directory on pages 56 to 251 you will find the standards broken down and annotated for each breed. Alternative standards set by other associations are listed separately.

The Introduction gives the background to the breed and how it developed

The Penalties box lists the features for which a cat will be penalized or disqualified in the show ring

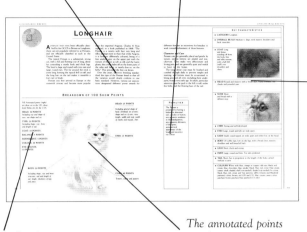

The Key Characteristics box gives specific descriptions

The listed points are those set by associations in other countries

The annotated points are those set in Britain, or set by the most relevant association for certain breeds

of shows take place in many different countries. Each country with an active band of cat fanciers has one or more governing bodies which accept cats for registration and promote the running of licensed cat shows.

Each registering body has its own rules and guidelines for breeding, registration and showing cats, and often publishes information on all aspects of cat care, breeding and exhibiting. In North America, cat lovers have a wide choice of cat organizations from which to choose.

The best way to enter the world of showing is to start by reading one of the specialist cat magazines available from large newsagents. Shows are listed, and a day or two watching the proceedings can be invaluable. Most exhibitors are more than delighted to talk about their cats, and about show procedures. All shows have information desks with helpful assistants, and once you become a member of an association you have access to a vast wealth of data. Each association has its own rules and methods of show organization, but in one aspect they are all identical – the cat's welfare is the first priority at all times.

Show procedures vary, but the end result is the same. Cats are assessed by qualified judges who relate each cat's qualities to an official standard of points for its breed or variety, and then rank each cat in a class in order of merit. Various bodies have their own

At GCCF shows, cats are individually judged at their show pens after the exhibitors have been asked to vacate the main body of the show hall.

nomenclature for top award-winning cats – Champion, Supreme Champion, and so on. Even non-pedigree domestic cats may be shown, and have a special section at most shows. As they cannot be assessed against any breed standard, they are judged on temperament, condition, and overall aesthetic appeal.

FELINE ASSOCIATIONS AND GOVERNING BODIES

Countries where pedigree cats are bred and exhibited have one or more associations or governing bodies which keep a register of cats and their lineage, and set down rules and regulations for cat shows. Britain has the Governing Council of the Cat Fancy (GCCF) and The Cat Association of Britain, which is the British member of FIFe. American cat fanciers have nine associations, the largest being the Cat Fancier's Association (CFA) which also has affiliated clubs in Canada and Japan.

In Europe, Australasia and South Africa, there are national bodies, and other associations, and generally, one in each country is a member of the Federation Internationale Feline (Fife) which is the largest and most powerful of the feline associations in the world. Fife has thousands of members, covering the entire world of cats and trains and licenses judges of high calibre throughout the world.

CANADA

- **CCA** The **Canadian Cat Association** is the only all-Canadian registry, with activities centred mainly in eastern Canada. It publishes a bi-lingual, quarterly newsletter in French and English.

UNITED STATES

- **ACA** America's oldest cat registry, having been active since 1899, the **American Cat Association** is a fairly small association which holds shows in the south-east and south-west of the United States.

- **ACC** Based in the south-west, the **American Cat Council** is a small association which has modified "English-style" shows in which exhibitors must vacate the show hall during judging.

- **CCFF** Although it is one of the smaller associations in the United States, the **Crown Cat Fanciers' Federation** has many shows each year in the north-east and south-eastern regions, and also in western Canada.

- **CFA** The **Cat Fanciers' Association** is America's largest association, incorporated and run by a board of directors. It produces an impressive annual yearbook full of articles, breeders' advertisements and beautiful colour photographs. There is a CFA show somewhere in the United States almost every weekend of the year.

- **CFF** With activities centred in the north-east region of the United States, the **Cat Fanciers' Federation** is a registering body of medium size.

- **UCF** A medium-sized association, the **United Cat Federation** is centred in the south-west of the United States.

UNITED KINGDOM

- **CA** Formed on 20 February 1983 as an alternative body to the GCCF, the **Cat Association of Britain** keeps a register of all pedigree, half-pedigree and non-pedigree cats belonging to its members, and holds cat shows all over Britain. Formerly run as an independent association, CA became a member of FIFe (below) in 1991.

- **GCCF** Formed on 8 March 1910, the **Governing Council of the Cat Fancy** is run by an executive committee, and its sixty or so affiliated clubs send delegates to represent their members at council meetings. Until 1983, GCCF was the sole body responsible for the registration of cats and licensing of cat shows in Britain.

WORLDWIDE

- **ACFA** An international association and run very democratically, the **American Cat Fanciers' Association** has affiliated clubs in the United States, Canada and Japan, and produces a monthly news bulletin for members.

- **FIFe** Most European countries have at least two bodies for the registration of cats, and licensing of shows. One body is almost certain to be affiliated to the **Federation Internationale Feline**, an enormous and well-organized incorporated and chartered society which also has affiliates in countries beyond Europe. Fully established in 1949, FIFe is today the largest cat body in the world uniting more than 150,000 breeders and exhibitors united in the love of the world of show cats.

- **TICA The International Cat Association** produces a bi-monthly newsletter and a yearbook. It has a modern approach to showing and has shows throughout the United States and affiliates in Canada and Japan.

CAT CARE

The domestic cat is quite easy to care for within the confines of the home. It must be provided with some basic equipment, such as feeding and drinking bowls, a comfortable bed, a litter tray and scratching post.

KEEPING YOUR CAT healthy is mainly a matter of commonsense and proper husbandry. In the first place, the cat needs to have been properly reared as a kitten, and should be regularly vaccinated against the most dangerous feline diseases such as panleukopaenia, or infectious enteritis, rhinotracheitis and calicivirus, often called cat 'flu, and feline leukaemia virus. All cats should be fed a well-balanced diet, and receive regular courses of anthelmintics to ensure that they are free from internal parasites. External parasites such as fleas should be controlled by the application of pest powder or sprays when necessary, or by dosing with a product designed to curtail the fleas' breeding cycle. The cat's toilet tray must be maintained in spotless condition at all times as must its food and water bowls. Given such care, and lots of love and attention, the cat should always remain in good health.

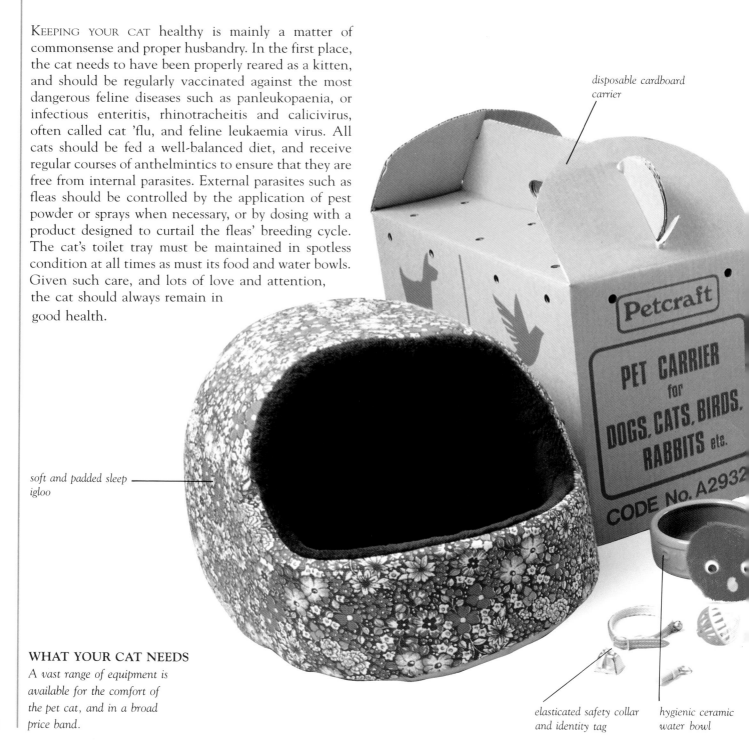

disposable cardboard carrier

soft and padded sleep igloo

WHAT YOUR CAT NEEDS
A vast range of equipment is available for the comfort of the pet cat, and in a broad price band.

elasticated safety collar and identity tag

hygienic ceramic water bowl

LIFESPAN OF A CAT

The length of a cat's life varies enormously. Those living wild as strays may only survive for two years or so, while a cherished pet may live well into its teens, an old age pensioner in human terms.

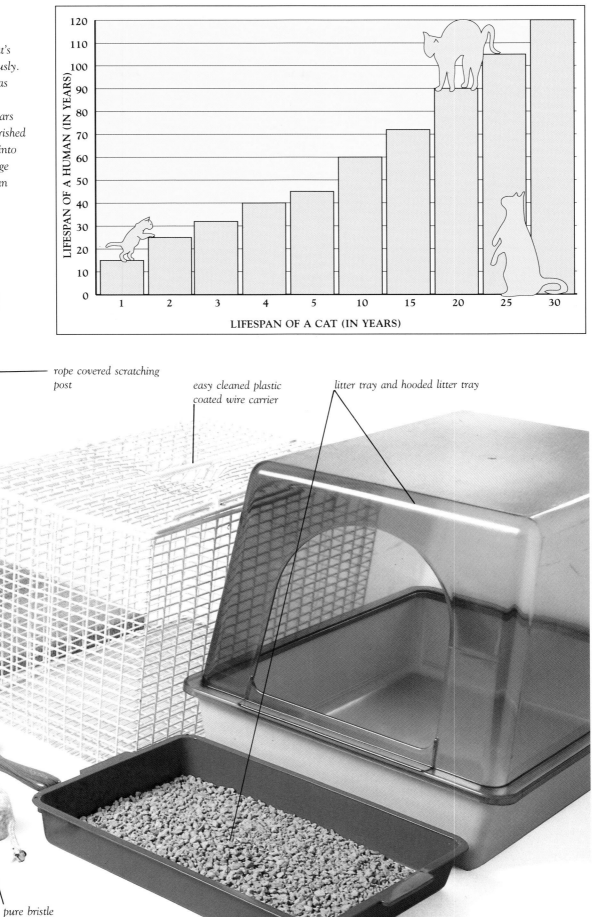

LIFESPAN OF A CAT (IN YEARS)

rope covered scratching post

easy cleaned plastic coated wire carrier

litter tray and hooded litter tray

non-toxic, unbreakable toys

pure bristle grooming brush

GROOMING

Most cats benefit from grooming and longhaired breeds such as the Persian must be groomed daily to keep the full coat in good condition and to prevent the soft undercoat from matting. Start grooming routines when the cat is very young. Weaning kittens should be gently brushed and handled all over so that they never resent being groomed in later life. It is essential to make the grooming routine a pleasant one, ensuring that the cat never becomes resentful, particularly when its tender parts, such as the inside of the thighs, are being combed through. Different coat types need different grooming tools, and these should be reserved for the cat's own use. A wide variety of equipment is available, and items of better quality are less likely to damage the cat's coat or skin.

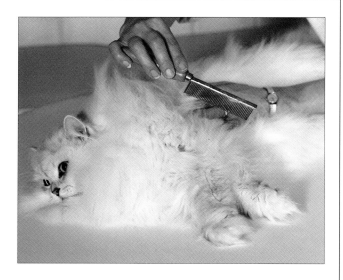

 1    2   3   4   5

GROOMING A LONGHAIRED CAT

1 Apply grooming powder to the coat.
2 Rub powder into the coat starting from the tail and working towards the head.
3 Brush the coat thoroughly, removing the powder and lifting the coat away from the skin.

4 Use a wide-toothed comb from tail to head to ensure there are no tangles; pay particular attention to the underparts.
5 Clean the eyes, nostrils and inside the ear flaps with a series of moist swabs or small brush.

 1   2    3    4   

GROOMING A SHORTHAIRED CAT

1 Remove dust, loose hairs and any debris or parasites, using a metal fine-toothed comb from head to tail.
2 A rubber brush may be used for cats with thick short coats.

3 A soft bristle brush is best for cats with very fine short coats.
4 Buff the coat with a special grooming mitt, a piece of silk or velvet, or a chamois leather.

wire and bristle brush — *wide- and fine-toothed comb*

slicker brush — *toothbrush*

HEALTH

Though basically strong, healthy and built for survival, the cat is susceptible to a range of diseases. Luckily the most deadly of these may be guarded against by means of effective vaccines, generally given from kittenhood.

GIVING A CAT the correct care is basically a question of common sense. A cat must be given a clean, warm environment in which to live, the correct amount of suitable, nourishing food, constant access to fresh, clean drinking water and facilities for play and exercise.

A cat should have a bed of its own, in a quiet, secluded place, and it should be left in peace to sleep for undisturbed periods during the day. Meals should be fed regularly, on clean dishes, and any food not eaten within a reasonable time, should be removed and disposed of. Cats will not eat stale food. Fresh water should be provided every day, and left down for the cat to drink whenever it wishes.

Even if the cat has access to the garden, it should be provided with a toilet tray and fresh litter at all times.

WATCHING OUT FOR PROBLEMS

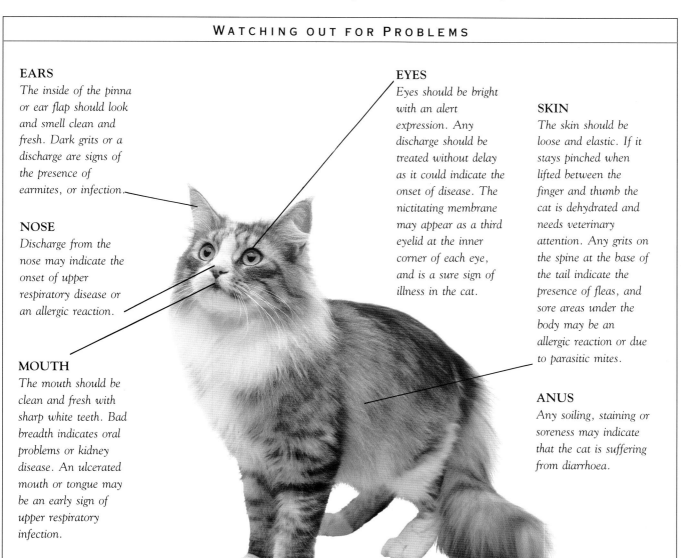

EARS
The inside of the pinna or ear flap should look and smell clean and fresh. Dark grits or a discharge are signs of the presence of earmites, or infection.

NOSE
Discharge from the nose may indicate the onset of upper respiratory disease or an allergic reaction.

MOUTH
The mouth should be clean and fresh with sharp white teeth. Bad breadth indicates oral problems or kidney disease. An ulcerated mouth or tongue may be an early sign of upper respiratory infection.

EYES
Eyes should be bright with an alert expression. Any discharge should be treated without delay as it could indicate the onset of disease. The nictitating membrane may appear as a third eyelid at the inner corner of each eye, and is a sure sign of illness in the cat.

SKIN
The skin should be loose and elastic. If it stays pinched when lifted between the finger and thumb the cat is dehydrated and needs veterinary attention. Any grits on the spine at the base of the tail indicate the presence of fleas, and sore areas under the body may be an allergic reaction or due to parasitic mites.

ANUS
Any soiling, staining or soreness may indicate that the cat is suffering from diarrhoea.

SIGNS OF ILL HEALTH

Pain Often the first sign of disease. Locating the site of pain may need diagnosis. Pain from skin, muscle or bone damage is easier to detect than that from the deeper structures.

Fever A rise in body temperature generally indicates infection, but may be caused by heatstroke. A cat's normal temperature at rest is 36.6°C (101.5°F) but 39.2°C (102.5°F) is not uncommon.

Change in Behaviour Often the first sign of a serious illness, a change in the personality or behaviour of a cat should be monitored.

Loss of Balance or Body Control Lameness is detected fairly easily, denoting an injury to a muscle, tendon or bone; other signs of painful movement may be more difficult to detect – the cat may just stop jumping up to or down from a chair.

Breathing Laboured breathing, wheezing, coughing or sneezing must not be ignored. Note changes in the cat's voice. Any of these symptoms could denote the onset of respiratory disease.

Defecation and Urination Any changes such as the presence of blood in the faeces or urine must be taken seriously. A cat straining on its litter tray without producing any results must see a veterinarian without delay.

Eating and Drinking A change in appetite may be transitory, but should not be disregarded. Constant drinking, vomiting, or dribbling are all symptoms of feline diseases. Take note of the cat's behaviour pattern and if it persists, seek veterinary advice. It may point to a dental problem or indicate the onset of illness.

Skin and Fur Most cats normally shed their coats twice a year, but any severe hair loss, perhaps leaving bald patches, should be reported to your veterinarian. If the cat scratches at its neck it may have a parasitic infestation of fleas, ticks or mites, which need to be treated. Ear mites infest the inside of the ear and must not be neglected. Ringworm, a fungal infection, often produces circular lesions, and is transmissable to humans. Cats are also susceptible to various allergies from such things as household disinfectants and flea bites. A skin condition should never be neglected.

CALL THE VET IMMEDIATELY IF THE CAT IS:
- Shocked or haemorrhaging
- Thought to have ingested a poisonous substance
- Partially or completely unconscious
- Falling about, with uncoordinated movements, or appears partly or completely paralysed
- Obviously injured
- Vomiting frequently or has constant diarrhoea

It is more hygienic for the cat's wastes to be disposed of than for it to soil the garden. Various types of litter boxes are available, some with hooded lids, and the wide range of cat litter includes some made from fresh smelling wood chips, as well as the original products made from Fuller's earth. The litter tray should be washed and dried when the litter is changed, and sterilized with diluted household bleach or a safe disinfectant recommended by the veterinary surgeon.

Cats need to strop their claws from time to time, to keep them in good condition and to remove any loose scale. Various types of scratching posts are available, from simple cardboard strips to ingenious constructions of shelves and posts covered with rope or carpet. A cat prefers to strop its claws on an upright post rather than one laid flat on the floor.

Although most cats which are correctly cared for and properly fed, housed and vaccinated remain fit and well, it is important to be able to recognize the first signs of infection or trauma. Any change in a cat's normal behaviour patterns should be treated with suspicion, for while this may be caused by something as simple as a change in the weather, it could also point to the first stages of a specific illness. All signs and symptoms should be carefully noted, and if necessary, veterinary advice should be sought. It is important to avoid any delay in seeking advice in the event of one of the more serious feline diseases, when early treatment is most effective.

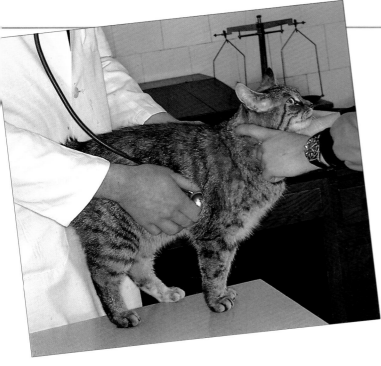

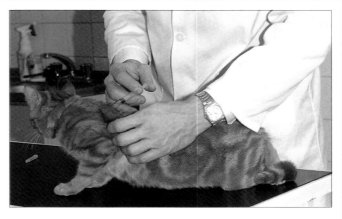

The veterinarian should be a cat's best friend, diagnosing and treating any problems and providing preventative care in the form of feline vaccinations and constructive advice.

FELINE DISORDERS

	Gynnecological disorder FP	Pregnancy	Queen in distress: 'calling'	Trauma: fracture, dislocation etc	Ear infection	Conjunctivitis	Dental problems	Incorrect diet	Fleas and other external parasites	Intestinal worms	Heat stroke	Kidney disease	Hairball	Gastroenteritis	Uroliathiasis FUS	Feline infectious peritonitis FIP	Feline leukaemia virus FeLV	Feline infectious anaemia FIA	Respiratory virus infection – cat 'flu, FOV, FVR etc	Feline infectious enteritis FIE
Vomiting	?	?		?				*		?		×	*	*	×	?	?	?		×
Diarrhoea		?						*		?			?	*		?	*	?		×
Apparent constipation				?				×					?	?	*					?
Excessive thirst	×											*	?	?		?		?		?
Loss of appetite	×	×	×	×		?		*	×			?	×	×	×	×	×	×	?	*
Abnormal urination	?			?								*			*					
Dehydration	?											×				?	×		×	*
Coughing/sneezing								?			?		?	?		?			*	
Breathing problems		?		×				?			?	*				×	×	?	?	
Fever	?					?						*			?		×		?	×	?
Lowered temperature	×	?		?									?	?	?	×	?	?	?	*
Pale lips/gums	?			×					?			×				?	?	*		×
Abdominal swelling	×	*		?				?			×		?			×	*	?		
Shaking head				?	*		?		?											
Scratching head/neck				?	×		×	?	*											
Apparent pain	?		*	*	×		×						?	?	×	?				×
Lameness			*				?					?								
Salivation				?			*	×				*		×	?					?
Localized discharge	*		×	*	*	*	?												*	
Noticeable weight loss	?							?		?		*				*	*	?	?	?

SYMPTOMS
* MAJOR
× COMMON
? POSSIBLE

Feeding Your Cat

An adult cat requires about 50 calories per 450 grams (one pound) of its body weight each day. Active cats may need more calories and sedentary cats may need less. Entire cats which are breeding require more calories than neutered cats, and a queen that is lactating, and feeding four or more kittens, may need as much as 150 calories for each 450 grams of her body weight.

Adult cats generally fare better when given two regular daily meals, and as they grow old, they are best fed three or four small meals daily. Old cats with digestive problems often need special diets as advised by a veterinary surgeon.

A cat's general appearance is the best guide to whether or not its diet is suitable for its size and lifestyle. The signs of a poor diet include dull eyes, a warm, dry nose, bad breath, a dry scurfy coat, flaking claws and diarrhoea or offensively smelling stools.

There are a number of excellent ways of feeding cats. Canned food is comparatively expensive, but it is formulated to be highly acceptable to cats, and a check on the label will ensure that the quality and nutritional components are adequate.

Semi-moist diets are very convenient to store and

Though adult cats do not need to drink milk, most cats, except those unable to digest it like many Orientals, really enjoy this special treat.

WHAT TO FEED

This chart shows you at a glance how many feeds to give your cat on a daily basis.

CAT DETAILS		FOOD REQUIREMENTS	
AGE of CAT	WEIGHT OF CAT IN GRAMS	FEEDS	GRAMS PER FEED
KITTEN			
Newborn	110	10	30
5 weeks	450	6	85
10 weeks	900	5	140
20 weeks	2000	4	170
30 weeks	3000	3	200
ADULT			
Male/Female	3000–4500	1–2	170–240
Pregnant	3500	2–3	240
Lactating	2500	4	400
Neuter	4000–4500	1–2	170–220

NUTRITIONAL REQUIREMENTS

Proteins are essential substances for growth and repair; they are found in muscle meat, fish, cheese, eggs and milk. At least 35–40 per cent of the entire cat's diet should consist of protein; neutered cats need 25 per cent. Cats which cannot digest milk or milk products may be able to accept yogurt as an alternative.

Carbohydrates are not essential in the cat's diet, and if fed, should consist of cooked grains and vegetable fibre.

Fats provide concentrated forms of energy, and the cat is capable of digesting a diet containing 25 to 30 per cent fat. Fats contain the fatty acids necessary for a healthy skin and coat, and fat-soluble vitamins A, D, E and K. Fats may be added to the cat's diet in the form of butter, margarine, bacon fat or pure vegetable oils.

Vitamins and minerals are found in a wide range of foods. Cats need a lot of Vitamin A, but too much can be dangerous. If using a proprietary brand of cat food, check the label for the Vitamin

A level. If feeding fresh meat, add 28 grams (one ounce) of lightly cooked liver on one or two days each week.

Vitamin B is important to cats, and you should check the labels of proprietary brands of food to ensure that the B group content is adequate.

Vitamin C is generally considered to be unnecessary in the feline diet, though it may help recovery after illness. Most cats accept Vitamin C in the form of an orange-flavoured syrup sold for human babies.

Vitamin D is essential, but cats need a very small amount compared to the requirements of dogs and humans, and most of this need is obtained from sunlight. It is rarely necessary to supplement the diet with additional vitamins and minerals provided an adequate diet is fed.

serve, and are highly acceptable to most cats. However, they contain humectants and preservatives which can cause digestive disturbances in some cats. Owners often get round this problem by feeding one meal of canned food and one of semi-moist food each day.

Dry diets are very popular, particularly for pet cats. They are inexpensive, and very easy to store and serve. It is important to ensure that cats fed solely on dry diets are seen to drink plenty of water every day. Some brands may be slightly deficient in fat, so extra fat may be given if necessary.

ENERGY REQUIREMENTS

An adult cat needs 200 to 300 kcal per day, depending on its size and amount of exercise. Kittens have a higher demand in relation to their body weight due to their rapid growth rate. Neutered cats need less energy in relation to their body weight as they are not reproducing and generally lead rather sedentary lives.

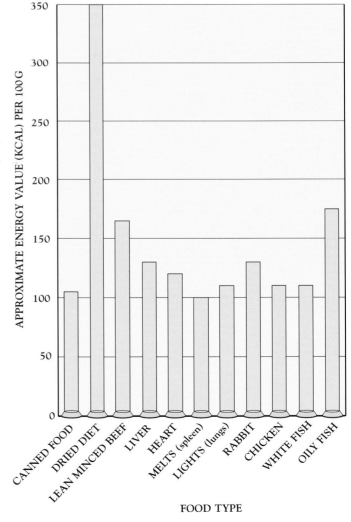

FOOD TYPE

KEEPING YOUR CAT HEALTHY

A regular regime of care for your cat will help to ensure it stays in good condition and be less likely to fall ill.

DAILY
- Observe the cat's general appearance and behaviour; any dramatic change may indicate the need for immediate veterinary attention.
- Feed a well-balanced diet of good quality food.
- Provide fresh water in a clean container.
- Dispose of soiled litter; clean toilet tray; check cat's stools (and urine if possible) for any sign of abnormality.
- Groom the cat according to its requirements in respect of coat type and hair length.
- In free-ranging cats, check the coat for the staining which could indicate diarrhoea and for foreign bodies such as grass seeds or parasites such as ticks; check the feet for sore or cracked pads and for foreign bodies such as splinters or thorns; check all over the head, body, underparts and legs for signs of fighting – bites and scratches can lead to abcesses if not treated with an antiseptic wash.

WEEKLY
- Examine ears and coat for parasites. If present check with the veterinary surgeon for appropriate treatment.
- Check mouth and throat; clean teeth if necessary.

MONTHLY
- Check the cat all over from head to tail with your fingertips, feeling for any lumps, bumps, lesions or foreign bodies. Any worrying anomalies should be discussed with the veterinary surgeon.

SIX-MONTHLY
- Check the cat's records to see if blood tests or vaccinations are due and mark the dates in your diary: free-ranging cats should have a sample of faeces analyzed for the presence of parasitic worms, and treatment administered where appropriate.

YEARLY
- Have a complete veterinary check carried out. This can be arranged in conjunction with an annual vaccination booster programme.

58 Persian
78 Colourpoint

LONGHAIRED BREEDS

LONGHAIR

ALTHOUGH THEY HAVE been officially classified by the GCCF in Britain as Longhairs, these cats are popularly referred to as Persians, and are officially classified as such in the United States.

The typical Persian is a substantial, strong cat, with a full and flowing coat of long, dense fur concealing a sturdy body and thick legs. The head is large and round with tiny ears and large, round eyes. The fur around the neck is extra long, forming the typical frill or ruff, and the long hair on the tail makes it resemble a fox's tail or brush.

Persian cats first arrived in Europe in the sixteenth century and became more popular than the imported Angoras. Charles H. Ross reported, in a book published in 1868: "The Persian is a variety with hair very long and silky; perhaps more so than that of the Angora; it is however differently coloured, being of a fine uniform grey on the upper part with the texture of the fur as soft as silk and the lustre glossy; the colour fades off on the lower parts of the sides and fades, or nearly does so, on the belly." This preceded the first cat shows.

Over the years, selective breeding standardized the type of the Persian breed so that all the varieties would closely conform to one basic standard. However, various cat associations designated different points awards for

BREAKDOWN OF 100 SHOW POINTS

NB Annotated points (right) are those set in the UK; those listed below are for the USA.

HEAD: 30 POINTS
Including size and shape of eyes, ear shape and set.

TYPE: 20 POINTS
Including shape, size, bone and length of tail.

COAT: 10 POINTS

BALANCE: 5 POINTS

REFINEMENT: 5 POINTS

COLOUR: 20 POINTS

**EYE COLOUR:
10 POINTS**

HEAD: 25 POINTS

Including general shape of head, forehead; set of eyes; shape and set of ears; nose length, width and stop; width of cheeks and muzzle; chin.

EYES: 15 POINTS

BODY: 20 POINTS

Including shape, size and bone structure, tail and length of tail, height, thickness of legs and paws.

COAT: 40 POINTS

Texture, colour and pattern.

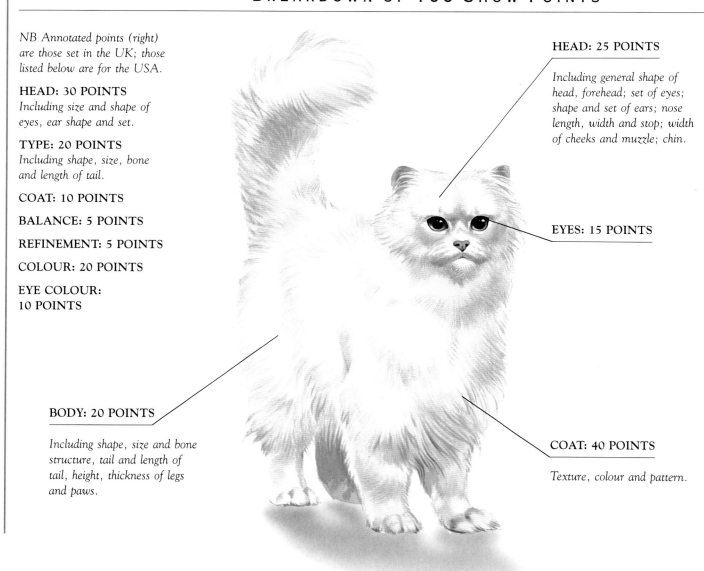

different features as incentives for breeders to work towards refinement of those features.

Character and Care

Persian cats are generally placid and gentle by nature, and as kittens are playful and mischievous. They make very affectionate and loving pets, and are generally quiet and restful to have in the home.

The long, dense coat must be brushed and combed through daily to prevent tangles and matting, and kittens must be accustomed to being groomed all over, including their underparts, from a very early age. In adults, particular attention must be paid to the frill or ruff, under the belly, and the flowing hair of the tail.

PENALTIES

The Persian is penalized for having a kinked or abnormal tail; a locket or button; any apparent weakness in the hindquarters; any apparent deformity of the spine; asymmetrical appearance of the head, and incorrect eye colour.

KEY CHARACTERISTICS

- **CATEGORY** Longhair.

- **OVERALL BUILD** Medium to large, with massive shoulders and back, muscular.

- **COAT** Long and dense, standing off from the body, fine and silky texture, with a full frill (ruff) over shoulders and chest.

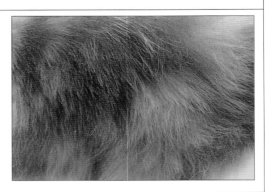

- **HEAD** Round and massive with a broad skull, round forehead, full cheeks and powerful jaws.

- **NOSE** Short and broad with a definite stop.

- **CHIN** Strong and well-developed.

- **EYES** Large, round and full, set wide apart.

- **EARS** Small, round-tipped, set wide apart and rather low on the head.

- **BODY** Of cobby type, low on the legs, with a broad chest, massive shoulders and well-muscled back.

- **LEGS** Short, thick and strong.

- **PAWS** Large, round and firm. Toe tufts preferred.

- **TAIL** Short, but in proportion to the length of the body, carried without a curve.

- **COLOURS** White with blue, orange or copper, odd eyes; black, red, cream, blue, chocolate, lilac; smoke: black, blue, red, tortie, blue-cream; cameo: shell, shaded, shell tortoiseshell, shaded tortoiseshell; bi-colour: black, blue, red, cream and Van patterns; tabby (Classic and Mackeral patterns): silver, brown, red (*UK and US*), blue, cream, cameo, silver patched, brown patched, blue patched (*US only*).

WHITE

ODD-EYED WHITE

In this variety of Persian one eye should be orange or copper, and the other deep blue, and both eyes should be of equal colour intensity.

THIS VARIETY HAS been popular for more than a hundred years, and is the result of matings between the earliest imported Angora and Persian cats. The original white longhairs had blue eyes. Because of a genetic anomaly connected to blue eye colour in cats, many of them were deaf. Eventually, efforts were made to improve the overall type and conformation of the whites, and cross-matings were made with Blue Persian and Black Persian show winners. Not only did the resulting offspring have more solid bone and better body and head type, some cats had orange or copper eye colour, and in some cases, were odd-eyed, having one blue eye and one of orange or copper. An added bonus was that these cats had

good hearing, although some of the odd-eyed whites were found to be deaf in the ear adjacent to the blue eye. Today's White Persians are judged as three separate varieties, according to eye colour, in Britain.

Special care is needed in grooming these white varieties as they can easily become soiled with yellow staining around the eyes, nostrils, lips and under the tail. If neglected the stains may prove impossible to remove, spoiling the beauty of the coat. Fanciers generally use a white grooming powder to clean and enhance their pets' white coats, and this helps to prevent staining.

Colouring

The coat should be pure glistening white, without markings or shadings of any kind. Nose leather and paw pads are pink. In the blue-eyed White eye colour is deep blue. In the copper-eyed (USA) or orange-eyed (UK) White eye colour is brilliant copper (USA) or orange or copper (UK). The odd-eyed White has one eye of deep blue, the other of orange or copper.

BLUE-EYED WHITE

These cats are sometimes found to be deaf, due to a genetic factor.

ORANGE-EYED WHITE

Cats with this orange or copper eye colour are not affected by problems with their hearing, and often appear more responsive than their blue-eyed cousins.

UK STANDARDS

COLOUR: 25 POINTS

COAT: 40 POINTS

BODY: 20 POINTS

HEAD: 25 POINTS

EYES: 15 POINTS

Europe and USA standard as for all Persians (see page 59).

BLACK

ONE OF THE oldest of the pedigree breeds, the Black Persian is one of the most difficult to produce in top show condition. It is a massive, handsome cat, and the glossy, raven-black coat is complemented by the large glowing eyes. The black hair is prone to developing rusty tinges, thought to be caused by strong sunlight or damp conditions, and periods of moulting cause brownish bars to appear in the flowing coat. Young black kittens are often quite disappointing, with lots of shading in the undercoat and rustiness in the top coat, but these defects usually disappear with maturity.

Colouring

The coat should be dense coal black from roots to tips of hair, free from any tinge or markings or shadings of any kind, and with no white hair. The nose leather is black, and the paw pads black or brown. Eye colour is brilliant copper (*USA*) or copper or deep orange (*UK*), with no green rim.

UK STANDARDS

COAT: 40 POINTS

BODY: 20 POINTS

HEAD: 25 POINTS

EYES: 15 POINTS

Europe and USA standard as for all Persians (see page 59).

BLACK PERSIAN

The eyes of the Black Persian should be brilliant copper or deep orange, setting off the jet-black coat to perfection.

RED

RED PERSIAN
Comparatively rare at cat shows, a good Red Persian has a rich red coat, free from ghost tabby markings.

ALTHOUGH THIS HAS been a favourite show breed for over a hundred years, in the days of the first cat shows there was some confusion in contemporary writings as to the true description of the variety's colour. Until 1894, shows at London's Crystal Palace offered classes for Brown or Red Tabby Persians, but in 1895 a class for Orange and Cream was added. The Orange, Cream, Fawn and Tortoiseshell Society revised the standard for the Orange Persian, requiring "the colour to be as bright as possible, and either self or markings to be as distinct as can be got". Judges obviously selected their winners irrespective of markings. Over the years breeders selected for either self-coloured or tabby in the reds and by 1912 they had separate classes, still being described as Orange Self or Orange Tabby. The deeper colour was selected, and although the Second World War

decimated the variety's numbers, the past fifty years have seen wonderful improvements in Red Persians in the world's show rings.

Colouring
The coat should be deep, rich, clear, brilliant red without markings or shadings or ticking. Lips and chin are the same colour as the coat. Nose leather and paw pads are brick red and eye colour is brilliant copper (*USA*) or deep copper (*UK*).

CREAM

IN THE EARLY DAYS, cream cats were often called "fawns" and were often discarded by keen exhibitors in favour of cats with stronger coat colours. Some of the first Angoras were probably cream, for Charles H. Ross, writing in 1868, describes the Angora as "a very beautiful variety, with silvery hair of fine silken texture . . . some are yellowish, and others olive, approaching the colour of a lion . . ."

In 1903, Frances Simpson wrote that creams were becoming fashionable, but the first cats of this variety had been considered "freaks or flukes" and were given away. Cream cats were eventually imported into the United States from Britain and soon established themselves as successful show winners. Today's exhibition Cream Persian is a refined and sophisticated breed, exemplifying all the best features of the typical Longhair.

Colouring

The requirements for coat colour differ between the United States, the United Kingdom and Europe in general. The CFA standard requires one level shade of buff cream, sound to the roots, without markings, and with lighter shades preferred. Britain's GCCF calls for pure and sound pale to medium colour, without shadings or markings. The FIFe standard requires pale, pure, pastel cream with no warm tone or any lighter shadings or markings, the colour to be sound and even from roots to tips. Nose leather and paw pads are pink; eye colour is brilliant copper (USA) deep copper (UK).

CREAM PERSIAN

This Cream Persian is of very good type and has the desired pale cream coat colour, free from lighter shading, and ghost marks.

UK STANDARDS

COAT 40 POINTS

BODY: 20 POINTS

HEAD: 25 POINTS

EYES: 15 POINTS

Europe and USA standard as for all Persians (see page 59).

BLUE

THE BLUE COLOUR in cats is caused by the action of the dilution factor on black, and some of the earliest Persian imports had this attractive coat colour. In the first cat shows lots of blue cats were exhibited, but they did not closely resemble the cats seen in the show rings today. By the turn of the century early show faults such as white lockets and tabby markings had been largely eliminated, and in 1901 the Blue Persian Society was founded to promote the breeding and exhibiting of cats of this variety. Members of society, including Queen Victoria, owned Blue Persian cats, and this added to their general status and popularity, which remains to this day.

Colouring

The blue coat should be of one level tone from nose to tail tip, and sound from roots to tips of hair. Any shade of blue is allowed, but in the USA the lighter shades are preferred. The coat must be free from all markings, shadings or white hairs. The nose leather and paw pads are blue; the eye colour is brilliant copper (*USA*) deep orange or copper without any trace of green (*UK*).

UK STANDARDS

COAT: 40 POINTS

HEAD: 25 POINTS

EYES: 15 POINTS

BODY: 20 POINTS

Europe and USA standard as for all Persians (see page 59).

BLUE PERSIAN

Most popular of all the Persian varieties is the Blue. Any shade of blue coat colour is allowed, but the lighter shades are preferred for showing.

BLUE-CREAM

BLUE-CREAM PERSIAN

In American shows, this variety is required to have cream patches on its blue coat, while the GCCF expects an intermingled coat.

UK STANDARDS

COLOUR:
30 POINTS

COAT and CONDITION:
20 POINTS

BODY: 15 POINTS

HEAD: 20 POINTS

EYES: 15 POINTS

Europe and USA standard as for all Persians (see page 59).

CONSIDERED TO BE a fairly new variety, the Blue-cream Persian was not recognized in Britain until 1930, although reports of kittens with blue and cream markings appeared at the turn of the century. Blue-cream colouring is the dilute equivalent of tortoiseshell. Just as a tortoiseshell has patches of black and red, so the blue-cream cat has corresponding dilute patches of blue (from black) and cream (from red). Although early cat fanciers understood little of feline genetics, some, by careful observation, were able to deduce some of the results to be expected by cross-matings between cats of various colours. The biggest problem to beset the early cat breeders was that they did not recognize the fact that the "marked blue cats", or blue-creams, were all female, and that the colour was sex linked. Breeders waited hopefully for similar male kittens to be born so that like-to-like matings could take place, to produce a "true" breed.

Colouring

The requirements for coat colour and pattern differ between the United States, the United Kingdom, and Europe in general. In North America the coat is required to be blue with clearly defined patches of solid cream, well broken on both body and extremities. Britain's GCCF requires the coat to consist of pastel shades of blue and cream, softly intermingled. In Europe, FIFe refers to Blue-cream as Blue Tortie, and the coat requirement is for light blue-grey and pale cream, patched and/or mingled, both colours to be evenly distributed over the body and extremities. Although breeders and show judges like the Blue-cream to have a facial blaze, USA and UK standards do not stipulate this, though it is featured as desirable by FIFe.

The eye colour is brilliant copper (*USA*) or deep copper or orange (*UK*).

SMOKE

UK STANDARDS

**COLOUR:
40 POINTS**
*Body, mask, feet, frill,
ear tufts, underbody*

HEAD: 20 POINTS
Including ears

COAT: 10 POINTS
Texture and condition

BODY: 15 POINTS

EYES: 10 POINTS

TAIL: 5 POINTS

*Europe and USA
standard as for all
Persians (see page
59).*

FIRST GIVEN A breed class at a British cat show in 1893, a contemporary author wrote of the Smoke Persian, "The Smoke is a cat of great beauty, but unfortunately is very rare". Sadly this remains as true today, though there was a time in the early 1900s when the variety enjoyed more popularity. One of the early successful breeders and exhibitors was Mrs H.V. James, who wrote about her beloved breed in 1903 and later supplied information for a cat book published in 1948, showing clearly her dedication to Smoke Persians. Mrs James bought a Blue Persian kitten which died, and the replacement she received from the breeder proved most disappointing, developing into a cat of "a deep cinder colour", nothing like a Blue Persian. Mrs James thought he looked rather smoky in colour and so entered him as a Smoke Persian in a show, where, to her surprise, he was placed first in all his classes.

The National Cat Club's stud book, published in Britain for the years 1900 to 1905, listed thirty Smoke Persians, but when the newly established GCCF published its first stud book in 1912, only eighteen such cats were

CREAM SMOKE PERSIAN

The cream variety is a dilute version of the Red Smoke. The cream colouring shades to white on the side and flanks.

BLACK SMOKE PERSIAN

The Smoke Persian's typical white undercoat shows only when the animal is in motion.

**BLUE SMOKE
PERSIAN**

*An excellent example
of this variety with a
full pale frill or ruff
and ear tufts as
required in the show
standard.*

listed. By the end of the Second World War, the Smoke Persian, like so many other minority breeds, had become practically non-existent.

Today's Smoke Persian is known as "the cat of contrasts" and though rare, is generally of excellent longhair type. The breed has always been popular in the United States, and in recent years has been bred in colours other than the original black.

BLACK SMOKE The undercoat is pure white, deeply tipped with black. In repose the cat appears black, but in motion the white undercoat is clearly apparent. The mask and points are black with a narrow band of white at the base of the hairs next to the skin, seen only when the hair is parted. The frill (ruff) and ear tufts are light silver. Nose leather and paw pads are black; eye colour is brilliant copper (*USA*) or orange or copper (*UK*).

BLUE SMOKE The white undercoat is deeply tipped with blue so that in repose the cat appears blue, but in motion the white undercoat is clearly apparent. Mask and points are blue with a narrow band of white next to the skin which is seen only when the hair is parted. The frill (ruff) and ear tufts are all white; the nose leather and paw pads are blue; the eyes are a brilliant copper or orange or copper.

RED SMOKE The undercoat is white, deeply tipped with red. In repose the cat appears red, but in motion the white undercoat is clearly apparent. Mask and points are red with a narrow band of white next to the skin, seen only when the hair is parted. The frill (ruff) and ear tufts are white, the eye rims, nose leather and paw pads rose; eye colour is brilliant copper.

**LILAC SMOKE
PERSIAN**

*Both Chocolate and
Lilac Smoke Persians
are accepted by several
feline bodies and apart
from colour, should
conform in every other
way to the basic
standard of points.*

SMOKE TORTOISESHELL The white under-coat is deeply tipped with black, with clearly defined, unbrindled patches of red and light red hairs in the pattern of a Tortoiseshell. In repose the cat appears to be tortoiseshell, but in motion the white undercoat is clearly apparent. The face and ears are tortoiseshell patterned with a narrow band of white next to the skin, seen only when the hair is parted. A blaze of red or light red tipping on the face is desirable. The frill (ruff) and ear tufts are white and the eyes a brilliant copper.

BLUE-CREAM SMOKE The white undercoat is deeply tipped with blue, with clearly defined, unbrindled patches of cream in the pattern of a Blue-cream. In repose the cat appears to be blue-cream, but in motion the white undercoat is clearly apparent. Face and ears are blue-cream patterned with a narrow band of white next to the skin, seen only when the hair is parted. A blaze of cream tipping on the face is desirable. The frill (ruff) and ear tufts are white, and the eye colour a brilliant copper.

CHOCOLATE SMOKE PERSIAN

Although only accepted as a provisional variety, this young cat has very good type and excellent eyes for both colour and shape.

LILAC TORTIE SMOKE

The dilute version of the Blue-Cream Smoke, just beginning to develop the desired pale frill or ruff.

RED SMOKE PERSIAN

An excellent example of a variety that is difficult to breed without tabby markings. This fine cat has a superb coat and has been perfectly groomed.

CAMEO

CAMEO PERSIAN

In kittens of the Cameo series, the full colour effect takes some time to develop. This youngster has very good type.

UK STANDARDS

COLOUR:
30 POINTS

COAT and CONDITION:
10 POINTS

BODY and LEGS:
15 POINTS

HEAD and EARS:
25 POINTS

EYES: 10 POINTS

TAIL: 10 POINTS

Europe and USA standard as for all Persians (see page 59).

FIRST BRED IN the United States in 1954, Cameo Persians were the result of matings between Smoke and Tortoiseshell cats of outstanding type. Cameo kittens are born almost white, and develop their subtle colour as they grow. There are three intensities of colouring within the Cameo group: Shell is very pale, Shaded somewhat darker, and Smoke is darker.

Cameo cats are naturally affectionate, and their unusual colouring soon gained popularity for the new varieties in countries outside the United States.

SHELL CAMEO (RED CHINCHILLA) The white undercoat must be sufficiently tipped with red on the head, back, flanks and tail to give the characteristic sparkling appearance of the variety. The face and legs may be lightly shaded with tipping. The chin, ear tufts, stomach and chest are white. Eye rims, nose leather and paw pads are all rose, and the eye colour a brilliant copper.

SHADED CAMEO (RED SHADED) A white undercoat has a mantle of red tipping shading the face, the sides and the tail. The colour ranges from dark on the ridge to white on the chest, stomach, under the tail and on the chin. The legs are the same tone as the face. The general effect is much more red than the Shell Cameo. Eye rims are rose; eye colour is a brilliant copper.

RED SHELL The white undercoat, delicately tipped with black, has well-defined patches of red and light red tipped hairs, in the tortoiseshell pattern, on the head, back, flanks and tail. The face and legs may be slightly shaded with tipping. The chin, ear tufts, stomach and chest are white. A blaze of red or light red tipping on the face is desirable. The eyes are brilliant copper.

RED SHADED The white undercoat has a mantle of black tipping and clearly defined patches of red and light red tipped hairs in the tortoiseshell pattern. This covers the face, down the sides and the tail, the colour ranging from dark on the ridge to white on the chest, stomach, under the tail and on the chin. The general effect is much darker than the Shell Tortoiseshell. Eye colour is a brilliant copper.

BLUE-CREAM CAMEO

The softly intermingled blue and cream tipping of this variety may be of any intensity, overlaying the white undercoat.

BI-COLOUR

THE EARLIEST RECORDS of fancy cats give several examples of two-coloured cats. Mainly Shorthairs, they include several colours, each with white. At the first cat shows, black and white cats were known as Magpies, and were expected to have very precise and even markings. Such precise markings proved very difficult to achieve, and few breeders were prepared to persevere in order to produce the perfect Bi-colour. Eventually, new standards were formulated by cat associations around the world.

The Bi-colour may be of any solid colour with white: black and white, blue and white, red and white, cream and white. In the United States, the cats are required to have white legs and paws, white on the chest, the underbody, and the muzzle, and an inverted "V" of white on the face is desirable. White is also allowed under the tail and as a marking resembling a collar around the neck.

The British standard is less precise in the requirements for the distribution of colour and white. The patches of colour should be clear and evenly distributed, with not more than two-thirds of the coat being coloured, and not more than one half of the coat being white. The face must be patched with colour and white. Faults in the bi-colour include tabby markings, a long tail or incorrect eye colour.

UK STANDARDS

COLOUR:
30 POINTS

COAT and CONDITION: 10 POINTS

BODY and LEGS: 15 POINTS

HEAD and EARS: 25 POINTS

EYES: 10 POINTS

TAIL: 10 POINTS

Europe and USA standard as for all Persians (see page 59).

RED AND WHITE BI-COLOUR
Red and Cream Bi-coloured cats should be free from any shading in the coloured areas of their coats.

BLACK AND WHITE BI-COLOUR
This massive cat has very good markings, particularly the desired white "collar".

BLUE AND WHITE BI-COLOUR

The inverted "V" on the face of this fine Persian is one of the features required for exhibition of this variety in the USA.

CREAM AND WHITE BI-COLOUR

In the Bi-colour, the face is required to show both coloured and white areas.

PERSIAN VAN BI-COLOUR

THIS SUB-VARIETY may be shown in black and white, blue and white, red and white or cream and white. The colour distribution is quite different from that of the Persian Bi-colour. The Van Bi-colour is basically a white cat with the colour confined to the extremities – head, legs and tail. Only one or two small coloured patches on the body are allowed.

VAN BI-COLOUR

The distribution of colour is unusual; the coat is basically white, with coloured areas confined to the head, ears and tail.

UK STANDARDS

COAT: 40 POINTS

BODY: 20 POINTS

HEAD: 25 POINTS

EYES: 15 POINTS

Europe and USA standard as for all Persians (see page 59).

71

TABBY

Pedigree tabby cats have always caused controversy over their standards of points throughout the cat world. In the early days of the development of breeds there were arguments about pattern and clarity of markings, and even more disagreement about the correct eye colour. Tabby Persians are quite rare in the show rings of the world, possibly because it is difficult to reach the high standard demanded.

In Britain, the Tabby Persian is shown in three colour varieties – Silver, Brown and Red, whereas the American show rings exhibit a wider range of colours.

Coat Patterns

The Classic Tabby pattern, sometimes referred to as the "marbled" or "blotched", calls for precise dense markings, clearly defined and broad. The legs must be evenly barred, with bracelets extending as far as the body markings. The tail should be evenly ringed. Several unbroken necklaces ring the neck and upper chest, frown marks form a letter "M" on the forehead, and unbroken lines run back from the outer corner of each eye. Swirls on the cheeks and vertical lines over the back of the head extend to the shoulder markings, which are in the shape of a butterfly with both upper and lower wings distinctly outlined, and marked with dots inside the outline. Three parallel lines run down the spine from the butterfly to the tail, well separated by stripes of the coat's ground colour. A large, solid blotch on each side is encircled by one or more unbroken rings. There should be a double vertical row of "buttons" on the chest and stomach.

In the Mackerel Tabby pattern, dense and clearly defined narrow pencilling marks the coat. The legs are evenly barred, with narrow bracelets extending as far as the body markings. The tail is barred, and distinct chain-like necklaces encircle the neck. The head is barred, with a distinct "M" on the forehead. Unbroken lines run back from the eyes, and lines run back from the head to meet the shoulders. The spine lines form a narrow saddle, and pencillings run round the body.

SILVER TABBY A ground colour of pure pale silver includes the lips and chin; the markings are dense black. Nose leather is brick red, paw pads black and eye colour green or hazel.

UK STANDARDS

COAT: 40 POINTS

BODY: 20 POINTS

HEAD: 25 POINTS

EYES: 15 POINTS

Europe and USA standard as for all Persians (see page 59).

SILVER TABBY
The dense black markings of the longhaired Silver Tabby show up clearly on the pale silver base coat.

TORTIE TABBY
The Tortie Tabby Persian is a cat in which the tabby pattern in the main coat colour, is overlaid with shading of red, while still allowing both tabby and tortie areas to remain clearly visible.

BROWN TABBY
A very good example of a variety rarely seen on the show benches of today.

RED TABBY
A deep red coat with even deeper red markings is required by the show standards for the Red Tabby Persian.

RED TABBY The ground colour is red, including the lips and chin; the markings deep rich red. Nose leather is brick red, paw pads black or brown and eyes brilliant copper.

BROWN TABBY The ground colour is a brilliant coppery brown; the markings dense black. The lips and chin are the same colour as the rings round the eyes. The backs of the legs should be black from the paw to the heel. Nose leather is brick red, paw pads black or brown and the eyes copper or hazel (UK).

BLUE TABBY The ground colour of pale bluish ivory includes the lips and chin; the markings are very deep blue, affording good contrast with the ground colour. A warm fawn patina covers the whole of the cat. Nose leather is old rose, paw pads rose and eye colour copper.

CREAM TABBY The ground colour is a very pale cream, and includes the lips and chin. The markings of buff or cream are sufficiently darker than the ground colour to afford good contrast. Nose leather and paw pads are all pink; eye colour is brilliant copper.

CAMEO TABBY The ground colour is off white, including the lips and chin. The markings are red. Nose leather and paw pads are rose and eye colour is brilliant copper.

SILVER TORTIE TABBY A pale silver ground colour includes the lips and chin. Classic or mackerel markings of black and patches of red and/or light red are clearly defined on the body and extremities. A blaze of red or light red on the face is desirable. Eye colour is a brilliant copper or hazel.

BROWN TORTIE TABBY The ground colour is a brilliant coppery brown with the lips and chin the same shade as the rings round the eyes; with classic or mackerel markings of dense black and patches of red and/or light red clearly defined on both body and extremities. Eye colour is brilliant copper.

BLUE TORTIE TABBY A pale bluish ivory ground colour includes the lips and chin. Classic or mackerel markings of very deep blue afford good contrast with the ground colour. There are clearly defined patches of cream on the body and extremities and a warm fawn overtone or patina over the whole of the cat. A blaze of cream on the face is desirable. Eye colour is brilliant copper.

LILAC TABBY

In the dilute range of Tabby longhairs, the markings are less distinct.

BLUE TABBY

The Blue Tabby's strong blue markings are set on an unusual grey base coat with a slight fawn colour cast, called "blue biscuit".

CHOCOLATE TORTIE TABBY

Warm markings on a bronze agouti base coat give this cat its glowing coat pattern.

TORTOISESHELL

THE FIRST RECORDED tortoiseshell cats were short coated, but around the early 1900s long-coated tortoiseshells were seen at cat shows, and have always been popular as pets. Breeders are intrigued by the female-only variety, and enjoy the range of colours a tortoiseshell queen can produce, depending on the recessive colour genes she carries, and the colour and genotype of the male to which she is mated. A similar situation exists with tortoiseshell-and-white cats, once known as Chintz cats in Britain, and referred to as Calico cats in the United States. In the Dilute Calico, the effect of the dilute gene replaces the black colour with blue, and the red patches with cream, giving a blue, cream and white cat. A dilute tortoiseshell (without white) is a blue-cream, which has been described on page 65. As there are no males in these varieties (very occasionally a male is born but invariably proves to be sterile at maturity), solid-coloured cats are generally used for stud purposes.

TORTOISESHELL The body colour is black with unbrindled and clearly defined patches of red and light red on both the body and extremities. A blaze of red or light red on the face is desirable. The eye colour is brilliant copper.

TORTOISESHELL and WHITE (UK) The body colour is black, red and light red, or their dilutions, blue, cream and light cream, with the colours well distributed and interspersed with white. The eye colour is deep orange or copper.

CALICO (USA) The body colour is white with unbrindled patches of black and red; white is predominant on the underparts. The eye colour is brilliant copper.

DILUTE CALICO (USA) The body colour is white with unbrindled patches of blue and cream; white is predominant on the underparts. The eye colour is brilliant copper.

TORTOISESHELL
Popular since the pioneer days of cat breeding, the Tortoiseshell Persian always attracts public interest at shows by its striking coat of black patched with areas of red.

TORTOISESHELL AND WHITE
In America, this variety is known as a Calico Cat.

UK STANDARDS

Tortoiseshell, and Tortoiseshell-and-white

COAT: 50 POINTS

BODY: 15 POINTS

HEAD: 20 POINTS

EYES: 15 POINTS

Europe and USA standard as for all Persians (see page 59).

CHOCOLATE TORTIE
The black and red areas of the Tortie are replaced with warm chocolate and light red.

BLUE TORTIE AND WHITE
The patches of colour are required to be distinct, and free from scattered white hairs.

SILVER AND GOLDEN

PERHAPS THE MOST glamorous of the Persians, the Chinchilla has a characteristic sparkling, silvery appearance. It has a long history, being first recorded by John Jennings in 1893, who described it as "a peculiar but beautiful variety; the fur at the roots is silver and shades to the tips to a decided slate hue, giving it a most pleasing and attractive appearance". Exhibitors at London's first Crystal Palace cat shows described their cats variously as "Silver Grey", "Blue or Silver Striped", "Chinchilla Tabby", or "Silver Chinchilla".

The first Chinchilla cats were born by accident when silver tabbies were mated with cats of other colours. Early Chinchillas were much darker than those seen today, having heavier tipping, tabby markings on the face and heavy barring on the legs. As the breed developed the lighter cats came to be known as Chinchilla, and the darker ones, when successfully bred to a different standard, were designated the Shaded Silver. The question of eye colour proved difficult to resolve, the early specimens having a range of colour from yellow, to amber and bright green. Chinchilla cats were imported into the United States from Britain from the early 1900s, and soon became well-established and popular on both sides of the Atlantic.

In recent years American breeders have found it possible to add the chinchilla and shaded silver appearance to other colours, and Chinchilla Golden and Shaded Golden cats have begun to appear at shows.

CHINCHILLA SILVER The cat has a pure white undercoat, sufficiently tipped with black on the head, back, flanks and tail to give the characteristic sparkling silver appearance of this variety. The legs may be slightly shaded with tipping. The chin, ear tufts, chest and stomach are pure white, and the rims of the eyes, lips and nose are outlined with black. The nose leather is brick red; the paw pads are black; the eye colour is green or blue-green.

SHADED SILVER/PEWTER The cat has a white undercoat with a mantle of black tipping shading down the face, sides and tail, from dark

UK STANDARDS

Chinchilla Silver

COLOUR:
25 POINTS

HEAD and EARS:
20 POINTS

BODY and LEGS: 15
POINTS

EYES: 15 POINTS

COAT and
CONDITION:
15 POINTS

TAIL: 10 POINTS

Pewter Longhair

COLOUR:
30 POINTS

COAT and
CONDITION:
10 POINTS

HEAD and EARS:
25 POINTS

BODY and LEGS: 15
POINTS

EYES: 10 POINTS

TAIL: 10 POINTS

*Europe and USA
standards as for all
Persians (see page
59).*

CHINCHILLA
Often thought rather too dainty and fairylike to be a Persian breed, the Chinchilla is perhaps the most glamorous of all the longhaired varieties.

on the ridge to white on the chin, chest, stomach and under the tail. The legs are the same tone as the face and the general effect is darker than the Chinchilla. The rims of the eyes, lips and nose are outlined with black. The nose leather is brick red; the paw pads are black; the eye colour is green or blue-green. Note that the Pewter Longhair (UK) eye colour is orange or copper with black rims.

CHINCHILLA GOLDEN The cat has a rich, warm cream undercoat, sufficiently tipped with seal brown on the head, back, flanks and tail to give a golden appearance. The legs may be slightly shaded with tipping, and the rims of the eyes, lips and nose are outlined with seal brown. The nose leather is deep rose; the paw pads are seal brown; the eye colour is green or blue-green.

SHADED GOLDEN The cat has a rich, warm cream undercoat and a mantle of seal brown

tipping shading down the face, sides and tail, from dark on the ridge to cream on the chin, chest, stomach and under the tail. The legs are the same tone as the face and the general effect is darker than the Chinchilla. The rims of the eyes, lips and nose are outlined with seal brown. The nose leather is deep rose; the paw pads are seal brown; the eye colour is green or blue-green.

GOLDEN PERSIAN

Seal brown tipping on a base coat of golden apricot produces this unusual variety. As with the Chinchilla, this cat should have eyes of green or blue-green.

COLOURPOINT

THIS BREED IS a cat of true Persian type with the markings first known in Siamese cats, where the true coat colour is restricted to the cooler areas of the cat's body, known as the "points". These comprise the face, or mask, the ears, the legs and paws, and the tail. This colouring is produced by a recessive gene, often referred to as the Himalayan factor, hence the name used by American fanciers for Persian cats of this pattern.

The first crosses between Siamese and Persian cats were made in Sweden as long ago as 1922. Further experimental matings were made in the United States during the 1920s and 1930s, but it was not until the 1950s that breeders on both sides of the Atlantic, working with carefully planned breeding programmes, produced cats with the desired type and coat pattern. In 1955, Britain's GCCF issued a breed number and approved a standard of points for the Himalayan-patterned Persians, but designated them as Colourpoint Longhairs. In the United States recognition of the Himalayan was approved by the CFA in 1957, and by the 1960s all other American associations

had accepted the variety. The Himalayan, or Colourpoint Longhair, in all its colour sub-varieties, soon became well established as one of the most popular of all the longhaired cats in the world's show rings.

Character and Care

The character of the Colourpoint combines the best traits of the cats used in its creation – the Siamese and the Persian. It is generally a little livelier and more entertaining than its solid-coloured Persian cousins, but less vocal and boisterous than the typical Siamese. The precocious breeding tendencies of its Siamese ancestry have been passed on, with Colourpoint females coming into season and "calling" as early as eight months of age, though the males often do not reach maturity until they are 18 months old.

Regular grooming is essential to keep the long full coat in good condition, paying particular attention to the underparts, between the hind and fore legs, under the tail and around the neck, thoroughly brushing out the frill or ruff.

BREAKDOWN OF 100 SHOW POINTS

NB Annotated points (right) are those set in the UK; those listed below are for the USA.

HEAD: 30 POINTS

TYPE: 20 POINTS
Including shape, size, bone, length of tail

COAT: 10 POINTS

BODY COLOUR: 10 POINTS

POINTS COLOUR: 10 POINTS

EYE COLOUR: 10 POINTS

BALANCE: 5 POINTS

REFINEMENT: 5 POINTS

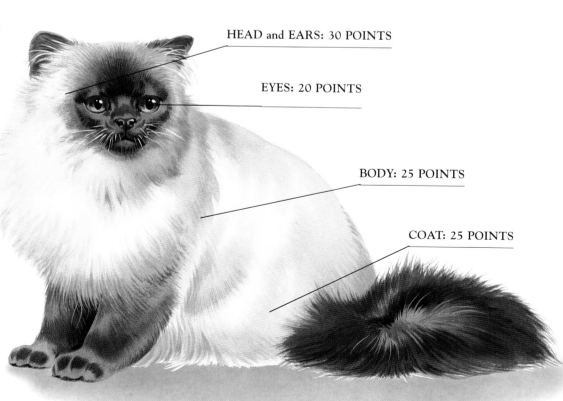

HEAD and EARS: 30 POINTS

EYES: 20 POINTS

BODY: 25 POINTS

COAT: 25 POINTS

KEY CHARACTERISTICS

- **CATEGORY** Longhair.

- **OVERALL BUILD** Medium or large, stocky.

- **COAT** Long and thick over the entire body, of fine texture and glossy; immense frill (ruff) around the neck and extending between the forelegs. Long tufts on the ears and between the toes.

- **HEAD** Round and massive, with very broad skull, round face, and set on a short, thick neck. Full cheeks.

- **NOSE** Short, broad nose with stop.

- **CHIN** Full, well-developed.

- **EYES** Large, full, round and set far apart.

- **EARS** Small, round-tipped, tilted slightly forward and set far apart on the head.

- **BODY** Of stocky type, low on the legs, with a deep chest and equally massive across the shoulders and rump.

- **LEGS** Short, thick and heavy; straight forelegs.

- **PAWS** Large, round and firm; toes not splayed.

- **TAIL** Short, but in proportion to body length; hair forms a "brush".

- **COLOURS** Seal point, blue point, chocolate point, lilac point, red point, cream point, seal tortie point, chocolate tortie point, blue-cream point, seal tabby point, blue tabby point, chocolate tabby point, lilac tabby point, lilac-cream point; red tabby point, cream tabby point, seal tortie tabby point, blue-cream tabby point, chocolate tortie tabby point, lilac-cream tabby point.

PENALTIES

The Himalayan is penalized for lack of pigmentation in paw pads and/or nose leather; a locket or button; any abnormality of the tail; a squint; white toes; eye colour other than blue; deformity of the skull and/or the mouth; any apparent weakness in the hindquarters.

SOLID POINTS

IN THE COLOURPOINTS with solid points colour, the standard requires that the colouring on all of the points should match in tone and be free from shadow markings or any patchiness.

SEAL POINT The body colour is an even, pale fawn or cream, warm in tone, which shades gradually into lighter colour on the chest and stomach. The points are deep seal brown. The nose leather and the paw pads are the same colour as the points; the eye colour is a deep, vivid blue.

BLUE POINT The body colour is bluish white,

cold in tone, which shades gradually to white on the chest and stomach. The points are blue. The nose leather and paw pads are slate grey; the eye colour is deep, vivid blue.

CHOCOLATE POINT The body colour is ivory, with no shading. The points are milk chocolate, warm in tone. The nose leather and paw pads are cinnamon pink; the eye colour is deep, vivid blue.

LILAC POINT The body colour is glacial white, with no shading. The points are frosty grey with a pinkish tone. The nose leather and

SEAL POINT COLOURPOINT

In Colourpoint kittens the facial markings or mask is not complete, leaving a typically pale forehead.

BLUE POINT COLOURPOINT

This cat has tiny and very well-set ears and the desired broad head.

CREAM POINT
*A very pale variety of
Colourpoint with the
cream points only
slightly darker than the
body.*

**RED POINT
COLOURPOINT**
*The Red Point has a
body of apricot-toned
white and points of a
deeper apricot-red. As
in all Colourpoints, the
eyes are ideally deep
blue.*

paw pads are lavender-pink; the eye colour is deep, vivid blue.

RED POINT The body colour is creamy white. The points colour ranges from deep orange flame to deep red. The nose leather and paw pads are flesh or coral pink; the eye colour is deep, vivid blue.

CREAM POINT The body colour is creamy white with no shading. The points are buff cream, and should have no apricot tinges. The nose leather and paw pads are flesh pink or salmon coral; eye colour is deep, vivid blue.

TORTIE POINT The body colour is creamy white or pale fawn; the points are seal brown, with unbrindled patches of red and light red. A blaze of red or light red on the face is desirable. The nose leather and paw pads are seal brown with flesh and/or coral pink mottling to conform with the points' colour; the eye colour is deep, vivid blue.

BLUE-CREAM POINT The body colour is bluish white or creamy white, which shades gradually to white on the chest and stomach. The points are blue with patches of cream. The nose leather and paw pads are slate-grey or pink, or a combination of slate-grey and pink mottling; the eye colour is deep, vivid blue.

TABBY POINTS

THE TABBY-POINTED varieties should have a clear "M" marking on the forehead, spotted whisher pads and typical "spectacle" marks around the eyes. Tips of the ears and tail should match.

SEAL TABBY POINT The body colour is pale cream to fawn, and warm in tone. The mask is clearly lined with dark stripes: vertical lines on the forehead form the classic "M" shape; horizontal lines bar the cheeks; dark spots appear on the whisker pads. The inner ear is light, and there is a "thumb-print" on the back of the outer ear. The legs are evenly barred with bracelets, and the tail is barred. All markings should be broad, dense and clearly defined. No striping or mottling is allowed on the body, but consideration is given to shading in older cats.

The points are beige brown ticked with darker brown tabby markings. The nose leather is seal or brick red; the paw pads are seal brown; the eyes deep blue.

BLUE TABBY POINT The body colour is bluish white, and cold in tone. The mask is clearly lined with dark stripes: vertical lines on the forehead form the classic "M" shape; horizontal lines bar the cheeks; dark spots appear on the whisker pads. The inner ear is light, and there is a "thumb-print" on the back of the outer ear. The legs are evenly barred with bracelets, and the tail is barred. All markings should be broad, dense and clearly defined. No striping or mottling is allowed on the body, but consideration is given to shading in older cats. The points are light silvery blue, ticked with

SEAL TABBY POINT

This variety is known as the Seal Lynxpoint in the United States, and this cat's head type conforms to the American standards.

RED TABBY POINT

In the red series, some slight shading similar to that of the Points' colour may be seen on the pale body.

COLOURPOINT KITTEN

Colourpoint kittens are very inquisitive, friendly and playful. The markings slowly develop, showing their true colour a few weeks after birth.

darker blue tabby markings. The nose leather is blue or brick red; the paw pads are blue; the eye colour is deep, vivid blue.

CHOCOLATE TABBY POINT The body colour is ivory. The mask is clearly lined with dark stripes: vertical lines on the forehead form the classic "M" shape; horizontal lines bar the cheeks; dark spots appear on the whisker pads. The inner ear is light, and there is a "thumbprint" on the back of the outer ear. The legs are evenly barred with bracelets, and the tail is barred. All markings should be broad, dense and clearly defined. No striping or mottling is allowed on the body, but consideration is given to shading in older cats. The points are warm fawn, ticked with milk-chocolate markings. The nose leather and paw pads are cinnamon pink; the eye colour is deep, vivid blue.

LILAC TABBY POINT The body colour is glacial white. The mask is clearly lined with dark

stripes: vertical lines on the forehead form the classic "M" shape; horizontal lines bar the cheeks; dark spots appear on the whisker pads. The inner ear is light, and there is a "thumbprint" on the back of the outer ear. The legs are evenly barred with bracelets, and the tail is barred. All markings should be broad, dense and clearly defined. No striping or mottling is allowed on the body, but consideration is given to shading in older cats. The points are frosty grey ticked with darker frosty grey tabby markings. The nose leather and paw pads are lavender pink; the eye colour is deep, vivid blue.

BLUE-CREAM POINT

Softly intermingled blue and cream pattern the points of this Colourpoint. It has a wonderfully full and well-groomed coat.

CHOCOLATE TORTIE COLOURPOINT

This cute kitten shows the warm chocolate and light red markings on its points that identify the chocolate tortoiseshell colouration. As with all Colourpoint kittens, the markings take some time to develop fully.

CHOCOLATE AND LILAC

DURING THE BREEDING and development of the Himalayan or Colourpoint Longhairs, breeders realized it might also be possible to produce self-coloured chocolate and lilac longhaired cats. This proved quite simple to put into practice, and cats with the desired coat colour were bred quite easily, but their body type and coat quality were extremely poor when judged against Persian standards. The pioneer breeders of these varieties also had to contend with the natural fading and bleaching effect on the coat colour caused by the chocolate gene, and some of the early chocolate and lilac cats were very disappointing. Never to be outdone, the breeders determined to select for the characteristics they most desired in their dreamed-of colour varieties, and eventually they succeeded in establishing chocolate and lilac longhaired cats of equal quality to their Himalayan cousins. Some North American associations decided to group the self-coloured chocolate and lilac longhairs under the breed name of Kashmir; others grouped them with the Himalayans. Britain's GCCF preferred to call them the Chocolate Longhair and the Lilac Longhair.

CHOCOLATE LONGHAIR The colour is a rich, warm, chocolate brown, sound from the roots to the tips of the hair, and free from markings, shading or white hairs. The nose leather and paw pads are brown; the eye colour is deep orange or copper (UK), or brilliant copper (USA).

LILAC LONGHAIR The colour is a rich, warm, lavender with a pinkish tone, sound from the roots to the tips of the hair, and free from markings, shading or white hairs. The nose leather and paw pads are pink; the eye colour is pale orange in the UK, brilliant copper in the USA.

CHOCOLATE PERSIAN

Known as the Kashmir in some associations, the self-coloured chocolate Persians is one of the most difficult cats to breed to the exacting standard of points.

LILAC-CREAM

This variety was created when the red or orange genetic factor was added to some breeding programmes.

LILAC PERSIAN

Often called the Lilac Kashmir, this cat has true Persian type and a full, flowing coat.

88   Birman

94   Maine Coon

100   Ragdoll

105   Snowshoe

106   Norwegian Forest Cat

112   Angora

116   Turkish Van

SEMI LONGHAIRED BREEDS

BIRMAN

ALSO KNOWN AS THE Sacred Cat of Burma, the Birman is quite unrelated to the Burmese, despite the similarity in names. It is a unique breed, for although it bears a superficial resemblance to the Himalayan, or Colourpoint Longhair, it has stark white paws on all four feet. Its coat is silky, more like that of the Turkish Angora than the Himalayan, and its body type differs from that of the Persian, being longer and less cobby.

Legends about explaining the origins of this beautiful breed, and one in particular attempts to explain the Birman's colouring. Before the time of Buddha, the Khmer people built temples in honour of their gods. One such temple was raised to Tsun-Kyan-Kse, where a golden statue of the goddess so named was worshipped.

In the early 1900s the temple was raided, but it was saved by Major Gordon Russell and Monsieur Auguste Pavie. As a gesture of thanks, a pair of temple cats were sent to the two men, now living in France. The male cat died en route, but the female arrived safely and gave birth to kittens which founded the Birman breed in Europe.

Whatever the true origins of the breed, it survived in Europe, and was imported into Britain and accepted for championship status by 1966. Separate breeding lines were established in the United States, with the first championship showing at the Madison Square Garden Cat Show, having been given official status by the CFA in 1967.

Character and Care
The Birman is quieter and more placid than a Siamese, but also less staid than a Persian. It is an inquisitive and affectionate cat, with a rather aloof appearance, giving the impression

BREAKDOWN OF 100 SHOW POINTS

NB Annotated points (right) are those set in the UK; those listed below are for the USA.

HEAD: 30 POINTS
Including size and shape of eyes and shape and set of ears.

TYPE: 25 POINTS
Including shape, size, bone, and length of tail.

COAT: 10 POINTS

COLOUR: 25 POINTS

**EYE COLOUR:
10 POINTS**

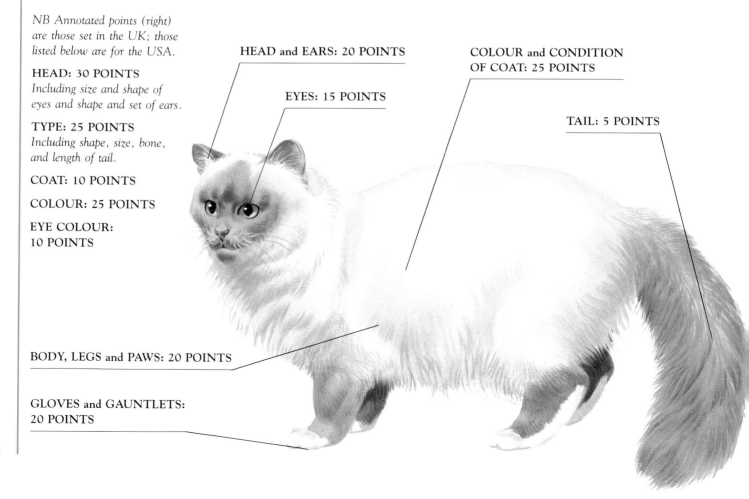

HEAD and EARS: 20 POINTS

EYES: 15 POINTS

COLOUR and CONDITION
OF COAT: 25 POINTS

TAIL: 5 POINTS

BODY, LEGS and PAWS: 20 POINTS

GLOVES and GAUNTLETS:
20 POINTS

that it is fully aware of its mystical origins. Unlike many other longhaired breeds, the Birman matures early and the females often start to "call" as early as seven months of age. The queens make excellent caring mothers, and males kept at stud are often renowned for their extra loving temperament.

The Birman coat is silkier and less dense than that of the Persian. It is comparitively easy to keep well groomed with regular brushing and combing. The white gloves and gauntlets must be kept free from staining by regular washing, careful drying and the application of white grooming powder which is rubbed in then completely brushed out, leaving the white areas spotlessly clean.

PENALTIES

The Birman is penalized for having white areas that do not run across the front paws in an even line; lack of white gloves on any paw; white shading on the stomach and chest; areas of pure white in the points (except the paws); a Siamese head type; and a squint.

KEY CHARACTERISTICS

- **CATEGORY** Longhair.

- **OVERALL BUILD** Medium sized, long but stocky.

- **COAT** Long, silky texture; heavy frill (ruff) round the neck; long on the back and flanks, may curl slightly on the stomach; little undercoat; rarely becomes matted.

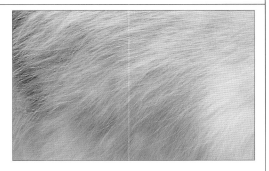

- **HEAD** Strong, broad, rounded skull with full cheeks.

- **NOSE** Medium length, roman in shape.

- **CHIN** Firm, with the lower lip forming a perpendicular line with the upper lip.

- **EYES** Almost round in shape.

- **EARS** Medium sized with rounded tips, set slightly tipped forward, not upright on the skull and with good width between.

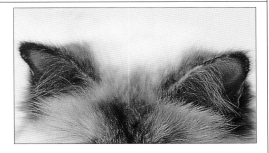

- **BODY** Fairly long but not stocky, males more massive than females.

- **LEGS** Short to medium in length, and heavy.

- **PAWS** Large and rounded.

- **TAIL** Medium length, forming a plume.

- **COLOURS** Seal point, blue point, chocolate point, lilac point, red point, cream point, seal tortie point, blue tortie point, chocolate tortie point, lilac tortie point solid points, tortie points, tabby points and tortie tabby all in the following colours: seal, blue, chocolate, lilac, red, cream.

SOLID POINTS

SEAL POINT BIRMAN

The characteristic white forepaws of this breed are called "gloves" and should end in a symmetrical line on or below the angle formed by the paw and leg.

A LITTER OF BIRMANS normally consists of three, four or five kittens which are born almost white all over. Within a few days the points colour starts to develop at the edges of the ears and on the tail. The eyes, when they open at seven to ten days, are a cloudy baby-blue which changes to the true blue colour as the kittens grow.

SEAL POINT The body is even fawn to pale cream, warm in tone shading to lighter colour on the stomach and chest. The points are deep seal brown apart from the gloves, which are pure white. The nose leather should match the points. The paw pads are pink, and eye colour is blue, the deeper and more violet the better.

BLUE POINT The body is bluish white, cold in tone, shading gradually to almost white on the stomach and chest. The points are deep blue except for the gloves, which are pure white. The nose leather is slate and the paw pads pink. Eye colour should be blue, the deeper and more violet the better.

CHOCOLATE POINT The body is ivory with no shading. Points are milk-chocolate of warm tone except for the gloves, which are pure white. The nose leather is cinnamon pink and the paw pads pink. Eye colour should be blue, the deeper and more violet the better.

BLUE POINT BIRMAN

The gloves on the hind paws are called "gauntlets". They cover the entire paw and taper up the back of the leg to a point just below the hock.

CREAM POINT BIRMAN
A slightly golden-hued white body and pale cream points are the hallmarks of the Cream Point Birman.

CHOCOLATE POINT BIRMAN
Warm toned milk-chocolate points identify this recently accepted colour variety in the Birman.

LILAC POINT BIRMAN
Apart from its four white paws, the Birman has normal Himalayan or Siamese colouring on the extremities of the body, known as the points.

LILAC POINT The body has a cold glacial tone verging on white with no shading. The points are frosty grey with a pinkish tinge, with pure white gloves. The nose leather is lavender pink, the paw pads pink and the eye colour blue, the deeper and more violet the better.
RED POINT The body is creamy white. The points, except for the gloves, are bright warm orange; the gloves are white. The nose leather and paw pads are pink; eye colour is blue.
CREAM POINT The body is creamy white. The points, except for the gloves, are pastel cream; the gloves are white. The nose leather and paw pads are pink; the eye colour is blue.

91

TABBY AND TORTOISESHELL POINTS

ALTHOUGH PURISTS CLAIM that only Seal Point and Blue Point Birman cats should be considered as the true Sacred Cats of Burma, the CFA in the United States also recognizes the Chocolate Point and Lilac Point varieties, and FIFe, in Europe has produced standards of points for both the tabby and red series, including tortoiseshell, and tortoiseshell–tabbies in the four basic colour combinations.

SEAL TABBY POINT The body is beige, with dark seal tabby points, except for gloves which are white. The nose leather is brick red, pink or seal brown and the paw pads are pink.

BLUE TABBY POINT The body is bluish white, with blue-grey tabby points, except for the gloves which are white. The nose leather is old rose or blue-grey.

CHOCOLATE TABBY POINT The body is ivory. The points, except for the gloves, are milk-chocolate tabby; the gloves are white. The nose leather is pale red, pink or milk-chocolate.

LILAC TABBY POINT The body is glacial white (magnolia) with lilac tabby (frosty grey with a slight pinkish tinge) points, except the gloves, which are white. The nose leather is pink or lavender-pink.

RED TABBY POINT The body is off-white with a slight red tinge. The points, except for the gloves, are warm orange tabby; the gloves are white. The nose leather is pink or brick-red.

CREAM TABBY POINT The body is off-white. The points, except for the gloves, are cream tabby; the gloves are white.

SEAL TORTIE POINT The body is beige, shading to fawn. The points, except for the gloves, are seal brown patched or mingled with red and/or light red. The gloves are white. The nose leather is pink and/or seal.

SEAL TORTIE TABBY POINT The body is beige. The points, except for the gloves, have tabby markings in seal brown patched or mingled with red and/or light red. The gloves are white and the nose leather seal, brick red or pink, or seal mottled with brick red or pink.

BLUE TABBY POINT BIRMAN

The Birman is alert and interested in everything that is going on. It makes an excellent pet, and its long coat is easier to care for than that of the cats of the Persian group.

SEAL TORTIE POINT BIRMAN

Seal brown overlaid and intermingled with red and light red produce the tortoiseshell colouring.

SEAL TABBY POINT BIRMAN
Tabby pointed Birman cats are now accepted with provisional status in Britain by GCCF.

BLUE TORTIE POINT The body is bluish white. The points, except for the gloves, are blue-grey patched or mottled with pastel cream. The gloves are white. The nose leather is blue-grey and/or pink.

BLUE TORTIE TABBY POINT The body is glacial white with a slight bluish tinge. The points, except for the gloves, have tabby markings in blue-grey patched or mingled with pastel cream. The gloves are white and the nose leather blue-grey, old rose or pink, or blue-grey mottled with old rose and/or pink.

CHOCOLATE TORTIE POINT The body is ivory. The points, except for the gloves, are milk-chocolate patched or mingled with red and/or light red; the gloves are white. The nose leather is milk-chocolate and/or pink.

CHOCOLATE TORTIE TABBY POINT The body is ivory. The points, except for the gloves, have tabby markings in milk-chocolate patched or mingled with red and/or light red; the gloves are white. The nose leather is milk-chocolate, light red or pink, or milk-chocolate mottled with light red and/or pink.

LILAC TORTIE POINT The body is glacial white (magnolia). The points, except for the gloves, are lilac (frosty grey with a slight pinkish tinge) patched or mingled with pale cream; the gloves are white. The nose leather is lavender pink and/or pink.

LILAC TORTIE TABBY POINT The body is glacial white (magnolia). The points, except for the gloves, have tabby markings in lilac (frosty grey with a slight pinkish tinge) patched or mingled with pale cream; the gloves are white. The nose leather is lavender pink or pale pink, or lavender pink mottled with pale pink.

RED TABBY POINT BIRMAN
The slight golden shaded effect on the coat of this colour variety is known as a "halo".

93

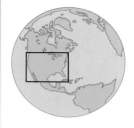

MAINE COON

ONE OF THE OLDEST NATURAL BREEDS of North America, the Maine Coon, or Maine Cat, has been known as a true variety for more than a hundred years. As its name implies, it originated in the north-eastern State of Maine. At one time it was thought that the cat was the product of matings between semi-wild domestic cats and raccoons, hence the name "coon", though this is now known to be a biological impossibility. Another legend tells how Marie Antoinette, in planning her escape from the horrors of the French Revolution, sent her pet cats to be cared for in Maine until she could find herself, and them, a new home. Today's more enlightened felinophiles believe that long-coated cats such as the Angora were introduced to coastal towns as trade goods by visting seamen, and these cats bred with the local domestic cats, resulting eventually in the large and handsome American longhaired breed we know today.

A tabby Maine Coon is recorded as having won the Best in Show at the Madison Square Garden Cat Show in 1895, but with the introduction of more striking breeds from Europe at the turn of the century, the popularity of the Maine Coon declined. Though the breed flourished as a popular and hardy pet for some years, it was not until 1953 that the Central Maine Coon Cat Club was formed to promote the breed. By 1967 a show standard was accepted by some American cat associa-

BREAKDOWN OF 100 SHOW POINTS

NB Annotated points (right) are those set in the UK; those listed below are for Europe.

HEAD: 30 POINTS
Shape: 15 points
Ears: 10 points
Eyes: 5 points

BODY: 35 POINTS
Shape: 20 points
Neck: 5 points
Legs and feet: 5 points
Tail: 5 points

COAT: 20 POINTS

COLOUR: 15 POINTS
Body colour: 10 points
Eye colour: 5 points

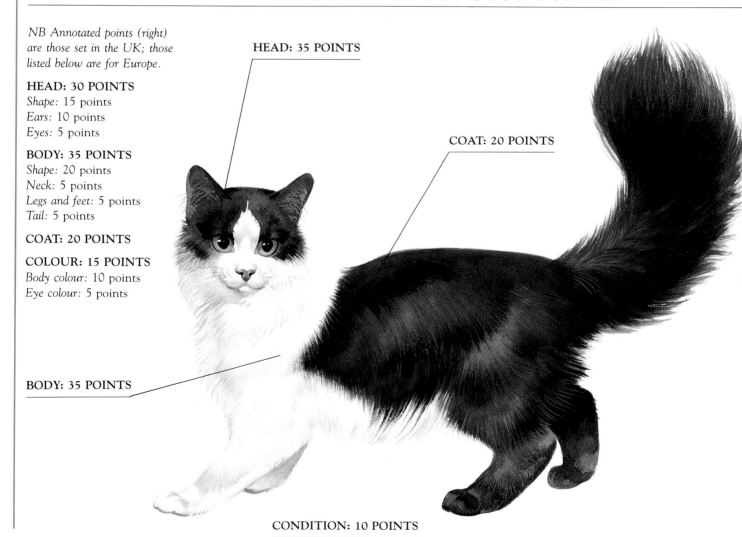

HEAD: 35 POINTS

COAT: 20 POINTS

BODY: 35 POINTS

CONDITION: 10 POINTS

tions. In 1976 the International Society for the Preservation of the Maine Coon was formed, and the Cat Fanciers' Association accepted the breed with full championship status.

Character and Care

Considered by their fans to be perfect domestic pets, typical Maine Coons have extrovert personalities and are very playful and amusing, often teaching themselves tricks. They may take three or four years to develop their full size and stature, being very slow to mature.

Although the coat is long and flowing, it rarely gets matted, and is easy to care for with occasional combing through.

KEY CHARACTERISTICS

- **CATEGORY** Longhair.

- **OVERALL BUILD** Medium to large.

- **COAT** Heavy and shaggy, with a silky texture. Short on the head, shoulders and legs, becoming gradually longer down the back and sides, shaggy on hind legs and belly fur; full frill (ruff).

- **HEAD** Medium sized with a squarish outline; gently concave in profile, with curved forehead and high, prominent cheekbones.

- **NOSE** Medium length.

- **CHIN** Firm, and in vertical alignment with the nose and upper lip.

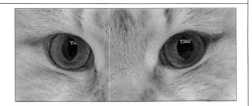

- **EYES** Large, slightly oval but not almond shaped, set slightly slanted towards the outer base of the ear.

- **EARS** Large, wide at the base, moderately pointed and with lynx-like ear tufts, set high but well apart.

- **BODY** Long with substantial bone, large framed and well proportioned, muscular and broad chested. Males are larger than females.

- **LEGS** Medium length.

- **PAWS** Large, round and tufted between the toes.

- **TAIL** At least as long as the body from shoulder-blade to the base of the tail; wide at the base tapering to the tip with full, flowing hair.

- **COLOURS** The Maine Coon is recognized in all colours except the Himalayan and Burmese patterns, and chocolate, cinnamon, lilac or fawn. There is no relationship between coat colour and eye colour, though brilliant eye colour is desirable. Any amount of white is allowed.

BLUE-CREAM AND WHITE

The Maine Coon originated in the American state of Maine where this cat would be known as the Dilute Calico variety.

GREEN-EYED WHITE

The Maine Coon is one of the few pedigree breeds in which the white variety may have green eyes.

THE STANDARD FOR solid colours insists on a coat that is sound to the roots and free from any shading, markings, or hair of another colour. The nose leathers and paw pads match the eye rims. Patterning should cover the coat, including the legs and tail in tortoiseshells, and in bicolour and particolours, any solid, tortoise-shell, tabby, shaded or smoke colour is accepted, combined with areas of white.

WHITE The coat is pure glistening white; and the nose leather and paw pads are pink. The eye colours may be blue, orange, odd, or green.

BLACK The coat is dense coal black, sound from the roots to the tips of the hair; with no sign of rustiness of colour on the tips, and no smoke undercoat. The nose leather is black; the pads are black or brown.

BLUE The coat is one even tone of grey-blue from nose to tail tip, and must be sound to the roots. Nose leather and paw pads are blue.

RED The coat is deep, clear, rich, brilliant red without any shading, markings, or ticking. The lips and chin must be the same colour as the coat. Nose leather and paw pads are brick red.

CREAM The coat is one even shade of buff cream, without any markings, and must be sound to the roots. The nose leather and paw pads are pink.

TORTOISESHELL The colour is black with unbrindled patches of red and light red, with the patches clearly defined and well broken on both the body and extremities. A blaze of red or light red on the face is desirable.

TORTOISESHELL-AND-WHITE There must be white on the bib, belly, and all four paws. White on one-third of the body overall is desirable.

BLUE-CREAM The colour is blue with clearly defined, unbrindled, well-broken patches of cream on the body and extremities.

BLUE-CREAM-AND-WHITE There must be white on the bib, belly, and all four paws. White on one-third of the body overall is desirable.

BICOLOUR This is a combination of a solid colour with white. The coloured areas predominate, with the white areas located on the face, chest, belly, legs, and feet. Colours accepted are black, blue, red, and cream.

SMOKE AND SHADED VARIETIES

ANY SOLID OR TORTIE colour is accepted in this group. The base coat should be as white as possible, with the tips of the hairs shading to the basic colour, darkest on the head, back and paws. The Smoke is densely coloured; while the shaded shows much more of the silver undercoat.

SHADED SILVER There is a white undercoat with a mantle of black tipping shading down the sides, face and tail, the colour ranging from dark on the ridge to white on the chin, chest, stomach and underside of the tail. The legs are the same tone as the face. The general effect is much darker than the Chinchilla. Eye rims, lips and nose are outlined with black; nose leather is brick red; paw pads are black.

SHADED RED There is a white undercoat with red tipping shading down the sides, face and tail, the colour ranging from dark on the ridge to white on the chin, chest, stomach and underside of the tail. Legs are the same tone as the face. Nose leather and paw pads are black.

BLACK SMOKE There is a white undercoat deeply tipped with black; in repose, the cat appears black; in motion, the white undercoat is clearly apparent. The points and mask are black, with a narrow band of white at the base of the hairs next to the skin. The frill (ruff) and ear tufts are light silver; the nose leather and paw pads are black.

BLUE SMOKE There is a white undercoat deeply tipped with blue; in repose, the cat appears blue; in motion, the white undercoat is clearly apparent. The points and mask are blue, with a narrow band of white hairs next to the skin. The frill (ruff) and ear tufts are white; nose leather and paw pads are blue.

RED SMOKE There is a white undercoat deeply tipped with red; in repose, the cat appears red; in motion, the white undercoat is clearly apparent. The points and mask are red, with a narrow band of white hairs next to the skin. The eye rims, nose leather and paw pads are rose.

CREAM SMOKE This is a dilute version of the Red Smoke in which the red tipping is reduced to pale cream.

RED SHADED

In shaded varieties, the undercoat should be as white as possible, and the basic colour should be deepest on the head, back and the paws.

TABBY VARIETIES

BOTH THE CLASSIC TABBY and Mackerel Tabby patterned cats are accepted in any of the following colours.

SILVER TABBY The cat has a pale, clear silver base coat with dense black markings; white is allowed around the lips and chin. The nose leather is brick red; the paw pads are black.

BROWN TABBY The cat has a brilliant coppery brown base coat with dense black markings. The backs of the legs from the paw to the heel are black; white is allowed around the lips and chin. The nose leather and paw pads are black or brown.

BLUE TABBY The cat has a pale bluish-ivory base coat with very deep blue markings affording good contrast with the base colour. There is a warm fawn patina over the whole coat. White is allowed around the lips and chin. The nose leather is old rose; the paw pads are rose.

RED TABBY The cat has a red base coat with deep rich red markings; white is allowed around the lips and chin. The nose leather and paw pads are brick red.

CREAM TABBY The cat has a very pale cream base coat with buff or cream markings sufficiently darker to afford good contrast with the base colour. White is allowed around lips and chin. Nose leather and paw pads are pink.

BROWN MACKEREL TABBY

In the mackerel tabby pattern the markings consist of fine lines running down the body.

MACKEREL TABBY AND WHITE

These markings are of the mackerel rather than the classic pattern.

SILVER TABBY

Cats with any either of the tabby patterns have similar head markings with the letter "M" etched on the forehead.

TORTIE TABBY

Full, round and luminous eyes set off the glowing coat to perfection.

SILVER TORTIE TABBY and WHITE

Some of the most unusual of all the feline colours are found in the Maine Coon. This pretty little cat has pale tortoiseshell markings mixed with silver tabby.

CAMEO TABBY The cat has an off-white base coat with red markings; white is allowed around the lips and chin. The nose leather and paw pads are rose.

TORTIE TABBY A Tortie Tabby or torbie is a silver or brown tabby with patches of red and light red, or a blue tabby with patches of cream. Nose leather of Tortie Tabby brick-red or pink; paw pads black and/or pink. Nose leather and pads of Blue Tabby blue and/or pink.

TABBY-AND-WHITE The cat may be any tabby colour as defined above – silver, brown, blue, red or cream – with or without white on the face, but with white on the bib, belly and all four paws; white on one-third of the body overall is desirable. The nose leather and paw pads are as for the colour described above.

TORTIE TABBY-AND-WHITE The colour is as described for the Tortie Tabby, but with white markings as defined for the Tabby-and-white (above). Colours accepted are silver, brown and blue. The nose leather depends on basic colour; paw pads are pink.

RAGDOLL

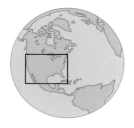

THE FIRST RAGDOLL cats were bred by an American, Ann Baker, whose white long-haired cat Josephine was involved in a road accident which left her with permanent injuries. When Josephine eventually had kittens, they were found to have particularly placid temperaments and would completely relax when picked up and cuddled, reminiscent of a rag doll.

The name was chosen and recognized in 1965 by the National Cat Fanciers' Association, and later by other associations. Although this breed's alleged inability to feel pain or fear, or to fight with other animals is claimed to be due to Josephine's accident, this goes against all genetic reasoning. The specialized temperament is almost certainly due to the fact that only cats of a loving disposition were selected in the first matings. The three patterns found in the breed could certainly have been produced by Josephine if the stud cat used had carried genes for the Himalayan pattern and long coat, and if either Josephine or her mate had also carried the gene for white spotting.

Though some controversy remains over the breed, the Ragdoll has gained popularity around the world, and it has become an interesting addition to the show scene.

BREAKDOWN OF 100 SHOW POINTS

NB Annotated points (right) are those set in the UK

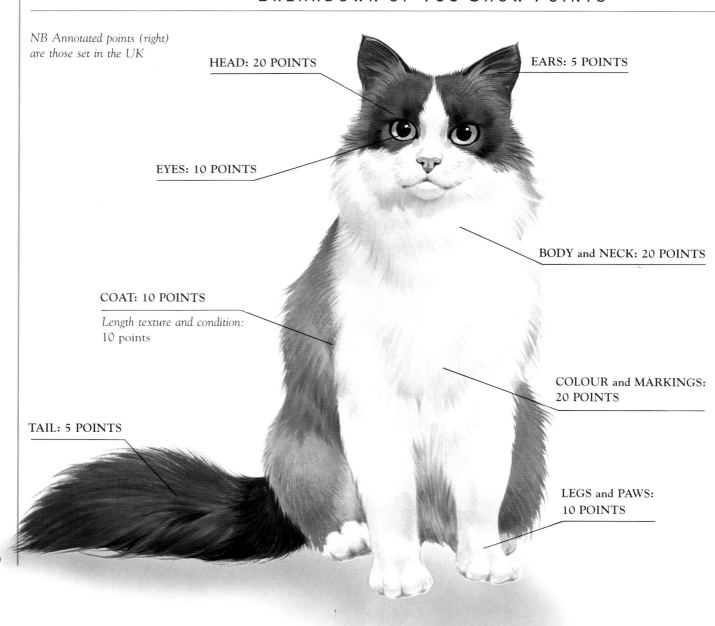

HEAD: 20 POINTS

EARS: 5 POINTS

EYES: 10 POINTS

BODY and NECK: 20 POINTS

COAT: 10 POINTS

Length texture and condition: 10 points

COLOUR and MARKINGS: 20 POINTS

TAIL: 5 POINTS

LEGS and PAWS: 10 POINTS

Character and Care

The Ragdoll is an exceptionally affectionate, loving and relaxed cat. Although it is generally calm and placid, with a quiet voice, it loves to play and to be petted. The thick coat does not form mats, and is therefore quite easy to groom with regular gentle brushing of the body and combing through the longer hair on the tail and around the neck.

PENALTIES

The Ragdoll is penalized for having a narrow head, roman nose, too large a stop in profile, too small or pointed ears; almond-shaped eyes; a neck too long or too thin; cobby body; narrow chest; short legs; splayed feet; lack of toe tufts; short or blunt tipped tail; eye colour other than blue.

KEY CHARACTERISTICS

- **CATEGORY** Longhair.

- **OVERALL BUILD** Large, solid appearance.

- **COAT** Medium long, dense, soft and silky in texture, lying close to the body and breaking as the cat moves. Longest around the neck and framing the face; short on the face; short to medium length on the front legs; medium to long over the body.

- **HEAD** Medium size, broad modified wedge shape with a flat plane between the ears; well-developed cheeks; medium long muzzle.

- **NOSE** Slightly curved in the upper third.

- **CHIN** Well developed.

- **EYES** Large and oval, with the outer corners being level with the base of the ears.

- **EARS** Medium size, broad-based, with rounded tips, set wide apart and tipped slightly forward.

- **BODY** Long, with medium bone structure. Muscular, broad chest, muscular hindquarters.

- **LEGS** Medium in length and of medium bone. Hind legs slightly higher than forelegs.

- **PAWS** Large, round and compact; with tufts between the toes.

- **TAIL** Long, but in proportion to the body, medium broad at the base and slightly tapered towards the tip; bushy.

- **COLOURS** Seal point, blue point, chocolate point and lilac point, all with clear blue eyes.

MITTED

SEAL MITTED RAGDOLL

Mitted Ragdolls may have a narrow white facial blaze in addition to white on the chin, chest, bib and underbody, and the obligatory four white paws.

BLUE MITTED RAGDOLL

In the mitted pattern of the Ragdoll breed, the four paws are white to the same degree as that found in the Birman.

THE BODY IS LIGHT in colour and only slightly shaded; the points (except the paws and chin) should be clearly defined, matched for colour and in harmony with the body colour. The chin must be white and a white stripe on the nose is preferred; white mittens on the front legs and back paws should be entirely white to the knees and hocks. A white stripe extends from the bib to the underside between the front legs to the base of the tail.

LILAC POINT The body colour is glacial white; the points are frosty grey of a pinkish tone, except for the white areas.

SEAL POINT The body colour is pale fawn or cream; the points are deep seal brown, except for the white areas.

BLUE POINT The body colour is cold-toned bluish-white; the points are blue, except for the white areas.

CHOCOLATE POINT The body colour is ivory; the points are milk chocolate, except for the white areas.

LILAC POINT The body colour is glacial white; the points are frosty grey of a pinkish tone, except for the white areas.

BI-COLOUR

THE BODY IS LIGHT in colour; the points – ears, mask and tail – should be well-defined. The mask has an inverted white "V"; the stomach is white; and the legs are preferably white. No white is allowed on ears or tail.

SEAL POINT The body colour is pale fawn or cream; the points are deep seal brown, except for the white areas.

BLUE POINT The body colour is cold-toned bluish-white; the points are blue, except for the white areas.

CHOCOLATE POINT The body colour is ivory; the points are milk chocolate, except for the white areas.

CHOCOLATE BI-COLOUR RAGDOLL
An inverted white "V" extending from the forehead to cover the nose is the identifying feature of the Colourpoint Ragdoll, in addition to the other required areas of white.

SEAL BI-COLOUR RAGDOLL
The Ragdoll is a large and very docile cat with a loving temperament and a sociable nature. Though long, its coat is easy to keep in good condition with little grooming.

COLOURPOINT

THE BODY IS LIGHT in colour and only slightly shaded; the points – ears, mask, legs and tail – should be clearly defined, matched for colour and in harmony with the body colour. No white hairs allowed.

LILAC POINT The body colour is glacial white; the points are frosty grey of a pinkish tone, except for the white areas.

SEAL POINT The body colour is pale fawn or cream; the points are deep seal brown, except for the white areas.

BLUE POINT The body colour is cold-toned bluish-white; the points are blue, except for the white areas.

CHOCOLATE POINT The body colour is ivory; the points are milk chocolate, except for the white areas.

SEAL COLOURPOINT
All the points are evenly matched, with no white markings anywhere.

BLUE COLOURPOINT
The basic Himalayan colours of seal, blue, chocolate and lilac are accepted in this breed.

LILAC COLOURPOINT
Even in the lilac variety good contrast between the body and points' colour is required. The coat itself should be dense, of silky texture and medium length.

SNOWSHOE

SNOWSHOE
*Sometimes called Silver
Laces, the Snowshoe is
a very rare cat indeed
and only recognized in
a few associations. It is
of the stocky build
found in the American
Shorthair.*

THE SNOWSHOE OR Silver Laces is a rare cat even in the United States where it was first bred. It combines the stocky build of the American Shorthair with the body length of the Siamese, and is Himalayan, or Siamese in colouring, but with the white paws which are also found in the Birman.

Character and Care
The Snowshoe is a robust and lively cat. It is highly intelligent and loving and, like the Siamese, enjoys human company.

Its coat needs the minimum of grooming, and the white paws may be kept immaculate by dusting with grooming powder from time to time to prevent discolouration.

KEY CHARACTERISTICS
● **CATEGORY** Shorthair.
● **OVERALL BUILD** The Snowshoe is of medium size and well muscled.
● **COAT** Short fine close-lying coat.
● **COLOURS** Any recognized points colour.
● **OTHER FEATURES** The head is triangular with large pointed wide-based ears and large oval eyes of brilliant blue. The long body is well-muscled with a strong back, the legs are of medium bone with compact oval paws, and the tail is thick at the base, tapering to a pointed tip. There are no standards set either for the nose or for the chin.

NORWEGIAN FOREST CAT

KNOWN AS THE *Norsk Skaukatt* in its native Norway, the Norwegian Forest Cat is very similar to the Maine Coon in many ways. It is a uniquely Scandinavian breed whose origins are shrouded in mystery, and is referred to in Norse myths and mid-nineteenth-century fairy stories. Having evolved naturally in the cold climate of Norway, it has a heavy, weather-resistant coat. The glossy, medium-length top coat hangs from the spine line, keeping out rain and snow, while the woolly undercoat keeps the body comfortably warm. Its strong legs, paws and claws make the Forest Cat an extremely good climber in trees and on rocky slopes. It is highly intelligent, nimble and an excellent hunter.

From these naturally evolved cats a group of breeders set out in the 1930s to develop a pedigree breed, starting with some hardy farm cats. As a breed, the Forest Cat gained in popularity during the 1970s and was granted full Championship status in FIFe in 1977.

The ideal show cat differs from the Maine Coon in having hind legs longer than the forelegs, and the standard of points specifies a double coat, which is permitted but not desirable in the American breed.

BREAKDOWN OF 100 SHOW POINTS

NB Annotated points are those set in Europe.

EARS: 10 POINTS

Shape and placement.

HEAD: 20 POINTS

General shape, nose, profile, jaw and teeth, chin.

EYE SHAPE: 5 POINTS

TAIL: 10 POINTS

Shape and length.

BODY: 25 POINTS

Shape, size, bone structure, leg length and height.

COAT: 25 POINTS

Quality, texture and length.

CONDITION: 5 POINTS

Character and Care

Strong and hardy, the Forest Cat can be very playful while retaining the strongly independent character of its semi-wild forbears. It enjoys human company, and can be very affectionate, but dislikes too much cosseting. The trouble-free coat periodically needs combing through to keep the undercoat in good condition and to tidy the flowing tail and full frill or ruff.

KEY CHARACTERISTICS

- **CATEGORY** Longhair.

- **OVERALL BUILD** Large.

- **COAT** Semi-long; a woolly undercoat is covered with a smooth, water-repellent upper coat. The glossy hair covers the back and sides. The cat has a full frill or ruff.

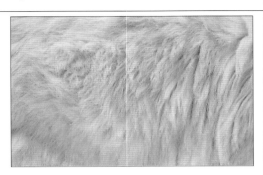

- **HEAD** Triangular, with a long, straight profile and no stop.

- **NOSE** Long and straight.

- **CHIN** Firm.

- **EYES** Large, open and set slightly obliquely.

- **EARS** Wide based, with lynx-like tufts, set high, the outer edges of the ears following the lines of the head down to the chin.

- **BODY** Long, strongly built, with solid bone structure.

- **LEGS** Long, the hind legs longer than the forelegs.

- **PAWS** Tufted.

- **TAIL** Long and bushy.

- **COLOURS** All colours except chocolate, cinnamon, lilac and fawn are accepted, though neither the Himalayan pattern nor the Burmese factor is allowed. Type always takes preference over colour. No relationship between coat and eye colour, but clear eye colour is desirable.

SOLID VARIETIES

WHITE
In the Norwegian Forest Cat, any eye colour is allowed, regardless of the coat colour.

IN THE SOLID COLOURED varieties of the Norwegian Forest Cat, the coat should be sound in colour and free from any shadings, markings, or colour other than the basic one.

WHITE The coat is pure glistening white; and the nose leather and paw pads are pink.

BLACK The coat is dense coal black, sound from the roots to the tips of the hair; with no sign of rustiness of colour on the tips, and no smoke undercoat. The nose leather is black; the pads are black or brown.

BLUE The coat is one level tone of grey-blue from nose to tail tip, and must be sound to the roots. Nose leather and paw pads are blue.

RED The coat is deep, clear, rich, brilliant red without any shading, markings or ticking. The lips and chin must be the same colour as the coat. Nose leather and paw pads are brick red.

CREAM The coat is one level shade of buff cream, without any markings, and must be sound to the roots. Both the nose leather and the paw pads are pink.

NORWEGIAN FOREST CAT
The coat is double, with a weatherproof, woolly undercoat covered with a smooth, almost waterproof top coat.

TABBY VARIETIES

ANY OF THE FOUR tabby patterns are accepted in the Norwegian Forest Cat, and a whole range of colours, except the chocolate and lilac series. Any amount of white on the body is also permitted.

SILVER TABBY The cat has a pale, clear silver base coat with dense black markings; white is allowed around the lips and chin. The nose leather is brick red; the paw pads are black.

BROWN TABBY Brilliant coppery brown base coat with dense black markings. The backs of the legs from paw to heel are black; white allowed around lips and chin. Nose leather and paw pads are black or brown.

BLUE TABBY The cat has a pale bluish-ivory base coat with very deep blue markings affording good contrast with the base colour. There is a warm fawn patina over the whole coat. White is allowed around the lips and chin. The nose leather is old rose; the paw pads are rose.

RED TABBY Red base coat with deep rich red markings; white allowed around lips and chin. Nose leather and paw pads are brick red.

CREAM TABBY The cat has a very pale cream base coat with buff or cream markings sufficiently darker to afford good contrast with the base colour. White is allowed around lips and chin. Nose leather and paw pads are pink.

TABBY-AND-WHITE May be silver, brown, blue, red or cream – with or without white on the face, but with white on the bib, belly and all four paws; white on one-third of the body overall is desirable. The nose leather and paw pads are as above.

BLUE SILVER TABBY

Any amount of white is permitted on the paws, chest, or underbody, or as a facial blaze.

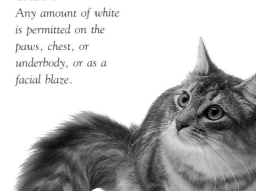

BROWN TICKED TABBY

All tabby patterns are accepted, including the Ticked as seen in this very full-coated cat.

BROWN TABBY

This handsome cat is marked with the Classic tabby pattern which shows clearly on the smooth semi-longhaired cat.

RED SILVER TABBY and WHITE

The addition of silver to other varieties adds to the range of pale, attractive shades.

RED AND WHITE
Although the amounts of white is not specified for this breed, this cat does look even more attractive having neatly matching white paws and a small bib.

DEVELOPED FROM THE indigenous domestic cat, the Norwegian Forest Cat is found in a wide range of coat colours and patterns. There is no relationship between coat colour and eye colour as expected in most other pedigree breeds.

TORTOISESHELL Black with unbrindled patches of red and light red, the patches clearly defined and well broken on body and extremities. A blaze of red on the face is desirable.

TORTOISESHELL-AND-WHITE Colour as for the Tortoiseshell with or without white on the face, but there must be white on the bib, belly and all four paws. White on one-third of the body overall is desirable.

BLUE-CREAM The colour is blue with clearly defined, unbrindled, well-broken patches of cream on the body and extremities.

BLUE-CREAM-AND-WHITE The colour is as defined for the Blue-cream, with or without white on the face, but there must be white on the bib, belly and all four paws. White on one-third of the body overall is desirable.

BI-COLOUR Combination of a solid colour with white. Colour predominates, with white areas located on the face, chest, belly, legs and feet. Colours are black, blue, red and cream.

TORTOISESHELL
All colours of torties are accepted in the breed and may be with or without white markings.

SMOKE AND CAMEO VARIETIES

THE LONG COAT OF the Norwegian Forest Cat is particularly attractive in the colours which have a silver undercoat, such as the smoke, shaded, tipped and cameo series in all colours.

CHINCHILLA There is a pure white undercoat, and the coat on the back, flanks, head and tail is sufficiently tipped with black to give the characteristic sparkling silver appearance. The legs may be slightly shaded with tipping. The chin, ear tufts, stomach, and chest are pure white; eye rims, lips and nose are outlined with black. Nose leather and paw pads are black.

SHADED SILVER There is a white undercoat with a mantle of black tipping shading down the sides, face and tail, the colour ranging from dark on the ridge to white on the chin, chest, stomach and underside of the tail. The legs are the same tone as the face. The general effect is much darker than the Chinchilla. The eye rims, lips and nose are outlined with black; nose leather is brick red; paw pads are black.

RED SHELL CAMEO There is a white undercoat, and the coat on the back, flanks, head and tail is sufficiently tipped with red to give the characteristic sparkling appearance. The face and legs may be very slightly shaded with tipping. The chin, ear tufts, stomach and chest are white; the eye rims, nose leather and paw pads are rose.

RED SHADED CAMEO There is a white undercoat with a mantle of red tipping down the sides, face and tail, the colour ranging from dark on the ridge to white on the chin, chest, stomach and underside of the tail. The legs are the same tone as the face. The nose leather and paw pads are black.

BLACK SMOKE There is a white undercoat deeply tipped with black; in repose, the cat appears black; in motion, the white undercoat is clearly apparent. The points and mask are black, with a narrow band of white at the base of the hairs next to the skin. The frill (ruff) and ear tufts are light silver; the nose leather and paw pads are black.

BLUE SMOKE There is a white undercoat deeply tipped with blue; in repose, the cat appears blue; in motion, the white undercoat is clearly apparent. The points and mask are blue, with a narrow band of white hairs next to the skin. The frill (ruff) and ear tufts are white; the nose leather and paw pads are blue.

RED SMOKE There is a white undercoat deeply tipped with red; in repose, the cat appears red; in motion, the white undercoat is clearly apparent. The points and mask are red, with a narrow band of white hairs next to the skin. The eye rims, nose leather and paw pads are rose.

BLACK SMOKE

The Forest Cats' eyes should be large, and held well opened, set slightly obliquely, and may be of any colour.

ANGORA

ONE OF THE MOST ANCIENT of cat breeds, originating in Turkey, the Angora was the first of the longhaired cats to reach Europe. In the sixteenth century, a naturalist called Nicholas-Claude Fabri de Peiresc imported several cats into France from Angora (now Ankara) in Turkey. They were described in contemporary literature as "ash-coloured dun and speckled cats, beautiful to behold". The cats were bred from, and some of the kittens went to England, where they were highly prized and known as French cats. When another type of long-coated cat arrived in Europe from Persia (now Iran), the Angora and the Persian were intermated quite indiscriminately.

The Persian type gradually superseded the Angora type in popularity, and by the twentieth century the Angora breed was virtually unknown outside its native land.

During the 1950s and 1960s North America, Britain and Sweden imported cats from Turkey to start breeding programmes for the development of the Angora breed. In the United States, the Turkish Angora was officially recognized and granted championship status by some associations in the early 1970s, but until 1978, the CFA only accepted the white variety. Eventually, however, a wide range of colours was accepted.

Character and Care

Precocious as kittens, Angoras are playful and athletic. They are generally affectionate with their owners but can be aloof with strangers.

Angoras moult excessively in summer and the loose hair should be combed out daily. The lack of a fluffy undercoat ensures that the coat does not become matted.

BREAKDOWN OF 100 SHOW POINTS

NB Annotated points (right) are those set in the UK; those listed below are for the USA.

HEAD: 35 POINTS

BODY: 30 POINTS

COLOUR: 20 POINTS

COAT: 15 POINTS

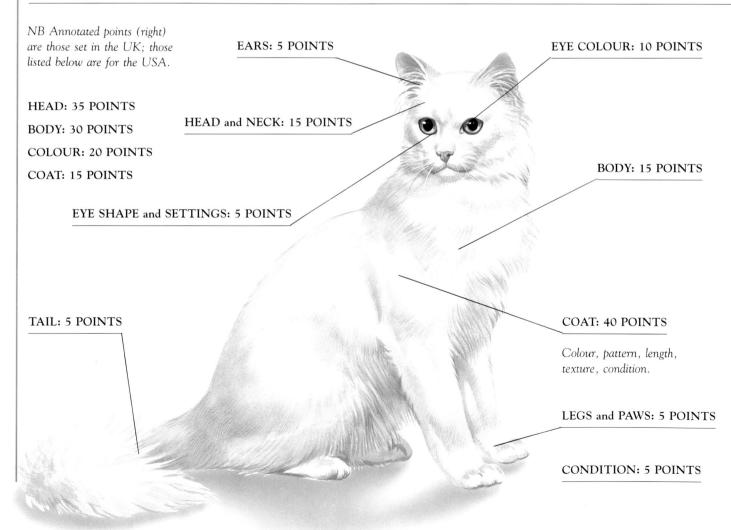

EARS: 5 POINTS

EYE COLOUR: 10 POINTS

HEAD and NECK: 15 POINTS

BODY: 15 POINTS

EYE SHAPE and SETTINGS: 5 POINTS

TAIL: 5 POINTS

COAT: 40 POINTS

Colour, pattern, length, texture, condition.

LEGS and PAWS: 5 POINTS

CONDITION: 5 POINTS

KEY CHARACTERISTICS

- **CATEGORY** Longhair.

- **OVERALL BUILD** Medium sized, and well-proportioned, with males larger than females.

- **COAT** Medium length, silky and sleek, with no undercoat. Long at the frill.

- **HEAD** Small to medium in size and wedge-shaped, wide at the top tapering towards the chin.

- **NOSE** Medium length, with a gentle slope and no stop or break.

- **CHIN** Gently rounded, the tip forming a perpendicular line with the nose.

- **EYES** Large, almond shaped, slanting slightly upwards.

- **EARS** Long and pointed, wide at the base, well furred and tufted.

- **BODY** Fine boned, with a light-framed chest and slender torso. Lithe, with the hind part higher than the front.

- **LEGS** Long, with hind legs longer than forelegs.

- **PAWS** Small, round and dainty with tufts between the toes.

- **TAIL** Long and tapering, wide at the rump and narrow at the tip; well furred. It is carried horizontally over the body, sometimes touching the head.

- **COLOURS** White with amber, blue green, or odd eyes; black, blue, chocolate red, cream, cinamon, caramel, fawn, blue-cream tabby in standard and silver, in any pattern and all colours; tortie, tortie tabby, smokes and shaded in all colours.

PENALTIES

The Angora (Turkish Angora) is penalized for having a kinked or abnormal tail.

DISQUALIFICATION FEATURES

- Persian body type

ANGORA VARIETIES

ODD-EYED WHITE

In the Angora, unlike most other Odd-Eyed cats, one eye should be blue and the other eye green.

IN THE BRITAIN, the Angora has been granted preliminary show status as the longcoated equivalent of the Oriental, the cat called Javanese by the Cat Association of Britain and FIFe of Europe.

WHITE The coat should be pure white with no other colouring, and the nose leather and paw pads pink. There are three sub-varieties – Amber-eyed, Blue-eyed and Odd-eyed.

BLACK The colouring must be dense coal black, sound from the roots to the tips of the hair and free from any tinge of rust on the tips, or a smoke undercoat. Nose leather is black and paw pads black or brown; eye colour is amber.

BLUE The denser shades of blue are preferred, the coat should be one level tone from nose to tail tip with the colour sound to the roots. The nose leather and paw pads are all blue and the eye colour is amber.

RED A deep, rich, clear, brilliant red is required, without shading, markings or ticking. Lips and chin should be the same colour as the coat. Nose leather and paw pads are brick red; the eye colour is amber.

CREAM One level shade of buff cream without markings must be attained, with the colour sound to the roots. Lighter shades are preferred. Nose leather and paw pads should be pink and the eye colour is amber.

BLUE-CREAM Blue should be the predominant colour with patches of solid cream. The patches should be clearly defined and well broken on both body and extremities. The eye colour is amber.

TORTOISESHELL Black is the dominant colour with unbrindled patches of red and light red. The patches should be clearly defined and well broken on both body and extremities. A blaze of red or light red on the face is desirable. The eye colour is amber.

CALICO The coat should be mostly white, with unbrindled patches of black and red, and white predominant on the underparts. Eye colour is amber. In the dilute calico the dominant colour is again white, with unbrindled patches this time of blue and cream; white is predominant on the underparts.

BI-COLOUR Varieties are black and white, blue and white, red and white or cream and

WHITE

The white coat should be free from any staining and a smudge of colour is permitted in kittens but not in adult cats.

LILAC ANGORA

This is an excellent example of the variety showing very good type and a true lilac coat which should be as the standard describes – frosty grey with a distinct pinkish tone, giving the overall appearance.

white. The muzzle, chest, legs, feet and underparts should all be white in each. White under the tail and a white collar are permissible. An inverted V-shaped blaze on the face is desirable. Eye colour is amber.

BLACK SMOKE The undercoat is white, deeply tipped with black. In repose the cat appears black, but in motion the white undercoat is clearly apparent. The narrow band of white hairs next to the skin may be seen only when the hair is parted. The mask and points, nose leather and paw pads are black and the eye colour is amber.

BLUE SMOKE The white undercoat is deeply tipped with blue. The cat in repose appears blue, but in motion the white undercoat is clearly apparent. Blue mask and points with a narrow band of white hairs next to the skin may be seen only when the hair is parted. The mask and points, nose leather and paw pads are blue, and the eyes amber.

Tabby

The following colours apply to both the Classic and Mackeral tabby patterns.

SILVER TABBY This cat has a pale, clear silver base coat including lips and chin, with dense black markings. Nose leather is brick red and paw pads black. The eyes are green or hazel.

BROWN TABBY The brilliant coppery brown base coat should have dense black markings. Lips and chin should be the same shade as the rings round the eyes, and backs of the legs black from paw to heel. Nose leather is brick red and

paw pads black or brown. The eyes are amber.

BLUE TABBY The pale bluish ivory base coat includes the lips and chin, with very deep blue markings affording a good contrast with the base colour. A warm fawn patina should cover the whole coat. Nose leather is old rose, the paw pads rose and the eyes amber.

RED TABBY The red base coat includes the lips and chin with deep, rich red markings. Nose leather and paw pads are all brick red; the eye colour is amber.

BLACK

The jet black coat that is required in this variety is often difficult to produce, particularly in the young cat, for which judges make allowances in the show situation.

TURKISH

T HE CAT KNOWN as the Turkish in Britain and the Turkish Van in Europe and the United States was first introduced to Britain and the cat fanciers of the world in 1955 by Laura Lushington. Travelling in the Lake Van district of Turkey, she and a friend were enchanted by these cats, and eventually acquired the first breeding pair. Others of the breed were imported into Britain and the necessary breeding programmes were completed in order to apply for official recognition of the cats as a pure breed in their own right. This was achieved in 1969, and the cats attracted considerable attention.

Turkish Van cats were also introduced independently from Turkey directly to the United States, where they are now recognized by some associations.

Character and Care

The first cats imported from Turkey were inclined to be slightly nervous of human contact, but today's Turkish cats generally have affectionate dispositions. They are strong and hardy, and breeders were intrigued by the animals' natural liking for water – they will voluntarily swim if given the opportunity, and have no objection to being bathed in preparation for show appearances.

The silky coat has no woolly undercoat, making grooming an easy task.

BREAKDOWN OF 100 SHOW POINTS

NB Annotated points are those set in Europe.

HEAD: 25 POINTS

General shape, nose, jaw and teeth, chin shape and size of eyes.

EARS: 10 POINTS

Shape and placement and colour.

BODY: 25 POINTS

Shape, size, bone structure, legs and shape of paws, shape and length of tail.

EYE COLOUR: 10 POINTS

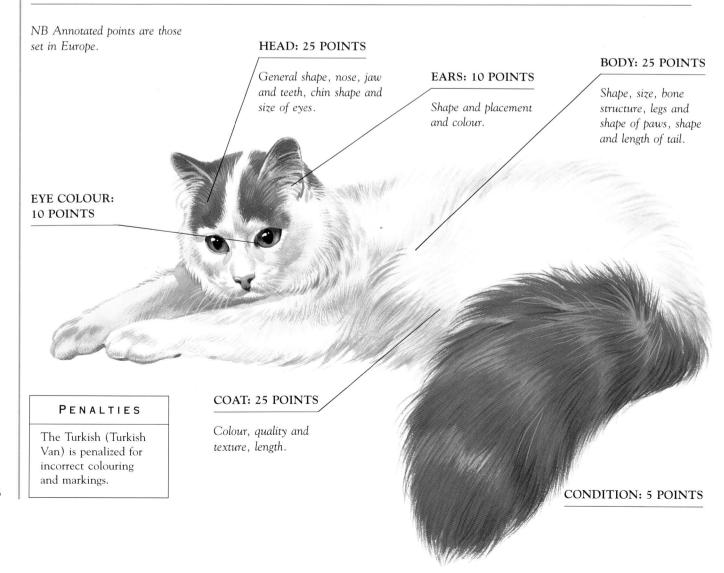

PENALTIES

The Turkish (Turkish Van) is penalized for incorrect colouring and markings.

COAT: 25 POINTS

Colour, quality and texture, length.

CONDITION: 5 POINTS

116

AUBURN TURKISH

The markings of the Turkish Van cat are responsible for the "Van" designation in other varieties which are mostly white, with small and discrete areas of colour.

KEY CHARACTERISTICS
● **CATEGORY** Longhair.
● **OVERALL BUILD** Of medium size and heavy build.
● **COAT** Fine and silky, semi-long on body, no woolly overcoat. **Pattern** Predominantly white, with auburn or cream markings on the face, and a white blaze; the tail is auburn or cream. Small, irregularly placed auburn or cream markings on the body are allowed in an otherwise good specimen.
● **COLOURS** Auburn – chalk-white coat with no trace of yellow; auburn markings on face with a white blaze; white ears. Eye rims, nose leather, paw pads and inside ears are shell pink; eye colour is amber (*UK*), plus blue and odd-eyed (*Europe*). Cream – chalk-white coat with no trace of yellow; cream markings on face with a white blaze; white ears. Eye rims, nose leather, paw pads and inside ears shell pink; eye colour amber, blue and odd-eyed.
● **OTHER FEATURES** Short, blunt head, triangular in shape. Straight nose, of medium length, with firm chin. Eyes are large and oval, set slightly obliquely. Ears are large and well-furred, wide-based with slightly rounded tips, set high and erect on the skull. The body is long, but sturdy and muscular, with medium-length legs and medium-length tail, well furred but without undercoat. Paws are round and dainty, and well tufted.

CREAM TURKISH

The cream Turkish cat may have light amber eyes, or blue eyes, and the odd-eyed variety is also accepted where there is one blue eye and the other of light amber.

120 British Shorthair

134 Chartreux

136 Manx

140 Scottish Fold

142 European Shorthair

146 American Shorthair

154 American Wirehair

156 Exotic Shorthair

SHORTHAIRED BREEDS

BRITISH SHORTHAIR

THIS BREED PROBABLY evolved from domestic cats introduced to the British Isles by the Roman colonists some 2000 years ago. However, today's pedigree Shorthairs must conform to strict standards of points, and differ quite considerably from the common

Shorthairs appeared in substantial numbers in the first cat shows held towards the end of the nineteenth century, then seemed to lose their popularity in favour of the Persian and Angora cats which were specially imported for the show scene.

It was not until the 1930s that a general resurgence of the breed began, and selective breeding produced cats of good type and the desired range of colours. In the early days solid colours were preferred to the patterned varieties, the most highly prized of all being the blue-grey, sometimes given solitary breed status as the British Blue.

British Shorthairs suffered a setback during the Second World War when many owners had to give up breeding pedigree kittens and neutered their cats. In the post-war years very few pedigree stud males remained, and the Shorthair's type suffered after outcrosses were made with shorthaired cats of Foreign type. Matters were redressed during the early 1950s by careful matings with Blue Persians, and within a few generations the British Shorthair was brought up to the exacting standards existing today.

American stock came from the best of the British catteries. At first the ACFA officially recognized only the blue and black varieties, and the CCA and CFF recognized only the British Blue. In 1976 the ACFA was the first to accept all colours, and was followed by the remaining associations. In the United States, as in Britain, British Shorthairs are bred only to

BREAKDOWN OF 100 SHOW POINTS

NB Annotated points (right) are those set in the UK for self-coloured cats. Those below are those set for patterned varieties.

HEAD and EARS:
25 POINTS

EYES: 10 POINTS

BODY, LEGS and PAWS:
20 POINTS

TAIL: 5 POINTS

COAT: 40 POINTS

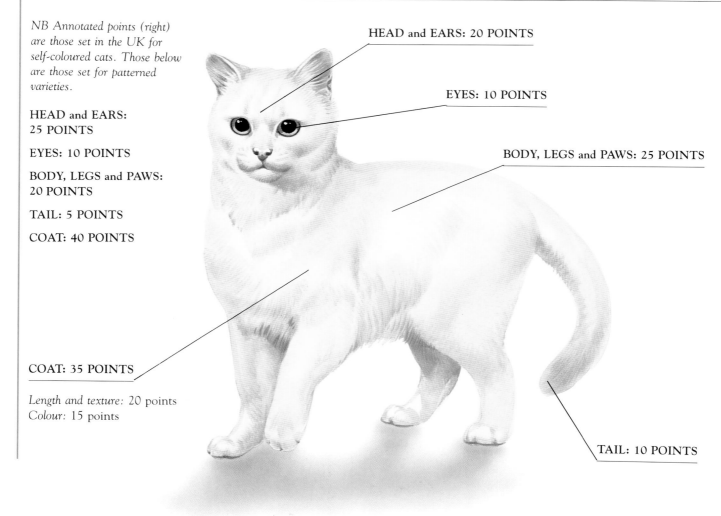

HEAD and EARS: 20 POINTS

EYES: 10 POINTS

BODY, LEGS and PAWS: 25 POINTS

COAT: 35 POINTS

Length and texture: 20 points
Colour: 15 points

TAIL: 10 POINTS

other British Shorthairs and back-crossing to Persians is no longer allowed.

Character and Care

The typical British Shorthair has a sweet and gentle nature and makes an undemanding, quiet-voiced pet. It is generally calm and intelligent, and readily responds to affection.

Although it has a short coat, this is quite dense and needs regular grooming by brushing and combing right through to the roots every day. It is particularly important to accustom all kittens to this daily procedure from a very early age so that it is not resented later. The eyes and ears should be gently cleaned with a cotton bud whenever necessary, and the coat may be polished with a grooming mitt or a silk scarf.

KEY CHARACTERISTICS

- **CATEGORY** Shorthair.

- **OVERALL BUILD** Large and chunky (not coarse or overweight).

- **COAT** Short and dense, not double or woolly. Firm and resilient to the touch.

- **HEAD** Very broad and round with well-developed cheeks, set on a short, thick neck.

- **NOSE** Medium broad with gentle dip in profile.

- **CHIN** Firm and well-developed.

- **EYES** Large, round and well opened.

- **EARS** Medium size, broad-based and round-tipped, set far apart.

- **BODY** Medium to large; powerful, with a level back and broad chest.

- **LEGS** Short to medium length, well boned.

- **PAWS** Round.

- **TAIL** Length in proportion to body, thick at the base and tapering to a rounded tip.

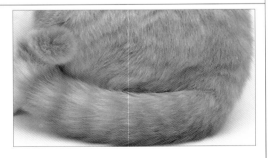

- **COLOURS** White, black, blue, cream tortoiseshell, blue-cream, black smoke, bi-colour, tortoiseshell-and-white, tabby (Classic, Mackerel and Spotted; all colours chocolate, lilac, smoke (all colours),tipped (all colours), Himalayan or Colourpoint (all colours).

SOLID VARIETIES

THE MOST POPULAR of the British Shorthairs is the self-coloured British Blue, the colour so well complemented by the orange or copper eyes. The Black and the British White have coats more difficult to produce to top show standard.

BLACK SHORTHAIR This is one of the oldest varieties known, and is often mismarked with a white locket. In the show specimen no white hairs are allowed anywhere. The true Black Shorthair must have a shining coat, jet black to the roots and with no rusty tinge. The nose leather is black, the paw pads black or brown and the eye colour gold, orange or copper with no trace of green.

WHITE SHORTHAIR The White Shorthair of good show type is one of the most striking of British Shorthairs. The coat must be pure white with no sign of yellow tingeing; the nose leather and paw pads are pink. The Blue-eyed White has eyes of a deep sapphire blue, and is penalized in the show ring for green rims or flecks in the eye. The Orange-eyed White has deep orange, gold or copper eye-colour.

BLACK

One of the oldest of the pedigree breeds, the Black British Shorthair is difficult to produce with the required black coat sound to the roots and with no white hairs.

BLUE-EYED WHITE

Occasionally found to be deaf, the Blue-Eyed White is a beautiful variety which, for showing, should have eyes of a deep blue.

CREAM BRITISH SHORTHAIR

The cream variety should be as free from tabby markings as possible, and without any white hairs. The eye colour may be copper, orange or gold.

BLUE

The "British Blue" is by far the most popular and best known of all the Shorthairs. Its large round and glowing eyes of copper, orange or gold perfectly complement the even blue coat.

CREAM SHORTHAIR A fairly rare variety, the Cream Shorthair is difficult to produce to the exacting show standard required without any shadowy tabby markings showing in the rich, light cream coat. There must be no white markings anywhere, and the cream colour should be sound to the roots. The nose leather and paw pads are pink, and the eye colour is orange or copper.

BLUE SHORTHAIR The British Blue is the most popular variety of the Shorthairs and is certainly the one that most closely meets the very exacting show standard. The coat should be very level in colour and of a light to medium blue tone, lighter shades being preferred. No tabby or white markings are allowed anywhere. Nose leather and paw pads are blue and the eye colour is gold, orange or copper.

BLUE-CREAM SHORTHAIR This is a female-only variety, being a dilute form of Tortoise-shell. It is bred from crosses between Blues and Creams, Creams and Tortoiseshells, or Blues and Tortoiseshells. In Britain, the standard calls for the coat to be softly intermingled with the two shades, but in the United States the variety is required to have a distinctly blue coat with cream patches. Nose leather and paw pads are blue and/or pink, and the eye colour should be gold, orange or copper.

BLUE-CREAM

A dilute variety of the tortoiseshell, the Blue-Cream British should have an evenly intermingled mixture of medium blue-grey and pale cream throughout its coat.

LILAC

A comparatively recent addition to the British Shorthair colour list, the Lilac conforms to the usual standard for conformation, and has an even coloured frosty grey coat with a distinctly pinkish cast.

BI-COLOUR VARIETIES

CREAM AND WHITE BI-COLOUR

Symmetry of colouring is desired in the British Bi-colour, with not more than half of the cat to be white.

BI-COLOUR SHORTHAIRS are cats of just two colours: a standard colour with white. It is important for the markings to be as symmetrical as possible to present a balanced impression. The cats may be black-and-white, blue-and-white, red-and-white or cream-and-white, and there must be no tabby markings in the self-coloured areas. The markings comprising the self-coloured portions should start immediately behind the shoulders round the barrel of the body and include the tail and hind legs, leaving the hind paws white. The ears and mask of the face should be in the self colour, while the shoulders, neck, forelegs and feet, chin, lips and blaze should be white. The white area also extends as a blaze up the face and over the top of the head in the ideal specimen. The nose leather and paw pads are generally pink and the eye colour is gold, orange or copper.

The Bi-colour is penalized for brindling or tabby markings and is disqualified if the white areas predominate.

BLUE AND WHITE BI-COLOUR

This cat is very evenly marked, with a good shade of medium blue in the basic coat colour.

TORTOISESHELL VARIETIES

BLACK AND RED markings, both dark and light, should be equally balanced over the cat's head, body, legs and tail. Colours should be brilliant, free from blurring, brindling and tabby patches, and with no white markings. A red blaze down the face is desired. The nose leather and paw pads should be pink and/or black. Eye colour is gold, orange or copper (hazel is also allowed by some associations).

This variety is penalized for brindling, tabby markings, unequal balance of colour and unbroken colour on the paws, and is disqualified for any white markings.

TORTOISESHELL
Here the characteristic black and red colours are intermingled evenly.

CHOCOLATE TORTIE
Warm chocolate mixed with red and light red make up the bright colouring of the chocolate-tortoiseshell coat.

LILAC TORTIE
In the lilac tortoiseshell there is an admixture of lilac and pale cream which produces a pleasing pastel effect over the body.

TORTOISESHELL AND WHITE

OFTEN CALLED THE calico cat, the Tortoise-shell-and-white is very difficult to breed to top exhibition standard. It should be equally balanced in black and red, both light and dark on white. The colours must be brilliant and the cat must have no sign of brindling or tabby markings. The patching should cover the top of the head, the ears and cheeks, the back and tail and part of the flanks. There should be a white blaze down the face. The nose leather and paws are pink and/or black and the eye colour is gold, orange or copper (hazel is also allowed by some associations).

This variety is penalized for brindling, tabby markings, unbroken colour on the paws and unequal markings, and is disqualified if the white areas predominate.

TORTIE AND WHITE
This cat is quite rare in the show rings since it is difficult to breed.

BLUE TORTIE AND WHITE
Bold areas of blue and cream patch the coat of this attractive cat and are highlighted by the white markings. In this variety, the eye colour can be copper, orange or gold.

TABBY VARIETIES

**BROWN
SPOTTED**

*Clearly defined black
spots on a brown
ground colour is the
requirement for this
variety.*

THERE ARE THREE acceptable tabby patterns in
the British Shorthair – the Classic, the Mackerel and the Spotted. All three are found in a
wide range of colours, only some of which are
recognized for show purposes, although associations around the world differ considerably in
their rules. Tabby varieties are penalized for
incorrect eye colour; white anywhere; and
incorrect tabby markings.

Patterns

In the Classic tabby markings should be dense
and clearly defined; the legs evenly barred with
bracelets and the tail evenly ringed, and the cat
should have several unbroken necklaces on the
neck and upper chest. On the head frown
marks form a letter "M", and an unbroken line
runs back from the outer corner of each eye.
There are swirl markings on the cheeks and
vertical lines run over the back of the head to
the shoulder markings, which resemble a butterfly, with both upper and lower wings distinctly outlined and marked with dots within
the outlines. The back is marked with a spine

**RED MACKEREL
TABBY**

*Lines run down from
the spine in the
mackerel Tabby, but
the markings on the
head are the same as
for the other tabbies.*

**BROWN CLASSIC
TABBY**

*This chunky British cat
shows the Classic
Tabby pattern which is
also known as the
Marbled or Blotched
Tabby.*

128

BLUE SPOTTED

In the Blue Spotted, the pattern consists of blue-grey spots on a lighter background, with enough difference in colour so to afford a good contrast between the markings and the base coat.

line and a parallel line on either side, all three lines being separated by stripes of the coat's ground colour. A large solid blotch on either side of the body should be encircled by one or more unbroken rings, and the side markings should be the same on both sides of the body. A double row of "vest" buttons should run down the chest and under the stomach.

In the Mackerel tabby, markings should be dense and clearly defined and all resemble narrow pencilling. The legs should be evenly barred with narrow bracelets, and the tail barred. There are several distinct narrow neck-laces around the neck. The head is barred, with a distinct "M" on the forehead, and unbroken lines running back from the eyes. More lines run back over the head to meet the shoulder markings. Along the spine the lines run together forming a dark saddle, and fine, pencil-like markings run down either side of the body from the spine. Clear spotting is

essential in the Spotted tabby: the spots can be round, oval, oblong or rosette-shaped. The head markings should be the same as those required for the Classic tabby. The legs should be clearly spotted and the tail spotted or with broken rings. Spotted cats are penalized when the spots are not distinct, and for having bars, except on the head.

SILVER SPOTTED

Perhaps the clearest of all the spotted coats is that of the Silver, which has dense black markings on a background of very pale silvery-white hair.

RED TABBY
This richly coloured Red Tabby has the typical Classic pattern on a slightly lighter red base. The desired unbroken "necklaces" can be seen quite clearly around the cat's neck.

SILVER TABBY
Like the Silver Spotted, the Silver Tabby's coat pattern shows up extremely well in black on pale silver. The necklaces and eye lines are easy to identify in this picture.

Colours

BROWN TABBY Ground colour should be rich sable or brown with dense black markings. Lips and chin should be the same as the rings around the eyes. Backs of the legs should be black from heel to paw. Nose leather must be brick red and the paw pads black or brown. Eye colour is gold, orange or copper. (Some associations also allow green or hazel eye colour.)

RED TABBY Ground colour is red, including lips and chin. Markings are a deep, rich red, quite distinct from the ground colour. Nose leather and paw pads are brick red. Eye colour is gold, orange or copper. (Some associations also accept hazel eye colour.)

SILVER TABBY Ground colour is a pale clear silver, including lips and chin, and markings are dense black. Nose leather is brick red; paw pads black. Eye colour may be green or hazel.

BLUE TABBY Accepted by some associations. Ground colour, including lips and chin, should be pale bluish ivory, and markings a very deep blue affording good contrast with the ground colour. There should be an overall warm fawn patina. Nose leather is old rose; paw pads rose. Eye colour is gold or copper.

CREAM TABBY Accepted by some associations. For this variety the ground colour, including lips and chin, is very pale cream. Markings are of buff or cream sufficiently darker than the ground colour to afford good contrast, while still remaining in the dilute colour range. Nose leather and paw pads are pink. Eye colour may be gold or copper.

BLUE TABBY

In dilute varieties like this blue tabby, the pattern is more diffused.

RED SILVER TABBY

The attractive base colour of a pale silvery cream is a warm-toned colour.

TORTIE TABBY

In the Tortie Tabby the tabby pattern is patched with red, light red or cream depending on the main colour of the cat's markings. This cat is a Tortie Silver Tabby.

OTHER VARIETIES

SMOKE-PATTERNED CATS are of standard feline colours but instead of the colour being sound to the roots, the undercoat is white or silver. In repose the cat at first appears to be self-coloured, but in motion the white or silver undercoat is apparent, giving a shot-silk appearance. In each sub-variety, the nose leather, paw pads and eye colour required is the same as for that of the relevant self-colour. British Shorthair Smoke cats are bred in a range of colours but the various associations each have a limited range of those which are officially recognized.

BLACK SMOKE The white or silver undercoat is deeply tipped with black. In repose the cat appears black; in motion the pale undercoat is clearly apparent. The nose leather and paw pads are both black and the eye colour may be either gold or copper.

BLUE SMOKE The undercoat is white or silver, deeply tipped with blue. The cat in repose appears blue; but as with the black, in motion the pale undercoat is clearly apparent. Nose leather and paw pads are blue and the eye colour may be gold or copper.

COLOUR POINTED

The general type of this group of Shorthairs is the same for the British Shorthair. A range of points colours is accepted including the Lilac Point.

RED COLOURPOINT

The mask, ears, legs and tail should be clearly defined and well matched.

CREAM COLOURPOINT

There should be good contrast between the points and the body colour and any shading on the body should be of the same tone as the points.

BLUE CREAM COLOURPOINT
Although the standard of points requires eye colour in the Colourpoint to be a clear definite blue, this has proved difficult to achieve in most varieties.

BLACK TIPPED SHORTHAIR
A genetically silver variety, the colour is restricted to the very tips of the hairs of the coat, while the undercoat is so pale that it appears to be pure white.

LILAC CREAM COLOURPOINT
Also called the Lilac Tortie, this is a very ethereal colour, the points being delicately mingled shades of palest lilac and delicate cream.

CHARTREUX

Native to France, the Chartreux is said to have been bred exclusively by Carthusian monks as long ago as the sixteenth century. The monks lived in the monastery near the town of Grenoble, world famous for its unique liqueur, known as Chartreuse. The naturalist Georges Louis Buffon's work *Histoire Naturelle*, published in 1756, records details of the self-blue feline, and in the 1930s a French veterinarian suggested that the breed should have its own scientific name *Felis catus cartusianorum*. Today's Chartreux should not be confused with the British Blue or the European Shorthaired

Blue. It is massively built, with a very distinctive jowled head, more pronounced in the male than in the female, and is a blue-only breed.

Character and Care
Self assured and affectionate, the Chartreux has always been considered a cat for the connoisseur. It is quiet-voiced and will happily live confined to the house. The dense coat needs regular combing to keep the woolly undercoat in good condition, and brushing enhances the way in which the coat stands away from the body – a breed characteristic.

BREAKDOWN OF 100 SHOW POINTS

NB Annotated points are those set in the UK.

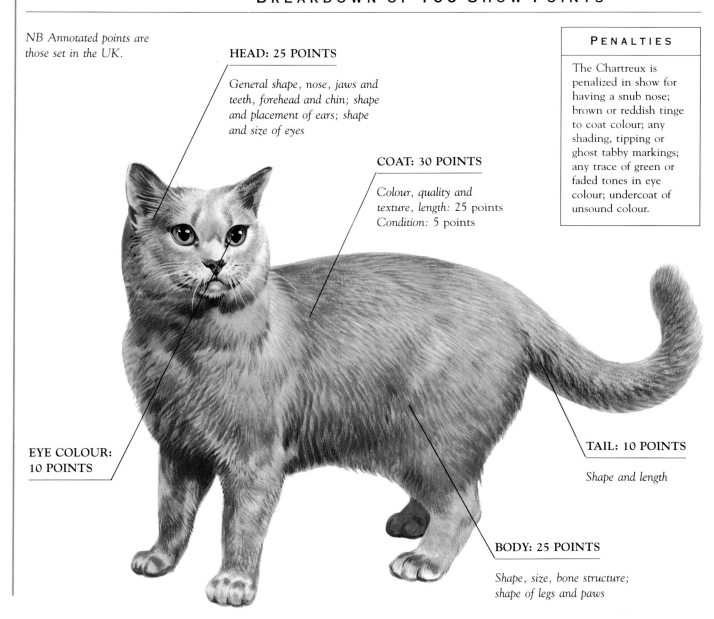

HEAD: 25 POINTS

General shape, nose, jaws and teeth, forehead and chin; shape and placement of ears; shape and size of eyes

COAT: 30 POINTS

Colour, quality and texture, length: 25 points
Condition: 5 points

PENALTIES

The Chartreux is penalized in show for having a snub nose; brown or reddish tinge to coat colour; any shading, tipping or ghost tabby markings; any trace of green or faded tones in eye colour; undercoat of unsound colour.

EYE COLOUR: 10 POINTS

TAIL: 10 POINTS

Shape and length

BODY: 25 POINTS

Shape, size, bone structure; shape of legs and paws

The strong head and broad skull of the blue cat known as the Chartreux.

KEY CHARACTERISTICS

- **CATEGORY** Shorthair.

- **OVERALL BUILD** Medium to large, firm and muscular.

- **COAT** Dense and with slightly woolly undercoat; double coat makes the hair stand out from the body; glossy appearance.

- **COLOUR** Any shade of blue from pale blue-grey to deep blue-grey, paler shades preferred. Uniform tone essential.

- **OTHER FEATURES** A wide head, with a narrow flat plane between the ears and wide jowls. The nose is broad and straight, and the chin firm and well developed. Eyes are large and open, not too rounded and with the outer corner slightly uptilted; eye colour is vivid deep yellow to vivid deep copper. The most intense colour is preferred. Ears are medium sized, set high on the head and slightly flaring, giving an alert expression. The body is solid and muscular with a broad chest; the legs are strong, medium length in proportion to the body. Paws are large and the tail is medium length in proportion to the body; it may taper, and has a rounded tip.

CHARTREUX

One of the true blue cats of the world, but not found in Britain, the Chartreux is a massive breed with a very gentle nature and a quiet voice.

MANX

LEGENDS AND FAIRY-TALES explaining the origins of this unique tail-less breed abound, but modern science agrees that its appearance is due to a mutant dominant gene. The original mutation must have occurred many years ago, for Manx cats have been known since 1900, with a specialist breed club being first established in Britain in 1901.

Although it is an old breed, Manx cats remain rare. The females produce small litters as a direct result of the gene for tail-lessness. This factor is a semi-lethal gene, and the homozygous Manx – one that inherits the tail-less gene from both parents – dies within the womb at an early stage of foetal development. The Manx that is born alive is the heterozygote – one that inherits only one gene for tail-lessness, the other member of the gene pair being for a normal tail. Breeders usually cross tail-less Manx with normal-tailed Manx off-spring to retain the correct body type.

Character and Care

Manx cats are highly intelligent, playful and affectionate, and make ideal and unusual pets. A good specimen generally takes top awards in show when competing against other breeds, particularly if it is easy to handle and performs wells for the judges.

The Manx's double coat repays good feeding and regular grooming. It should be combed through to the roots over the entire body, and given a final sheen by polishing with the hands, a grooming mitt or a silk scarf.

BREAKDOWN OF 100 SHOW POINTS

NB Annotated points are those set in the UK.

HEAD and EARS:
20 POINTS

TAILLESSNESS:
25 POINTS

EYES: 5 POINTS

COAT: 20 POINTS

BODY, LEGS and PAWS: 30 POINTS

KEY CHARACTERISTICS

- **CATEGORY** Shorthair.

- **OVERALL BUILD** Medium sized with a general impression of roundness.

- **COAT** *Manx* Short, dense and double, giving a padded quality due to the comparatively long, open outer coat and the close, cottony undercoat. *Cymric* Of medium length, with close dense undercoat and longer outer coat standing away from the body; full around the neck and on the breeches; tufted ears and toes.

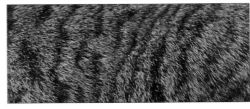

- **HEAD** Round, though slightly longer than it is broad, with a rounded forehead, prominent cheeks and a jowly appearance. The definite whisker break enhances large, round whisker pads and the muzzle is well developed.

- **NOSE** In profile there is a gentle nose dip.

- **CHIN** Firm and strong.

- **EYES** Large, round and full.

- **EARS** Medium size, set wide apart and slightly turned outwards.

- **BODY** Solidly muscled and compact with sturdy bone structure. The chest is broad and the back short, forming a smooth, continuous arch from the shoulders to the rump, where it curves to give the desirable round look.

- **LEGS** The legs and feet are heavily boned. The hind legs are much longer than the forelegs, causing the rump to be higher than the shoulders in the standing cat.

- **PAWS** Neat and round.

- **TAIL** Tail-lessness is absolute in the perfect Manx, with a definite hollow at the end of the spine where, in a tailed cat, the tail would begin. A rise of bones at the end of the spine is not always penalized, depending on the amount of bone present.

- **COLOURS** All colours and patterns are acceptable with the exception of the Himalayan (Siamese) coat pattern.

PENALTIES

The Manx cat is severely penalized in the show ring if the judge is unable to make it stand or walk properly.

DISQUALIFICATION FEATURES

- poor physical condition
- the incorrect number of toes
- colour or pattern indicates hybridization

The cat is transferred from the Manx breed class to that for Any Other Varieties if it has long or silky fur, or there is a definite, visible tail joint.

MANX VARIETIES

THE MANX IS accepted in the following colour varieties by most American associations. Each of the varieties listed has identical colour requirements to its equivalent in the American Shorthair, with the exception of eye colour. In American Shorthair varieties with brilliant gold eye colour, the Manx should have eyes of brilliant copper.

The accepted varieties are: Black; Blue; Red; Cream; Tortoiseshell; Blue-cream; Calico; Dilute Calico; Chinchilla; Shaded Silver; Black Smoke; Blue Smoke; Classic and Mackerel Tabby in the following colours: Brown Tabby; Blue Tabby; Red Tabby; Cream Tabby; Cameo Tabby; Silver Tabby; Patched Tabby in Brown, and Blue and Silver.

Other Manx Colours

Any other colour or pattern with the exception of those showing hybridization resulting in the the Himalayan pattern. The eye colour should be appropriate to the predominant colour of the cat.

TORTIE TABBY & WHITE MANX

This adorable little Manx kitten has adopted the typical natural stance of the breed. Manx kittens are precocious and very playful and inquisitive, making wonderful pets.

RED SPOTTED MANX

All colours are accepted in the Manx except those in the Himalayan or Siamese pattern.

BROWN TABBY AND WHITE MANX

All tabby patterns are allowed, including those with the addition of white areas. Taillessness is a high scoring feature.

BLUE TORTIE & WHITE MANX

The solid compact body and a short back makes the typical Manx a sturdy compact cat, and the hind legs are longer than the forelegs. The rump is firm and rounded.

CYMRIC

IN THE LATE 1960s breeders of Manx cats in the United States were intrigued to discover that long-coated kittens occasionally appeared in otherwise normal litters from their Manx queens. Although there were no longhaired cats in any of the pedigrees, it is possible that the recessive gene for causing long hair had been inherited from some of the tailed short-haired cats used as outcrosses in past generations. Although the first reaction of the breeders was to let such kittens go as neutered pets, it was decided that the variety could be developed as a separate, and very attractive breed in its own right. When choosing a name for the breed some associations preferred Long-haired Manx, while others accepted Cymric (pronounced koom-rik), the Welsh word for "Welsh". The breed is recognized by some associations, and apart from the coat, has the same standard requirements for show purposes as the Manx cat. The coat is of medium length, soft and full, giving a padded, heavy look to the body. The same coat colours and patterns are accepted as for the Manx.

TORTOISESHELL CYMRIC

The longcoated version of the Manx cat is not accepted by all associations.

139

SCOTTISH FOLD

A LITTER OF OTHERWISE normal kittens born on a farm in Scotland contained the first Scottish Fold in 1961. A shepherd, William Ross, noticed the kitten with the quaint, folded ears and expressed an interest in acquiring such a cat. Two years later, the mother cat, Susie, gave birth to two kittens with folded ears, and William Ross was given one. A breeding programme was begun in Great Britain, but when it was discovered that a small proportion of cats with folded ears also had thickened tails and limbs, the governing registration body banned Scottish Folds from all shows. The British breeders, who were dedicated to breeding only sound cats, resorted to registering their cats in overseas associations, and the main centre of activity for the breed switched to the United States. Today's Scottish Fold cats are bred to British Shorthairs in Britain and to American Shorthairs in the United States, or back to the prick-eared offspring of Folds. The folded ears are due to the action of a single dominant gene, and all Scottish Folds must have at least one folded-eared parent.

Character and Care
The Scottish Fold is a loving, placid and companionable cat which loves both humans and other pets. The female makes a superb mother and the kittens are quite precocious.

The short, dense coat is kept in good condition with the minimum of brushing and combing, and the folded ears are kept immaculate by gently cleaning inside the folds with a moistened cotton bud.

BREAKDOWN OF 100 SHOW POINTS

NB Annotated points are those set in the UK.

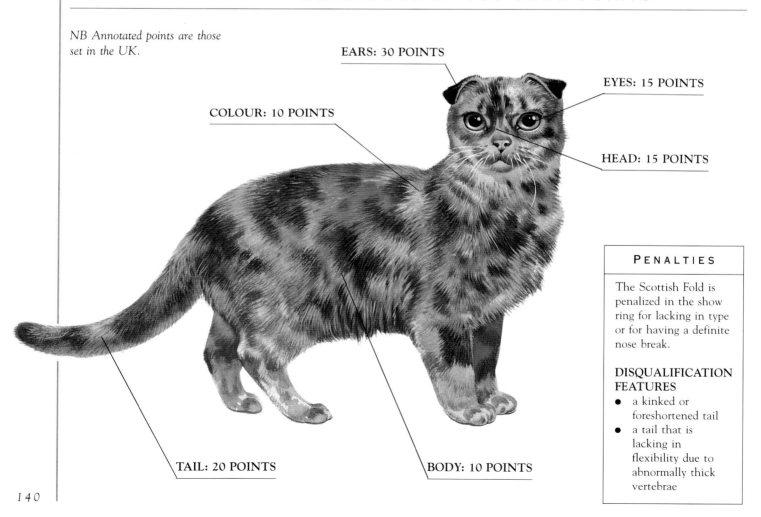

EARS: 30 POINTS

EYES: 15 POINTS

COLOUR: 10 POINTS

HEAD: 15 POINTS

TAIL: 20 POINTS

BODY: 10 POINTS

PENALTIES

The Scottish Fold is penalized in the show ring for lacking in type or for having a definite nose break.

DISQUALIFICATION FEATURES
- a kinked or foreshortened tail
- a tail that is lacking in flexibility due to abnormally thick vertebrae

CALICO FOLD
The colour requirements for the Scottish Fold are the same as for the American Shorthair.

BLACK & WHITE SCOTTISH FOLD
This cat illustrates the caplike attitude of the folded ears in a good example of this breed.

KEY CHARACTERISTICS

- **CATEGORY** Shorthair.

- **OVERALL BUILD** Medium size, well rounded with medium bone.

- **COAT** Short, dense and resilient.

- **COLOURS** White, black, blue, red, cream, tortoiseshell, calico, dilute calico, blue-cream, chinchilla, shaded silver, shell cameo, shaded cameo, black smoke, blue smoke, cameo smoke, bicolor; Classic and Mackerel Tabby in brown, blue, red, cream, cameo, silver; Patched Tabby in brown, blue, silver; any other colour or pattern with the exception of those showing evidence of hybridization resulting in the colours chocolate or lavender, the Himalayan pattern or these combinations with white. The eye colour should be appropriate to the coat colour. Each variety has identical colour requirements to its equivalent variety in the American Shorthair.

- **OTHER FEATURES** Well-rounded head with a firm chin and jaw, and muzzle with well-rounded whisker pads. Short nose with a gentle curve, and with a slight stop at eye level. The ears are small and fold forwards and downwards, and are set in a caplike fashion to expose a rounded cranium. The ear tips are rounded. The eyes are large and round with a sweet expression. The firm body of medium size has legs of medium bone and neat round paws. The tail is medium to long, flexible and tapering.

A LONGHAIRED VARIETY
This is one of the longcoated cats which have appeared from time to time in litters of Scottish Fold kittens.

PATCHED SILVER TABBY & WHITE
The ears of the Scottish Fold are small and fold forwards and downwards on the top of the head.

141

EUROPEAN SHORTHAIR

THIS SHOW BREED has been naturally developed from the indigenous cat of continental Europe. Its standard of points is similar to that of the British Shorthair, and it is presumed to be totally free of any admixture of other breeds. The first European Shorthairs were descended from cats introduced to Northern Europe by invading armies of Roman soldiers, who brought their cats with them to keep down vermin in their food stores.

Character and Care

The European Shorthair is a placid, good-natured breed which makes an ideal family cat. It also accepts the time it spends in the show ring and the demands of being judged with a quiet, dignified tolerance.

The short dense coat is easy to maintain with a few minutes' daily combing to keep the undercoat in good condition. The eyes and ears should be cleaned regularly with a slightly moistened cotton bud.

BREAKDOWN OF 100 SHOW POINTS

*NB Annotated points are those
set in Europe.*

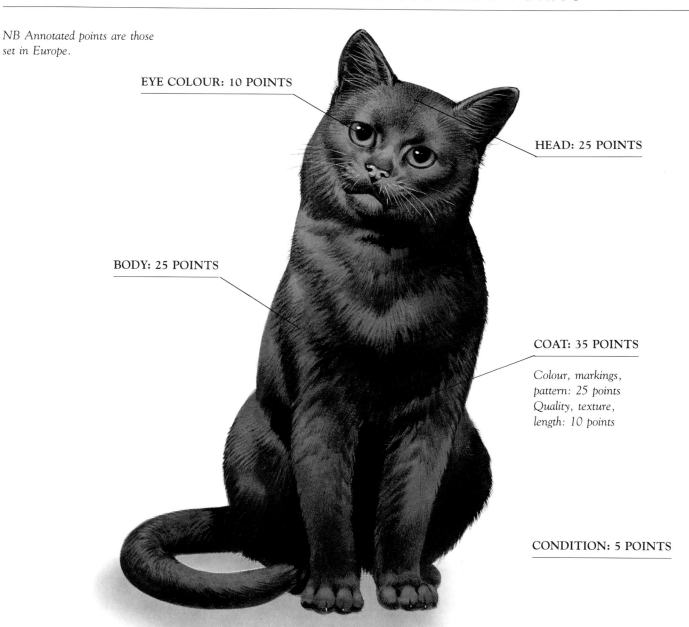

EYE COLOUR: 10 POINTS

HEAD: 25 POINTS

BODY: 25 POINTS

COAT: 35 POINTS

*Colour, markings,
pattern: 25 points
Quality, texture,
length: 10 points*

CONDITION: 5 POINTS

KEY CHARACTERISTICS

- **CATEGORY** Shorthair.

- **OVERALL BUILD** Medium to large (not over-large).

- **COAT** Short and dense, tight and glossy, not woolly.

- **HEAD** Fairly large; it appears round but is a little longer than its breadth; slightly rounded forehead and skull and well-developed cheeks. Neck muscular and of medium length.

- **NOSE** Medium length and straight.

- **CHIN** Firm.

- **EYES** Round and open, widely separated and set slightly obliquely.

- **EARS** Medium size, slightly rounded at the tips, set upright and well apart.

- **BODY** Robust, strong and muscular with well-developed chest.

- **LEGS** Medium length, strong and sturdy, narrowing gradually to paws.

- **PAWS** Firm and round.

- **TAIL** Medium length, thick at the base, tapering gradually to a rounded tip.

- **COLOURS** White with blue, green, yellow, orange or odd eyes; black, blue, red, cream, black tortie, blue tortie; smoke: black, blue, red, cream, black tortie, blue tortie; non-silver tabby: black, blue, red, cream , black tortie, blue tortie (all accepted in Classic, Mackerel and Spotted); silver tabby: black, blue, red, cream, black tortie, blue tortie (all accepted in Classic, Mackerel and Spotted); bi-colour: black, blue, red, cream, black tortie, blue tortie (all accepted in van, harlequin and bi-colour).

PENALTIES

The European Shorthair is penalized in the show ring for being too large in overall size or being either too cobby or too slender.

DISQUALIFICATION FEATURES
- hanging jowl pouches
- a definite nose stop
- over-long or woolly appearance to coat
- any signs of crossbreeding in its ancestry

EUROPEAN SHORTHAIR VARIETIES

MANY EUROPEAN SHORTHAIRS have British Shorthair ancestors and are found in a similar range of coat colours and patterns. Tabbies are popular, particularly in the silver range, plus the typy reds and creams, and pretty blue-creams.

EUROPEAN WHITE There are three sub-varieties of the European White, and all must have pure white coats without any sign of yellow tingeing or coloured hairs. The first sub-variety should have eyes of deep blue; the second may have either green, yellow or orange eye colour; the third, the White Odd-eyed, has one eye of deep blue and the other eye either green, yellow or orange.

EUROPEAN SOLID The Solid-coloured European may be black, blue, red or cream. All must have a coat colour sound to the roots. The eye colour may be green, yellow or orange.

EUROPEAN TORTIE These patched varieties may be either black and red, giving the Black Tortie, or blue and cream, giving the Blue Tortie. For both the eye colour may be green, yellow or orange.

EUROPEAN SMOKE Cats in this group have a white or silver undercoat, and the six accepted varieties are Black Smoke, Blue Smoke, Red Smoke, Cream Smoke, Black Tortie Smoke and Blue Tortie Smoke. All may have either green, yellow or orange eye colour.

Tabby Varieties

The non-silver tabby group may have a coat pattern blotched (also known as the Classic tabby), Mackerel, or Spotted. The six accepted varieties are Black Tabby, Blue Tabby, Red Tabby, Cream Tabby, Black Tortie Tabby and Blue Tortie Tabby. All may have green, yellow or orange eye colour.

In the silver tabby group, the markings are of the main varietal colour etched on a base colour of pure pale silver. There should be no ticked hairs or brindling in the pattern. The three tabby patterns – Classic, Mackerel and Spotted – are accepted, and the six accepted varieties are Black Silver Tabby, Blue Silver Tabby, Red Silver Tabby, Cream Silver Tabby, Black Tortie Silver Tabby and Blue Tortie Silver Tabby. Eye colour may be green, yellow or orange, but green is preferred.

SILVER SPOTTED EUROPEAN
This typical European Shorthair shows the black version of the silver spotted which is well marked on the flanks but with the pattern tending to form mackerel stripes over the ribs.

Non-tabby Bi-colour Varieties

Three patterns are accepted, van, harlequin and bi-colour. The markings may be black, blue, red, cream, black tortie or blue tortie.

In van and harlequin, the eye colour may be deep blue, green, yellow or orange; or odd-eyed with one eye deep blue and the other green, yellow or orange. In the Bi-colour pattern, the eyes may be green, yellow or orange. For judging purposes the van and harlequin cats are grouped together by eye colour.

Van-patterned cats are basically white, with two coloured patches on the head, separated by a white blaze down the nose, and a tail coloured from rump to tip. The ears may be coloured, but white ears with a pink inner surface to the pinna are preferable; the chest and stomach must be white but up to three small irregularly distributed colour patches on the body and/or legs are tolerated for judging purposes. There must be no white hairs in the coloured areas of the coat.

Tabby Van cats have the same basic requirements, and may have patches of any of the three basic tabby patterns – all Tabby Van cats are judged in the same class regardless of pattern. Tortie Van cats also have the same basic requirements, but have tortie markings on the patched areas.

Nose leather may be pink or as expected for the colour of the patterned areas. In the Tabby Van the nose leather should be pink or pinkish-red outlined with the appropriate colour for the patterned areas; in the Tortie Van the nose leather should be patched with pink.

Harlequin-patterned cats are basically white with solid coloured patches over at least one quarter, but not more than one half, of the body surface. The coloured parts should consist of various patches surrounded by white, and there must be no single white hairs present in the coloured areas. Tabby and Tortie Harlequin cats are also accepted. The nose leather and paw pads are as for the van pattern.

The bi-coloured cat is basically white with coloured patches which must be clearly separated from one another. At least one half, but not more than two-thirds, of the cat must be coloured; the colour must be even and harmoniously distributed over the cat's body. A white blaze down the face and some white on the back are desirable characteristics. There must be no single white hairs in the coloured areas.

The Tabby Bi-colour may be either Classic (blotched), Mackerel or Spotted; the Tortie Bi-colour should have large, well-defined patches of clear, bright colours. The nose leather and paw pads are as specified for the van pattern.

CLASSIC TABBY
The Classic tabby pattern consists of a precise set of clearly defined, dense markings on a paler ground colour.

MACKEREL TABBY
A beautiful example of a well marked mackerel tabby, this red cat has excellent type, matching the European Shorthair standards of points.

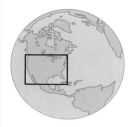

AMERICAN SHORTHAIR

AT THE BEGINNING of the twentieth century an English cat fancier gave a pedigree Red Tabby Shorthair male to a friend in the United States, to be mated with some of the indigenous shorthaired felines. This cat was registered in the name of Belle, and was the first pedigree cat to appear in the records of the Cat Fanciers' Association. Other British cats followed, including a male Silver Tabby named Pretty Correct, and the register grew with listings of "home-grown" cats as well as imports. At first the breed was called the Shorthair, then its name was changed to Domestic Shorthair, and in 1966 it was renamed the American Shorthair. To gain it credence as a natural American breed, registration bodies accepted applications of non-pedigree cats and kittens conforming to the required breed standards, and in 1971 one such cat won the ultimate accolade of the best American Shorthair of the Year in CFA.

Despite the influence of the introduction of the British Shorthair imports in the breeding programmes, the American Shorthair has retained its distinctive characteristics.

Character and Care

A cat of very even temperament, the American Shorthair makes an ideal family pet. It is an intelligent and good-natured animal which gets on well with other breeds and with dogs.

Its short, thick coat is quite easy to keep in good condition with a simple grooming routine. Combing keeps the coat neat, and stroking with the hand or a silk scarf imparts a healthy sheen. The eyes and ears are easily cleaned with a cotton bud, and a scratch post helps the indoor cat to trim its claws.

BREAKDOWN OF 100 SHOW POINTS

NB Annotated points are those set in the USA.

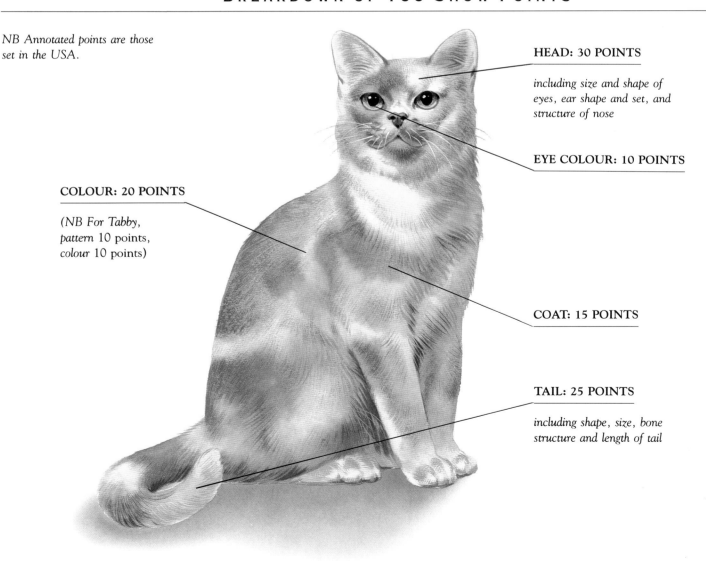

HEAD: 30 POINTS

including size and shape of eyes, ear shape and set, and structure of nose

EYE COLOUR: 10 POINTS

COLOUR: 20 POINTS

(NB For Tabby, pattern 10 points, colour 10 points)

COAT: 15 POINTS

TAIL: 25 POINTS

including shape, size, bone structure and length of tail

KEY CHARACTERISTICS

- **CATEGORY** Shorthair.

- **OVERALL BUILD** Medium to large, well-knit and powerful, not excessively cobby or rangy.

- **COAT** Short, thick and even, hard in texture, somewhat heavier and thicker in winter.

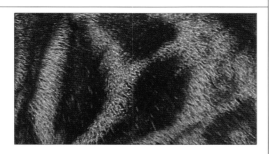

- **HEAD** Large, with full cheeks giving an oblong effect, head very slightly longer than it is wide, with square muzzle. Set on a medium-length, muscular neck.

- **NOSE** Medium length.

- **CHIN** Firm and well developed.

- **EYES** Round, wide-set, with a very slight slant to the outer aperture.

- **EARS** Medium size with rounded tips, set wide apart.

- **BODY** Well-knit, powerful body with well-developed chest and heavy shoulders.

- **LEGS** Firm-boned and heavily muscled.

- **PAWS** Firm, full and rounded paws with heavy pads.

- **TAIL** Medium length, heavy at the base, tapering to an apparently blunt end.

- **COLOURS** White, black, blue, red, cream, chinchilla, shaded silver, shell cameo, shaded cameo, black smoke, blue smoke, cameo smoke, tortoiseshell smoke, brown patched tabby, blue patched tabby, silver patched tabby, silver tabby, red tabby, brown tabby, blue tabby, cream tabby, cameo tabby, tortoiseshell, calico, dilute calico, blue-cream, bi-colour, van bi-colour, van calico, van blue-cream-and-white.

PENALTIES

The American Shorthair is penalized in the show ring for excessive cobbiness or ranginess in conformation; for obesity or boniness; or for having a very short tail.

DISQUALIFICATION FEATURES
- long or fluffy fur
- a kinked or abnormal tail
- a deep nose break in profile
- the incorrect number of toes.

AMERICAN SHORTHAIR VARIETIES

AMERICAN SHORTHAIR

Developed from the American domestic "working" cat, the American Shorthair has been refined and standardized into an attractive and viable breed of show cat in a wide range of coat colours and patterns.

IN THE CFA STANDARD of points, the American Shorthair is lovingly described. It says that some naturalists believe the breed to be the original domestic cat, which has, for centuries, adapted itself willingly and cheerfully to the needs of man, without allowing itself to become effete, or its natural intelligence to diminish.

The standard goes on: "Its hunting instinct is so strong that it exercises the skill even when well provided with food. This is our only breed of true working cat ... This is a cat lithe enough to stalk its prey, but powerful enough to make the kill easily. Its reflexes are under perfect control. Its legs are long enough to cope with any terrain and heavy and muscular enough for high leaps. The face is long enough to permit easy grasping by the teeth with jaws so powerful they can close against resistance. Its coat is dense enough to protect from moisture, cold, and superficial skin injuries, but short enough and of sufficiently hard texture to resist matting or entanglement when slipping through heavy vegetation. No part of the anatomy is so exaggerated as to foster weakness. The general effect is that of the trained athelete, with all muscles rippling easily beneath the skin, the flesh lean and hard, and with great latent power held in reserve."

Because the American Shorthair was developed from domestic cats in all colours and coat patterns, which were crossed with show quality imported British Shorthairs, today's cats are seen in a wide range of accepted coats.

The best known and most popular of the American Shorthair varieties is undoubtedly the silver tabby, with the Classic, Marbled or Spotted pattern being the favourite among fanciers. Other tabby colours are also very popular, but each of the accepted varieties has its own following of ardent fans.

TABBY VARIETIES

AMERICAN SHORTHAIR TABBY varieties may have the Classic or Mackerel pattern. In the Classic tabby markings should be dense and clearly defined; the legs evenly barred with bracelets and the tail evenly ringed, and the cat should have several unbroken necklaces on the neck and upper chest. On the head frown marks form a letter "M", and an unbroken line runs back from the outer corner of each eye. There are swirl markings on the cheeks and vertical lines run over the back of the head to the shoulder markings, which resemble a butterfly, with both upper and lower wings distinctly outlined and marked with dots within the outlines. The back is marked with a spine line and a parallel line on either side, all three lines being separated by stripes of the coat's ground colour. A large solid blotch on either side of the body should be encircled by one or more unbroken rings, and the side markings should be the same on both sides of the body. A double row of "vest" buttons should run down the chest and under the stomach.

In the Mackerel tabby, markings should be dense and clearly defined and all resemble narrow pencilling. The legs should be evenly barred with narrow bracelets, and the tail barred. There are several distinct narrow necklaces around the neck. The head is barred, with a distinct "M" on the forehead, and unbroken lines running back from the eyes. More lines run back over the head to meet the shoulder markings. Along the spine the lines run together forming a dark saddle, and fine, pencil-like markings run down either side of the body from the spine.

BLUE TABBY Base colour of coat for the blue tabby, including lips and chin, is pale bluish ivory with very deep blue markings. The whole coat colour has warm fawn overtones. Nose leather "old rose" in colour; paw pads are rose and the eye colour is brilliant gold.

BLUE TABBY AMERICAN

This classic tabby with its typical full-cheeked face is showing a good example of the "M" on the forehead, formed by the clearly marked frown lines.

MACKEREL TABBY

In the mackerel tabby, the body markings take the form of clear narrow pencillings running down from the spine and with narrow bracelets on the legs.

CLASSIC TABBY

The classic, blotched or marbled tabby has markings in a standardized patterns on the head, body legs and tail which show judges assess with great care when selecting the final winners.

BROWN TABBY Base colour of coat is a brilliant coppery brown with dense black markings. Lips and chin should be the same shade as the rings around the eyes, and backs of legs black from paw to heel. Nose leather is brick red; paw pads black or brown. Eye colour is brilliant gold.

RED TABBY Base colour of coat, including lips and chin, is red with deep rich red markings. Nose leather and paw pads are brick red and the eye colour brilliant gold.

CREAM TABBY Base colour of coat, including lips and chin, is very pale cream with buff or cream markings sufficiently darker than the base colour to afford good contrast. Nose leather and paw pads are pink and the eye colour is brilliant gold.

CAMEO TABBY Base colour of coat is off-white with red markings. Nose leather and paw pads are rose-coloured and the eye colour is brilliant gold.

RED TABBY

This fine cat is very well marked in the classic pattern and the red colour of both the base coat and the markings is correctly defined.

CAMEO TABBY

The Cameo is a soft and delicate colour. This classic tabby exhibits the intricacies of the pattern on the sides and flanks and shows good contrast between the colours of the base coat and markings.

BROWN TORBIE
The tortoiseshell tabbies are often called "torbies" for convenience, and in the United States some associations refer to the colouration as patched tabby.

SILVER TABBY
Perhaps the most striking of all the tabbies is the classic or marbled silver tabby with its dense black markings clearly etched on a pale silver base coat.

SILVER TABBY Base colour, including lips and chin, is pale clear silver with dense black markings. Nose leather brick red, paw pads black and eye colour may be green or hazel.

PATCHED TABBY or TORBIE The Patched Tabby or Torbie is similar to the established varieties of tabby, but with the addition of patches of red and light red, or cream.

BROWN PATCHED TABBY Base colour of coat is brilliant coppery brown with Classic or Mackerel markings of dense black and patches of red and/or light red clearly defined on both body and extremities; a blaze of red or light red on the face is desirable. Lips and chin to be the same shade as the rings around the eyes; the eye colour is brilliant gold.

BLUE PATCHED TABBY Base colour of coat, including lips and chin, is pale bluish ivory, with Classic or Mackerel markings of very deep blue and patches of cream clearly defined on both body and extremities; a blaze of cream on the face is desirable and warm fawn overtones suffuse the whole body. The eye colour is brilliant gold or hazel.

SILVER PATCHED TABBY Base colour, including lips and chin, is pale clear silver with Classic or Mackerel markings of dense black and patches of red and/or light red clearly defined on both body and extremities; a blaze of red and/or light red on the face is desirable. Eye colour may be hazel or brilliant gold.

BLUE TORBIE
Still clearly marked but with paler colouring, the blue patched tabby or torbie is the dilute version of the brown torbie, having blue and cream markings instead of black and red.

AMERICAN WIREHAIR

IN VERMONT, USA, in 1966, one of a litter of farm kittens was born with an unusual sparse and wiry coat. An experienced cat breeder acquired the kitten and one of its plain-coated litter-mates and sent hair samples from both for analysis by a British expert in feline genetics. The coat was of a different type to anything previously encountered in the domestic cat, and a breeding programme was soon established to develop the wirehaired trait.

The first wirehaired cat was a red and white male named Adam. He was first mated to his normal-coated litter-mate, and then to other unrelated shorthaired cats, and from these beginnings a new breed was born. All American Wirehair cats are descended from Adam,

and breeding stock has been very carefully selected over the years to ensure refinement and viability of the breed. Championship status was granted by the CFA in 1977.

Character and Care

The Wirehair is said by its owners to rule the home and cats of other breeds with an "iron paw", but to make a devoted parent. They are affectionate and playful, with a strongly independent character.

The unusual wiry coat is easy to maintain in peak condition by correct feeding, and needs the minimum of grooming.

BREAKDOWN OF 100 SHOW POINTS

NB Annotated points are those set in the USA.

HEAD: 25 POINTS

including size and shape of eyes, ear shape and set

COLOUR and EYE COLOUR: 10 POINTS

TYPE: 20 POINTS

including shape, size, bone, length of tail

COAT: 45 POINTS

PENALTIES

The American Wirehair is penalized in the show ring for having a deep nose break, or a long or fluffy coat.

DISQUALIFICATION FEATURES

- absence of wire hair
- a kink or other abnormality in tail
- the incorrect number of toes
- any evidence of hybridization resulting in the Himalayan pattern
- the colours chocolate or lavender
- any of these combinations with white

KEY CHARACTERISTICS

- **CATEGORY** Wirehair.

- **OVERALL BUILD** Medium to large, with medium bone. Males larger than females.

- **COAT** Springy, dense and resilient, feels coarse and hard. The hairs are crimped and wiry, hooked at the tips. The facial hairs and whiskers are crimped and often set at odd angles.

- **COLOURS** Requirements as for the American Shorthair (see pages 146–153). White, black, blue, red, cream, tortoiseshell, calico, blue-cream, dilute calico, chinchilla, shaded silver, shell cameo, shaded cameo, black smoke, blue smoke, cameo smoke, bi-colour; Classical or Mackerel tabby in brown, blue, red, cream, cameo, silver.

- **OTHER FEATURES** Round head with prominent cheekbones and a well-developed muzzle with a slight whisker break. Nose shows a gentle, concave curve in profile. The chin is firm and the eyes are large, round, bright and clear, set wide apart, with a slightly tilted aperture. The ears are medium sized with rounded tips, set wide apart on the head. Body is medium to large with a level back and well-rounded rump. Legs are well muscled and paws oval and compact. Length of tail in proportion to body, tapering from the rump to a rounded tip, neither blunt nor pointed.

BLACK AND WHITE
This cat is very well marked and with an inverted "V" on the forehead and the white area continuing right over the chin onto the chest.

AMERICAN WIREHAIR
All colours accepted for the American Shorthair are accepted in the Wirehair.

EXOTIC SHORTHAIR

IN THE DEVELOPMENT of British and American Shorthairs, and during the introduction of alternative colour factors in the Persians, breeders occasionally mated together pedigree cats of longhaired and shorthaired varieties. This was generally done as a single exercise, the offspring being back-crossed to the main breed in successive generations to strengthen the desired traits.

During the 1960s, cats of mixed Shorthair and Persian lineage were, with the approval of the board of the CFA, given the breed name Exotic Shorthair. The breed is, in essence, a short-coated version of the typical Persian, with the conformation of the latter, but the added bonus of a coat that is relatively easy to care for. The coat stands out from the body and is longer than that of the British or American Shorthair cat breeds.

Character and Care

In temperament the Exotic Shorthair is quiet, gentle and placid. It is an ideal show cat, being easy to prepare for the show ring, and enjoys being handled and admired.

The medium-length coat is quite easy to comb through and being groomed from the tail towards the head encourages the plush fur to stand away from the body. Body condition and shining fur is achieved by correct feeding, and the eyes and ears are kept immaculate by gentle cleaning with a cotton bud.

BREAKDOWN OF 100 SHOW POINTS

NB Annotated points are those set in the USA.

HEAD: 30 POINTS

including size and shape of the eyes; ear shape and set

EYE COLOUR: 10 POINTS

COLOUR: 20 POINTS

COAT: 20 POINTS

TYPE: 20 POINTS

including shape, size, bone and length of tail

- **CATEGORY** Shorthair.

- **OVERALL BUILD** Medium to large, cobby.

- **COAT** Medium length, dense and plush, soft-textured, standing well away from the body due to its density, never flat or close-lying.

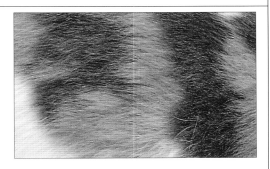

- **HEAD** Round and massive, with great depth of skull, set on a short, thick neck. Round face, full cheeks, broad and powerful jaws.

- **NOSE** Short and stubby with a definite "break".

- **CHIN** Full and well developed.

- **EYES** Large, round and set wide apart.

- **EARS** Small, round-tipped, set wide and low on the head.

- **BODY** Cobby, with a deep chest, massive shoulders and rump and a level back.

- **LEGS** Short and thick.

- **PAWS** Large and round.

- **TAIL** Short.

- **COLOURS** White (blue eyed and orange red), black, blue, chocolate, lilac, red, cream: tabby in Classic or Mackerel pattern: silver, brown, blue chocolate, lilac, red, cream: tortie tabby: black, chocolate, lilac: tortie, blue-cream, chocolate tortie, lilac-cream. Tortie and white, blue tortie and white, chocolate tortie and white, lilac tortie and white; bi-colour and Ban Bi-colour and Tri-colour: any recognized colour with white; spotted tabby: brown, blue chocolate, lilac, red, cream, silver; smoke: any recognized colour with silver-white undercoat:

SOLID VARIETIES

CREAM EXOTIC
The coat of the Exotic Shorthair is very dense and plush-like, soft in texture and stands out and away from the body.

BLUE EXOTIC
The head type of the Exotic Shorthair is almost identical to that of a show standard Persian.

SELF-COLOURED EXOTIC cats are bred to a very exacting standard and are penalized at shows for having incorrect or extremely pale eye colours or for flects of incorrect colour in either of the eyes' irises. Oriental or almond-shaped eyes or those set on the slant are also unacceptable.

WHITE The colour is pure glistening white with pink nose leather and paw pads. Eye colour is deep blue or brilliant copper. Odd-eyed Whites should have one blue and one copper eye of equal colour intensity.

BLACK The dense coal-black coat should be sound from roots to tips of fur. Nose leather is black and paw pads black or brown. Eye colour is brilliant copper.

BLUE A level tone of blue stretches from the nose to the tip of the tail, and is sound to the roots. Lighter shades are preferred. Nose leather and paw pads are blue and the eye colour is brilliant copper.

RED A deep, rich, brilliant red is required, without any shading, markings or ticking. Lips and chin should be the same colour as the coat. The nose leather and paw pads are brick red and the eye colour is brilliant copper.

CREAM One level shade of buff cream throughout should have no shading or markings, with lighter shades preferred. The nose leather and paw pads are pink and the eye colour is brilliant copper.

CHOCOLATE The coat is warm-toned medium to dark chocolate, free from shading or markings. The nose leather and paw pads are chocolate. Eye colour is copper or orange.

LILAC The warm-toned lilac coat is sound and even in colour. Lilac nose leather and paw pads and copper or orange eye colour.

TABBY AND BI-COLOUR VARIETIES

THE EXOTIC SHORTHAIR is accepted in the Classic and Mackerel patterns with the following colours allowed: silver, brown, blue, chocolate, lilac, red and cream. They have identical colour requirements to the equivalent varieties in the British Shorthair, except for eye colour, which in the Exotic Shorthair is brilliant copper..

Tortie tabbies are accepted in brown, blue, chocolate and lilac. The Spotted Tabby Exotic, in the same colour range as the Classic and Mackeral Tabbies, is very attractive with numerous well-defined round, oval or rosette-shaped marks clearly etched in distinct colour on the lighter base coat.

BI-COLOUR The coat of the Bi-colour is white with unbrindled patches of either black, blue, red or cream, as seen in the American Shorthair. Nose leather and paw pads colour corresponds with the basic coat colour. The eye colour is brilliant copper.

VAN BI-COLOUR The coat of the Van Bi-colour is white with unbrindled patches of either black, blue, red or cream confined to the head, tail and legs, although one or two small coloured patches on the body are allowed.

VAN TRI-COLOUR The coat of the Van Tri-colour is white with unbridled patches of both black and red confined to the head, tail and legs, although up to three small coloured patches on the body are allowed.

VAN BLUE-CREAM AND WHITE The coat of this variety is white with unbrindled patches of both blue and cream confined to the head, tail and legs, although one or two small coloured patches on the body are allowed.

BLUE AND WHITE EXOTIC
Bi-coloured Exotic cats should have clear and well distributed patches of colour as in this fine blue and white. The face should be patched with colour and with white.

BLUE TABBY COLOURPOINT EXOTIC
In the colourpointed range of the Exotic, the six main points colours are accepted.

OTHER VARIETIES

BLUE TORTIE AND WHITE EXOTIC

Well distributed patches of light to medium blue, pale cream and white form the pattern of this colour variety, known as the dilute calico in the USA.

THE EXOTIC SHORTHAIR is the ideal breed for the owner who craves for a cat with true Persian type, but does not have the time necessary to care correctly for the demanding Persian coat. Exotics are indeed a short-coated version of their Persian ancestors, and show standards for the two breeds, apart from the coat, are almost identical

TORTOISESHELL The coat is black with clearly defined, well-broken, unbrindled patches of red and light red on the body and extremities. A red or light red blaze on the face is desirable. Eye colour is brilliant copper.

TORTIE-AND-WHITE The coat is white with unbrindled patches of black and red, with white predominant on the underparts. Eye colour is brilliant copper.

BLUE-CREAM The coat is blue with clearly defined, well-broken patches of solid cream on the body and the extremities. The eye colour is brilliant copper.

BLUE-CREAM AND WHITE The coat is white with unbrindled patches of blue and cream, with white predominant on the underparts. Eye colour is brilliant copper.

CHINCHILLA The undercoat is pure white. The coat on the back, flanks, head and tail is sufficiently tipped with black to give a characteristic sparkling silver appearance. The legs may be slightly shaded with tipping. Chin, ear tufts, stomach and chest are pure white, and the rims of the eyes, lips and nose are outlined with black. Nose leather brick red, paw pads black, eye colour green or blue-green.

SHADED SILVER The undercoat is pure white and the coat heavily shaded with black to form a mantle over the spine, sides and on the face and tail, gradually shading from very dark on the spine to white on the chin, chest, stomach and under the tail. Legs are the same tone as the face. The general effect is much darker than the Chinchilla. Rims of the eyes, lips and nose are outlined with black. Nose leather brick red, paw pads black, eye colour green or blue-green.

CHINCHILLA GOLDEN The undercoat is a rich warm cream. The coat on the back, flanks, head and tail is sufficiently tipped with seal brown to give a golden appearance. The legs may be slightly shaded with tipping. Chin, ear tufts, stomach and chest are cream, and the rims of the eyes, lips and nose are outlined with seal brown. Nose leather is deep rose, paw pads are seal brown and the eye colour green or blue-green.

SHADED GOLDEN The undercoat is a rich warm cream and the coat is heavily shaded with seal brown to form a mantle over the spine, sides and on the face and tail, gradually shading from dark on the spine to cream on the chin, chest, stomach and under the tail. Legs

BROWN TABBY EXOTIC

The head has the frown lines created by the dark "M" marking on the forehead.

SILVER TABBY EXOTIC

The intensity of the dark markings is reduced by the density of the coat when etched on a silver base coat. This cat has the required brick red nose leather for its variety.

SHADED TORTOISESHELL The undercoat is white and the coat is heavily shaded with black tipping and clearly defined patches of red and light red tipped hairs as in the pattern of the Tortoiseshell, to form a mantle over the spine, sides and on the face and tail. The general effect is much darker than the Shell Tortoise-shell. A blaze of red or light red tipping on the face is desirable. The nose leather and paw pads are black, pink or mottled.

SMOKE EXOTIC The Smoke Exotic may be of any colour accepted in the Exotic Group, but instead of being sound in colour from the tips to the roots of the coat, the base of each hair is silvery white. There must be no tabby mark-ings, and the contrast between the top coat and the undercoat should be pronounced. The nose leather and paw pads should correspond with the coat colour and the eye colour should be copper, orange or deep gold.

TIPPED EXOTIC The tipping may be of any colour accepted in the Persian varieties. The undercoat must be as white as possible and the tips of each hair lightly coloured, giving a characteristic sparkling effect. Nose leather in cats with black tipping is brick red, and in all other colours, to correspond with the coat colour. Paw pads in black tipped may be either black or seal brown. In other colours, to correspond with the coat colour. Paw pads in black tipped may be either black or seal brown. In other colours, to correspond with the coat colour.

COLOUR POINTED EXOTIC This variety exhibits the Himalayan effect with a pale body and colour on the points – face, tail legs and paws. There must be good contrast between the body and points colour; the points should be free from white hairs, and the body ideally free from shading, which if present should tone with the points. Nose leather and paw pads correspond with individual points' colour. Eye colour decidedly blue.

BLUE-CREAM SMOKE EXOTIC

The undercoat of the Smoke Exotic is silvery white but only shows when the dense coat is parted.

SHADED SILVER

The pure white undercoat has a mantle of black tipping and more tipping on the face and tail producing the characteristically sparkling effect.

164	Abyssinian	192	Devon Rex
168	Somali	196	Sphynx
174	Russian Blue	198	Japanese Bobtail
176	Korat	200	Burmese
178	Havana Brown	206	Tiffanie
180	Egyptian Mau	207	Singapura
182	Ocicat	208	Tonkinese
184	Bengal	214	Bombay
188	Cornish Rex	216	Burmilla

Foreign Shorthaired Breeds

ABYSSINIAN

NO EVIDENCE EXISTS to connect an Abyssinian cat, recorded as having been taken from Ethiopia to England in 1868, with today's pedigree cats. Recognized as a true breed in 1882, the Abyssinian was also known as the Spanish, Russian, Ticked, Hare or Bunny Cat – it was once thought that it had resulted from a cross between a cat and wild rabbit!

The modern Abyssinian is a well-established breed world-wide. It has been referred to as the Child of the Gods because of its close resemblance to the sacred cats of the Ancient Egyptians. Whatever their colour, all Abyssinian cats have unusual ticked coats, known as the agouti, or wild-type pattern. Selective breeding over many generations has resulted in a reduction of the natural tabby bars normally found on the face, neck, tail and underparts, so that today's show cat has a clear, glowing ticked coat, rather like that of a Belgian hare.

The Abyssinian is another foreign shorthaired breed which is judged by slightly different standards in Europe and North America. The American Abyssinian has a shorter head and a more rounded profile than its European counterpart. In the allocation of show points, the American fancy gives most weight by points to body type, while the European standards place more emphasis on coat colour.

BREAKDOWN OF 100 SHOW POINTS

NB Annotated points (right) are those set in the UK; those below are for the USA.

HEAD: 25 POINTS
Muzzle: 6 points
Skull: 6 points
Ears: 7 points
Eye shape: 6 points

BODY: 30 POINTS
Torso: 15 points
Legs and feet: 10 points
Tail: 5 points

COAT: 10 POINTS
Texture: 10 points

COLOUR: 35 POINTS
Colour: 15 points
Ticking: 15 points
Eye colour: 5 points

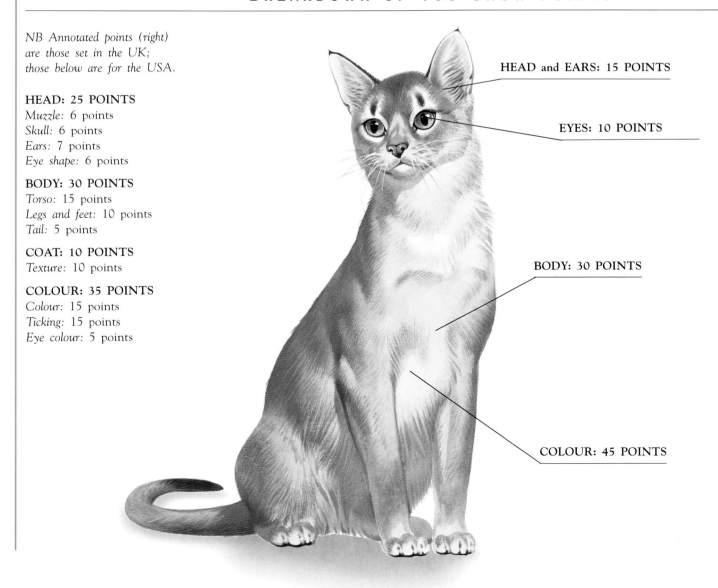

HEAD and EARS: 15 POINTS

EYES: 10 POINTS

BODY: 30 POINTS

COLOUR: 45 POINTS

Character and Care

The Abyssinian cat is typically quiet and gentle. It can be shy and reserved, mistrusting strangers, but it generally gets along well with other cats and adores its owner.

The coat is simple to keep immaculate with the minimum of grooming, and the large ears must be kept clean at all times, by regular use of moistened cotton buds.

KEY CHARACTERISTICS

- **CATEGORY** Foreign Shorthair.

- **OVERALL BUILD** Medium size, lithe and muscular.

- **COAT** Soft, silky, fine textured; medium in length to accommodate two or three bands of ticking.

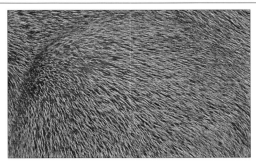

- **HEAD** Slightly rounded and wedge shaped with gentle contours, gently curved in profile. The muzzle is neither pointed nor square.

- **NOSE** Medium length.

- **CHIN** Firm.

- **EYES** Almond shaped, large, brilliant and expressive.

- **EARS** Large and alert.

- **BODY** Long, lithe and graceful.

- **LEGS** Slim and fine boned.

- **PAWS** Small and oval.

- **TAIL** Thick at the base, fairly long and tapering.

- **COLOURS** Usual, blue, red or sorrel, chocolate, lilac, cream, beige-fawn, tortie in all these colours. (Note that not all varieties are recognized by all associations.)

ABYSSINIAN VARIETIES

THE USUAL OR RUDDY is the normal coat colour for the Abyssinian, and is genetically black – the rich golden hairs having two or three bands of black ticking. The Red or Sorrel is produced by the action of the light-brown gene.

RUDDY (USA, Europe) **USUAL** (UK–GCCF) The coat is warm ruddy brown with black ticking; the base colour deep apricot or orange. The tail tip, ear tips and eye rims are black; the nose leather brick red (may be outlined with black). Paw pads, back of feet and toe tufts are seal brown or black. The eye colour is gold or green; rich deep colours are preferred.

BLUE The coat is warm blue-grey with dark, steel blue-grey ticking; the base colour pale fawn/cream. The tail tip and ear tips are dark steel blue-grey; the eye rims blue-grey. Nose leather is old rose (may be outlined with blue-grey); paw pads are old rose/blue-grey; backs of feet and toe tufts are deep steel blue-grey. Eye colour is as Ruddy Abyssinian.

SORREL or RED The coat is a bright, warm, copper red with chocolate brown ticking; the base colour deep apricot. The tail tip, ear tips, eye rims, backs of feet and toe tufts are red-brown. Nose leather is pale red (may be outlined with red-brown); paw pads cinnamon to chocolate. Eye colour is as Ruddy Abyssinian.

USUAL ABYSSINIAN

The rich golden brown coat ticked with bands of black gives the Usual Abyssinian its unusual appearance. It is known as the Ruddy Abyssinian in Europe and America.

BEIGE-FAWN The coat is dull beige with deep, warm, fawn ticking; the base colour pale cream. The tail tip, ear tips, backs of feet and toe tufts are dark warm cream; the eye rims old rose. Nose leather is pink (may be outlined with old rose); paw pads are pink. Eye colour is as Ruddy Abyssinian.

BLACK SILVER The coat is pure silver-white with black ticking; the base colour pure silver-white. The tail tip and eye rims are black; the ear tips, paw pads, backs of feet and toe tufts are black or seal brown. Nose leather is brick red (may be outlined with black). Eye colour is as Ruddy Abyssinian.

BLUE SILVER The coat is pure silver-white with dark steel blue-grey ticking; the base colour pure silver-white. The tail tip, ear tips, eye rims, backs of feet and toe tufts are dark steel blue-grey. Nose leather is old rose (may be outlined with dark steel blue-grey); paw pads are old rose or blue-grey. Eye colour is as Ruddy Abyssinian.

FAWN ABYSSINIAN

Beige with bands of warm fawn ticking makes up the rare and attractive coat of this variety.

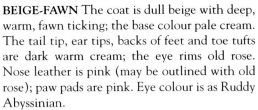

BLUE ABYSSINIAN

Abyssinians with this colouring turned up in otherwise usual litters from time to time, but until recent years were not accepted for showing.

SORREL ABYSSINIAN

Bright copper red and warm chocolate bands of ticking give the Sorrel or Red Abyssinian its rich glowing appearance.

SOMALI

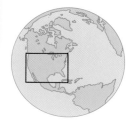

THIS BREED IS the longhaired version of the Abyssinian cat, and its coat colour is typically Abyssinian. It was thought that the long coat was due to a spontaneous mutation occurring within the Abyssinian breed, but genetic investigation of the history of the Somali showed that the gene for long hair was probably introduced when cats of Abyssinian type and lineage were out-crossed to others in the early days of breeding and showing.

When the first long-coated kittens appeared in otherwise normal litters of Abyssinian kittens they were discarded and given away as pets, but later, having seen some of these cats at maturity, when the full beauty of the ticked longhaired coat was apparent, breeders decided to develop the longhaired Abyssinian as a separate variety. A world-wide network of breeders – in North America, Europe, New Zealand and Australia – worked together and agreed on Somali as the cats' name. The breed was granted full championship status by the CFA in 1978.

Character and Care
Like the Abyssinian, the Somali is gentle and receptive to quiet handling and affection. It is soft-voiced, playful and athletic, and makes a perfect companion pet.

The coat, though full, is not woolly and is therefore very easy to groom. The full frill (ruff) and tail need regular combing through, and the large ears must be gently cleaned and kept free from dust.

BREAKDOWN OF 100 SHOW POINTS

NB Annotated points (right) are those set in the UK; those below are set in Europe.

HEAD: 15 POINTS

BODY: 20 POINTS

EYES: 10 POINTS

COAT: 50 POINTS
Body colour: 15 points
Ticking: 10 points
Texture: 10 points
Length: 15 points

CONDITION: 5 POINTS

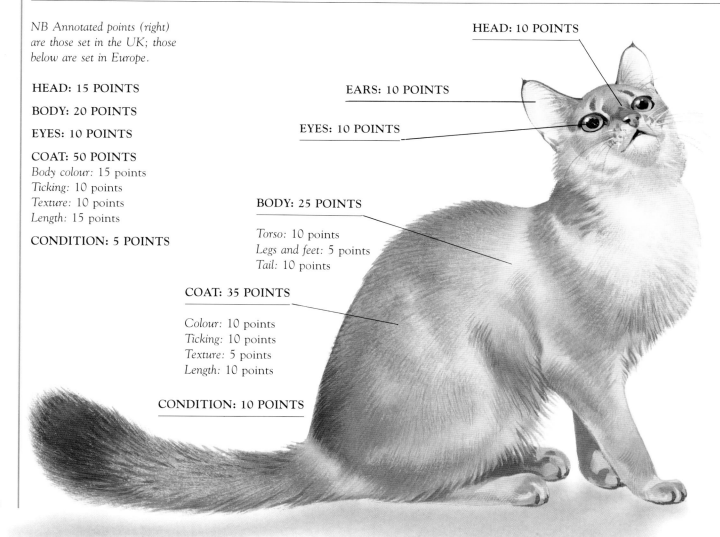

HEAD: 10 POINTS

EARS: 10 POINTS

EYES: 10 POINTS

BODY: 25 POINTS

Torso: 10 points
Legs and feet: 5 points
Tail: 10 points

COAT: 35 POINTS

Colour: 10 points
Ticking: 10 points
Texture: 5 points
Length: 10 points

CONDITION: 10 POINTS

KEY CHARACTERISTICS

- **CATEGORY** Foreign Longhair.

- **OVERALL BUILD** Medium to large.

- **COAT** Extremely fine and very dense, of medium length but shorter on the shoulders. A well-developed frill (ruff) and breeches are desirable.

- **HEAD** Wedged shaped and of medium proportions; wide at the top with soft contours.

- **NOSE** Medium long with a soft curve in profile, with neither a stop nor a straight nose.

- **CHIN** Firm and well developed.

- **EYES** Large, almond shaped and set well apart.

- **EARS** Large and broad at the base, slightly rounded at the tips, with lynx-like tufts, set well apart and pricked.

- **BODY** Of medium length. Bone structure firm, lithe and muscular.

- **LEGS** Long and fine boned, in proportion to the body.

- **PAWS** Small and oval.

- **TAIL** Fairly long and tapering; broad at the base and well furred.

- **COLOURS** As for the Abyssinian: ruddy, blue, red or sorrel, beige-fawn, black, silver, blue silver, sorrel silver, beige-fawn silver.
  Note Not all associations recognize all colour varieties.

PENALTIES

The Somali is penalized for having a cold grey or sandy tone to the coat colour; mottling or speckling in unticked areas; black roots to body hair; incorrect markings; a white locket or white anywhere other than the upper throat, chin or nostrils; incorrect colour of paw pads and/or nose leather; Siamese type and a whip tail.

NON-SILVER VARIETIES

ALTHOUGH DIFFERENT CAT associations have their own rules for acceptance of new varieties, the Somali is recognized in most of the regular Abyssinian colour varieties by most registering bodies. In the United Kingdom, the Cat Association of Britain accepts all colours, while the GCCF has granted full Championship status to the Usual and Sorrel in the non-Silver group; and has given preliminary status only to the blue, chocolate, lilac and fawn non-Silvers and to all the Silver Somali cats in the full range of colours.

LILAC USUAL The coat is rich and glowing golden brown ticked with black. The tail is tipped with black; the ears with black or dark brown. Nose leather is tile red; the paw pads and heels, and toe tufts are black or dark brown.

BLUE Any shade of blue ticked with darker blue is allowed, and the base hair is cream or oatmeal. The ears and tail are tipped with the same colour as the ticking. The nose leather is blue-mauve, and the blue-mauve paw pads have deeper blue between the toes and extending up the heels. The toe tufts are deep blue.

CHOCOLATE The coat is rich golden coppery

BLUE SOMALI
In this variety, the ticking may be any shade of blue on a base coat of cream or oatmeal, complemented by the delicate mauvish-pink nose leather.

USUAL SOMALI
This variety's other name of "Ruddy" sums up its appearance very well. The black ticking on the rich apricot base coat combines to give a rich golden and ruddy overall glow.

CHOCOLATE SOMALI

Somali kittens are slow to mature both in size and in developing the full ticked effect of the typical coat.

brown ticked with dark chocolate, with paler base hair. The ears and tail are tipped with the same shade as the ticking. The nose leather is pinkish chocolate. The paw pads are chocolate with darker chocolate between the toes and extending up the heels. The toe tufts are dark chocolate.

LILAC The pinkish dove-grey coat is ticked with a deeper shade of the same colour and a paler base coat. This variety has a powdered effect to the coat. The ears and tail are tipped with the same colour as the ticking. The nose leather is pinkish mauve; the pinkish mauve paw pads have deeper dove grey between the toes and extending up the heels. The toe tufts are deep dove grey.

SORREL The warm glowing copper coat is ticked with chocolate and a base coat of deep apricot. The ears and tail are tipped with chocolate. The nose leather is pink; the paw pads are pink with chocolate between the toes and extending up the heels; the toe tufts are chocolate.

FAWN The warm fawn coat is ticked with a deeper shade of the same colour and a paler base coat. The ears and tail are tipped with the same colour as the ticking. The nose leather is pink; the pinkish mauve paw pads have deep fawn between the toes and extending up the heels. The toe tufts are deep fawn.

FAWN SOMALI

A diluted version of the red or sorrel, the fawn Somali has an attractive "powdered" effect to its warm fawn coat, ticked with a deeper fawn colour. This is an elegant young kitten.

SILVER VARIETIES

A YELLOWISH EFFECT on the body, known as "fawning", is an undesirable trait in the Silver series of Somali cats. It occurs particularly in the usual silver, and blue silver varieties especially on the face and paws.

USUAL SILVER The white base coat is ticked with black; the tail and ears are tipped with black. The nose leather is light brick red. The paw pads are black or brown with black between the toes and extending up the heels with black toe tufts.

BLUE SILVER The white base coat is ticked with blue giving an overall sparkling silver-grey effect. The ears and tail are ticked with blue. The nose leather is blue-mauve. The blue-mauve pads have blue between the toes, extending up the heels; the toe tufts are blue.

USUAL SILVER
The coat gives an overall appearance of silver produced by black ticking on a white base coat.

RED SILVER
The Sorrel or Red Silver has a sparkling coat of a silvery peach shade. The ticking is a medium chocolate shade.

CHOCOLATE SILVER The white base coat has dark chocolate ticking giving an overall sparkling silvery chocolate effect. The nose leather is pinkish chocolate and the ears and tail are tipped with dark chocolate. The paw pads are chocolate with dark chocolate between the toes and extending up the heels. The ear tufts are dark chocolate.

LILAC SILVER The white base coat is ticked with dove-grey giving an overall sparkling dove-grey effect. The nose leather is pinkish mauve; pinkish mauve pads have dove grey between the toes and extending up the heels. The toe tufts are dove-grey.

SORREL SILVER The white base coat has chocolate ticking giving the overall sparkling silvery peach effect. The ears and tail are tipped with chocolate. The nose leather is pink. The pink paw pads have chocolate brown between the toes and extending up the heels. The toe tufts are dark chocolate.

FAWN SILVER The white base coat is ticked with fawn giving an overall sparkling silvery fawn effect. The ears and tail are tipped with fawn. The nose leather is pink. The pinkish mauve paw pads have fawn between the toes and extending up the heels. The toe tufts are fawn.

BLUE SILVER

Another striking colour in the Silver Somali range, where the white base coat is ticked with blue giving a sparkling silvery blue-grey coat pattern. As in all Somali varieties, the ears and tail colour should match that of the ticking.

RUSSIAN BLUE

THE VERY HANDSOME and unique Russian Blue is a natural breed with a unique combination of conformation, colour and coat that make it a striking animal.

The first Russian Blue cats are thought to have originated near the White Sea port of Archangel, just outside the Arctic Circle, and were carried as trade goods by merchant sailors on ships trading with England. The cats were shown extensively in England during the latter part of the nineteenth century, but differed from those of today in having bright orange eyes. The breed was exhibited under a number of names, including the Spanish Blue, the

Archangel and the Maltese. In the first cat shows, all shorthaired blue cats competed in one class, regardless of type. In 1912, the Russian Blue was given its own classes, but during the Second World War, the breed almost became extinct, being saved only by outcrossing to Siamese. Cats of foreign type were then shown as Russian Blues, but eventually breeders made a co-ordinated attempt to return to the pre-war characteristics of the breed, and in 1966 the show standard was changed to state specifically that Siamese type was undesirable in the Russian Blue.

BREAKDOWN OF 100 SHOW POINTS

NB Annotated points (right) are those set in the UK; those below are for the USA.

HEAD and NECK:
20 POINTS
Eyes: 15 points
Shape: 5 points
Colour: 10 points
Ears: 5 Points

BODY TYPE:
20 POINTS

COAT: 20 POINTS

COLOUR:
20 POINTS

BODY, LEGS and TAIL:
20 POINTS

COAT: 30 POINTS

COLOUR: 15 POINTS

HEAD and EARS:
20 POINTS

EYES: 15 POINTS

PENALTIES

The Russian Blue is penalized in the show ring for any white or tabby markings, or for having a kinked or abnormal tail.

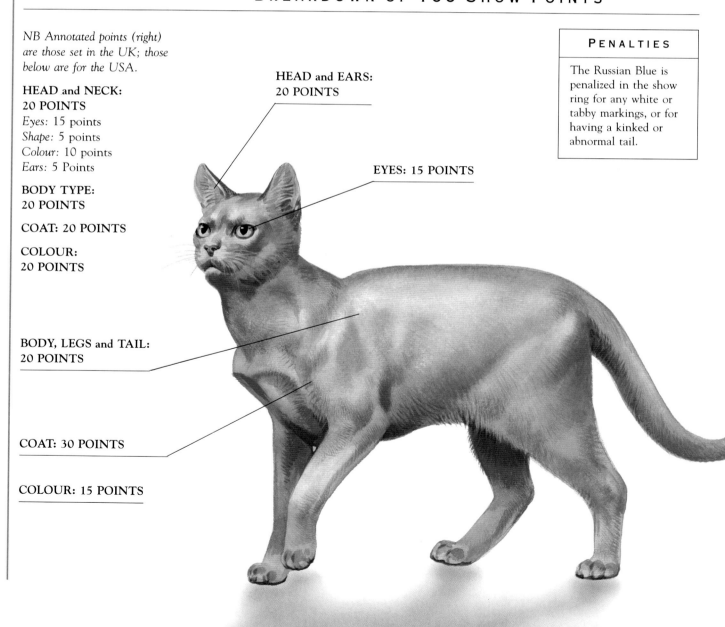

Maltese or Russian Blue cats are recorded in the United States as long ago as 1900, but only in 1947 did breeders really start work with these unique cats, and even today the breed is rare in the show rings of the world.

Character and Care

The Russian Blue has a delightful temperament, being quiet-voiced and very affectionate. It does not like to be left alone for long periods and needs the company either of a human being, or other pets.

The unique coat, with its short, thick, double fur, should be regularly combed through, and may be stroked both ways without exposing the blue skin. The sparsely furred ears must be kept clean at all times.

KEY CHARACTERISTICS
• **CATEGORY** Foreign Shorthair.
• **OVERALL BUILD** Medium in size, lithe and muscular.
• **COAT** Short, fine and plush, its density causes the double-textured coat to stand out from the body.
• **COLOUR** Blue only (some associations in Australia and New Zealand recognize a Black Russian and a White Russian.) A clear, even blue, the guard hairs being silver-tipped giving the cat an overall lustrous silvery sheen. Lighter blue shades are preferred in the United States, and medium blue shades in Britain. Nose leather is slate grey; paw pads, lavender-pink or mauve; eye colour, vivid green.
• **OTHER FEATURES** Wedge-shaped head with flat skull, broad at eye level with nose of medium length and level chin. Wide-based ears with very little hair inside or out. In the United States the ears should be set far apart on the head, in Britain the ears must be set vertically. Wide set eyes of vivid green and a rounded aperture in the United States, but almond shaped in Britain. Fine boned, long and muscular body with long slender legs and small paws. The tail should be long and tapered.

RUSSIAN BLUE
A natural breed with a long and interesting history, the Russian Blue standard has developed differently on either side of the Atlantic.

KORAT

THE BREED ORIGINATED in Thailand where it is called Si-Sawat, a descriptive compound word referring to its silver grey coat and luminous, light green eyes. The thirteenth-century *Book of Cat Poems* in the National Library of Bangkok illustrates the breed with the caption: "The cat Mal-ed has a body like Doklao, the hairs are smooth with roots like clouds and tips like silver, the eyes shine like dewdrops on a lotus leaf." *Mal-ed* refers to the seed of the Look Sawat, a silvery grey fruit lightly tinged with green. *Dok* is a flower, and *lao* a plant with silver tipped flowers. Highly prized in its native land, the Si-Sawat is considered a harbinger of good fortune, and a pair of these cats is a traditional wedding gift, intended to bring longevity, wealth and happiness to the couple.

First exhibited in London in 1896, the Korat was disqualified, being judged as a Siamese cat and not having the desired fawn coat, dark points and blue eyes! In 1959 Korat cats arrived in the United States, where they were officially recognized in 1966. The cat fanciers of South Africa and Australia officially accepted the breed in 1968 and 1969 respectively, but Britain's Governing Council of the Cat Fancy delayed recognition until 1975, and then withheld championship status. In 1983, the Cat Association of Britain finally accepted the Korat for full status, and Britain's first champion was chosen by judges from England, Belgium and Australia.

Character and Care

The Korat is a dainty, quiet-voiced little cat, generally alert, inquisitive and affectionate.

Its short, dense coat is easily cared for with a weekly brushing and buffing with a silk scarf.

BREAKDOWN OF 100 SHOW POINTS

NB Annotated points are those set in the UK.

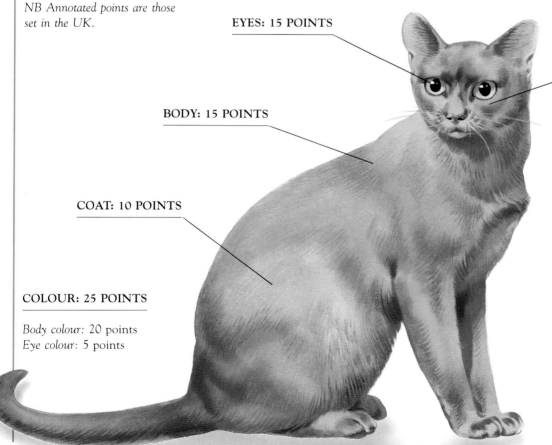

EYES: 15 POINTS

HEAD: 20 POINTS

Broad head: 5 points
Profile: 6 points
Breadth between eyes:
4 points
Ear set and placement:
5 points

BODY: 15 POINTS

COAT: 10 POINTS

COLOUR: 25 POINTS

Body colour: 20 points
Eye colour: 5 points

PENALTIES

The Korat is penalized if it is any colour but silver blue; has a visible tail kink; or white spot or locket. Kittens and young cats are not penalized for incorrect eye colour; this is not set until maturity in the Korat.

KEY CHARACTERISTICS

- **CATEGORY** Foreign Shorthair.

- **OVERALL BUILD** Small to medium size.

- **COAT** Short to medium length, fine textured and glossy.

- **COLOUR** Blue only. Silver blue tipped with silver. Nose leather and lips, dark blue or lavender; paw pads, dark blue ranging to lavender with a pinkish tinge. Eye colour, luminous green preferred, amber acceptable.

- **OTHER FEATURES** Heart-shaped head with large, round-tipped ears set high, giving an alert expression. Slight stop in profile of nose and a firm chin, lion-like in profile. The eyes are luminous and oversized for the face, and with an Asian slant when closed. The body is muscular and supple, midway between the Shorthair and the Siamese in type, with females being daintier than males. Well-proportioned legs with neat oval paws, and a tail of medium length heavier at the base and tapering to a rounded tip.

PROFILE
Always blue and with a fine short coat, the Korat is a dainty, quiet little cat.

KORAT
A natural breed discovered in Thailand, the Korat was considered as a good luck charm, and often given as a wedding gift.

HAVANA BROWN

THIS UNIQUE, MAN-MADE breed came into being when British breeders were working with Russian Blue and Shorthair cross-matings during the early 1950s, and self-coloured chocolate brown kittens were occasionally produced. At that time the science of feline colour genetics was in its infancy, but it was soon established that chocolate kittens could only occur when both parents carried the chocolate factor, and when two chocolate cats were mated, chocolate kittens always resulted.

Cats from these early matings were developed in Britain as the Chestnut Brown Foreign Shorthair, and were out-crossed to Siamese to establish Oriental type and conformation. Others were sent to the United States to establish a new breed, and were bred to a unique standard of points as the Havana Brown.

Character and Care

This breed is highly intelligent, affectionate and very agile. Less vocal than the Siamese, it is playful and craves human company. It makes a superb pet.

The coat is easy to maintain in good condition with the minimum of grooming. Combing removes any loose hairs, and buffing with the hand or a silk scarf produces a sheen on the glossy brown coat.

BREAKDOWN OF 100 SHOW POINTS

NB Annotated points are those set in the USA.

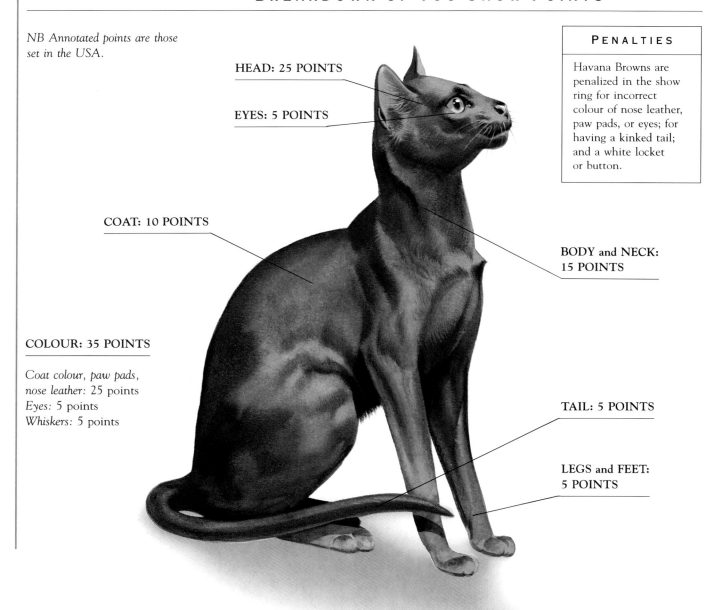

HEAD: 25 POINTS

EYES: 5 POINTS

COAT: 10 POINTS

BODY and NECK: 15 POINTS

COLOUR: 35 POINTS

Coat colour, paw pads, nose leather: 25 points
Eyes: 5 points
Whiskers: 5 points

TAIL: 5 POINTS

LEGS and FEET: 5 POINTS

PENALTIES

Havana Browns are penalized in the show ring for incorrect colour of nose leather, paw pads, or eyes; for having a kinked tail; and a white locket or button.

HAVANA BROWN

The Havana Brown as shown in the United States was developed from early imports of Chestnut Brown Foreign Shorthairs from Britain. It is a unique breed and bears very little resemblance to the Havana, or Oriental Chocolate found in Europe and Britain.

KEY CHARACTERISTICS

- **CATEGORY** Foreign Shorthair.

- **OVERALL BUILD** Medium size, muscular build.

- **COAT** Short to medium length coat, smooth and lustrous.

- **COLOUR** Warm brown only. Coat of a rich and even shade of warm brown throughout. Kittens are not penalized for showing ghost tabby markings. The nose leather is brown with a rosy flush; the paw pads must have a rosy tone. The eye colour is a vivid green.

- **OTHER FEATURES** Head slightly longer than it is wide with a distinct change in slope or 'stop' at eye level, when viewed in profile. The rounded muzzle has a definite break on either side behind the whisker pads, well developed chin. Large round tipped ears, wide set but not flaring and slightly pricked forward giving an alert appearance. Oval eyes of vivid green. Firm muscular body of medium length with legs in proportion and neat oval paws. A medium length tail, tapering gently to a slightly pointed tip.

HAVANA BROWN

Large pricked ears and vivid green oval eyes give the face of the Havana Brown its typical, sweet expression. The smooth lustrous coat is evenly coloured in warm brown.

EGYPTIAN MAU

NOT TO BE CONFUSED with cats of the same name bred experimentally in Britain during the 1960s and now called Oriental Tabbies. The Egyptian Mau was bred in the United States, and came from foundation stock brought there from Egypt via Rome in 1953. It is a spotted cat, very similar to those pictured in Ancient Egyptian scrolls and cartoons. It gained official recognition from the CFF in 1968; and finally from the CFA in 1977.

Character and Care

Rather shy but very loving, the Mau tends to attach its affections to only one or two people. It is naturally active and may be taught one or two party tricks.

Although the short coat is easy to keep in good condition, regular combing is required to remove dead hair.

BREAKDOWN OF 100 SHOW POINTS

NB Annotated points are those set in the USA.

HEAD: 20 POINTS

Muzzle: 5 points
Skull: 5 points
Ears: 5 points
Eye shape: 5 points

COAT: 5 POINTS

Texture and length: 5 points

PATTERN: 25 POINTS

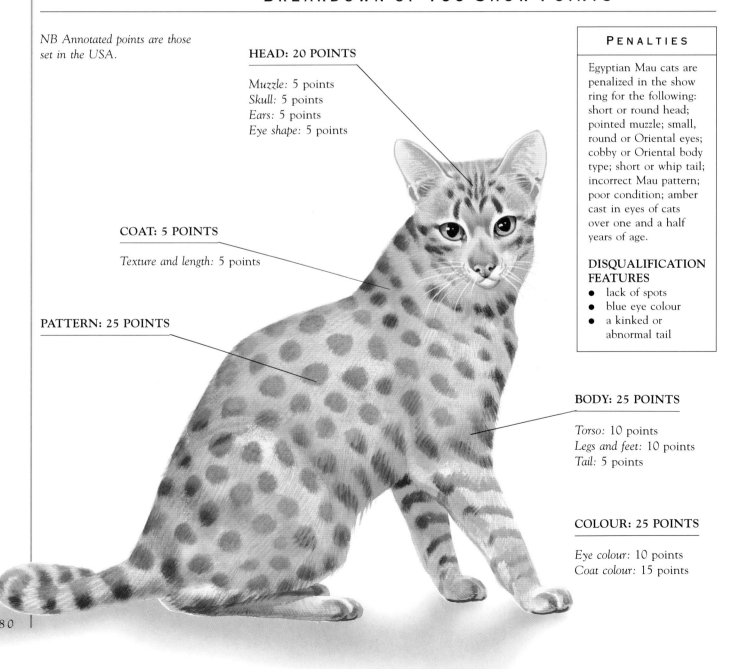

PENALTIES

Egyptian Mau cats are penalized in the show ring for the following: short or round head; pointed muzzle; small, round or Oriental eyes; cobby or Oriental body type; short or whip tail; incorrect Mau pattern; poor condition; amber cast in eyes of cats over one and a half years of age.

DISQUALIFICATION FEATURES
- lack of spots
- blue eye colour
- a kinked or abnormal tail

BODY: 25 POINTS

Torso: 10 points
Legs and feet: 10 points
Tail: 5 points

COLOUR: 25 POINTS

Eye colour: 10 points
Coat colour: 15 points

SILVER MAU

The silver Egyptian Mau has clear markings in dark charcoal on a pale silver ground colour. The gooseberry green eyes complete the rather exotic effect.

BRONZE MAU

The Bronze Egyptian Mau is perhaps the cat that most resembles the colour of the cats of the Ancient Egyptians. Dark brown markings show up clearly on the light bronze base coat. The whole coat has a warm glowing appearance.

SMOKE MAU

Unusual black markings on a charcoal grey base and with a silver undercoat give this unusually coloured cat the appearance of shot silk, the colour changing almost imperceptibly as it moves.

KEY CHARACTERISTICS

- **CATEGORY** Foreign Shorthair.

- **OVERALL BUILD** Medium size, long and graceful; muscular strength.

- **COAT** Silky and fine coat, dense and resilient to touch, with a lustrous sheen. Medium length hair, two or more bands of ticking, separated by lighter bands.

- **COLOURS**
  Silver Pale silver ground colour; dark charcoal markings contrasting with ground colour. Backs of the ears are greyish pink tipped in black; the nose, lips and eyes are outlined in black. The upper throat, chin and around the nostrils is pale clear silver, appearing white. Nose leather is brick red; paw pads are black; eye colour is light gooseberry green. *Bronze* Light bronze ground colour with creamy ivory underparts, dark brown markings against the ground colour. Backs of the ears are tawny pink tipped in dark brown; the nose, lips and eyes are outlined in dark brown, with ochre on the bridge of the nose. The upper throat, chin and around the nostrils is pale creamy white. Nose leather is brick red; paw pads are black or dark brown; eye colour is light gooseberry green. *Smoke* Charcoal grey ground colour with silver undercoat, the jet black markings plainly visible. Nose, lips and eyes outlined in jet black; upper throat, chin and around the nostrils are lightest in colour. Nose leather and pads black: eye colour light gooseberry green.

- **OTHER FEATURES** Slightly rounded wedge head of medium length. Muzzle neither short nor pointed. Medium to large ears alert and slightly pointed. Inner ear delicate shell pink. Ears tufts accepted. Legs in proportion to body, with higher hind legs and small, slightly oval paws. Medium long tail thick at the base, slightly tapered.

OCICAT

THE FIRST KITTEN of this breed appeared in the litter of an experimentally bred hybrid queen, from an Abyssinian-pointed Siamese breeding programme, mated with a chocolate-pointed Siamese male. The kitten, which was called Tonga, reminded its breeder of a baby ocelot, and she decided to produce similar cats which were eventually recognized as a separate breed called Ocicats.

Apart from the Ocicat itself, out-crosses to Abyssinian, American and Siamese are allowed in the pedigree. The Ocicat is a rather large, but well-proportioned cat, muscular and agile, with a typically "wild-cat" appearance. It is remarkable for its very clear spotted pattern and its striking golden eyes.

Character and Care
Ocicats are loving and gentle, inquisitive and playful and make excellent pets.

Their coats are groomed by gentle brushing and combing through on a regular basis to remove dead hair.

TYPICAL OCICAT
All the hairs except for those at the tip of the tail are banded. Within the markings each hair is tipped with darker colour. The overall effect is that of a small spotted and graceful wild cat.

BREAKDOWN OF 100 SHOW POINTS

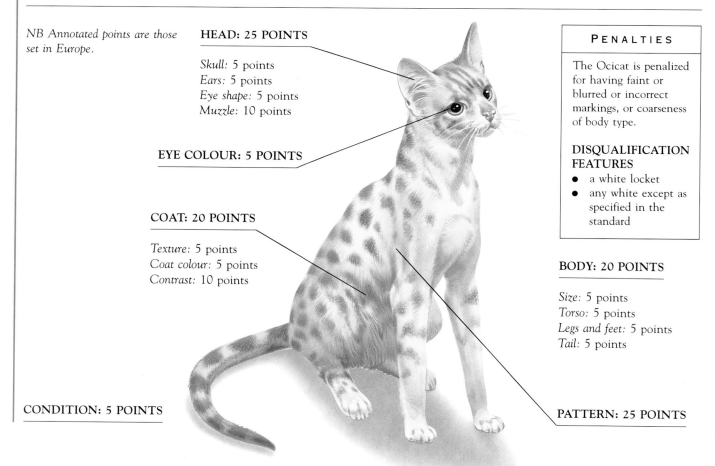

NB *Annotated points are those set in Europe.*

HEAD: 25 POINTS

Skull: 5 points
Ears: 5 points
Eye shape: 5 points
Muzzle: 10 points

EYE COLOUR: 5 POINTS

COAT: 20 POINTS

Texture: 5 points
Coat colour: 5 points
Contrast: 10 points

PENALTIES

The Ocicat is penalized for having faint or blurred or incorrect markings, or coarseness of body type.

DISQUALIFICATION FEATURES
● a white locket
● any white except as specified in the standard

BODY: 20 POINTS

Size: 5 points
Torso: 5 points
Legs and feet: 5 points
Tail: 5 points

CONDITION: 5 POINTS

PATTERN: 25 POINTS

CHOCOLATE SILVER

In this variety the tabby markings are in a warm shade of chocolate on a pure silver base coat.

KEY CHARACTERISTICS

- **CATEGORY** Foreign Shorthair.

- **OVERALL BUILD** Medium to large, athletic build.

- **COAT** Short smooth coat, satiny and lustrous, yet long enough to accommodate the necessary bands of colour.
  Ticking All hairs except those on the tip of the tail are banded. Within the markings, hairs are tipped with the darker colour; hairs in the ground colour are tipped with a lighter colour.
  Markings Distinctive markings must be clearly seen from any angle. Markings on the face, legs and tail may be darker than those on the body. The ground colour may be darker on the saddle and lighter on the underside, chin and lower jaw.
  Pattern The pattern is that of a spotted cat. This breed is noted for its powerful, graceful "wild cat" appearance.

- **COLOURS** Black spotted; blue spotted; chocolate spotted; lavender spotted; cinnamon spotted; fawn spotted; black silver spotted; blue silver spotted; chocolate silver spotted; lavender silver spotted; cinnamon silver spotted; fawn silver spotted. All colours should be clear. The lightest colour is on the face, around the eyes, on the chin and the lower jaw; the darkest colour is at the tip of the tail.

- **OTHER FEATURES** Modified wedge shaped head with a broad, well-defined muzzle and strong chin. Alert, moderately large ears preferably with ear tufts, set fairly wide apart on the head. Large, almond-shaped eyes. Long solid body, athletic with substantial bone and muscle structure; medium long legs with compact oval paws and a fairly long, slightly tapered tail.

BLUE SPOTTED

Markings on the face, legs and tail may be darker than those on the body and the ground colour may be darker on the saddle.

BLACK SILVER

This kitten is very well patterned with clear spots the correct head markings and pleasing type.

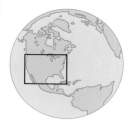

BENGAL

BASED ON CROSSES between Asian leopard cats which live wild in south east Asia, and domestic cats, the Bengal was first produced in the United States. It seems to have preserved the self-assurance and confidence of the Asian Leopard Cat in conjunction with the affectionate disposition of the domestic, producing a miniature leopard with a loving nature. The appearance of the Bengal should be as close as possible to that of the first cross, but without the possibility of its being mistaken for an actual Asian leopard cat. The texture of this breed's coat is unique, having the feel of satin or silk, and a glittering appearance as if sprinkled with gold dust or fragments of pearl.

Its cooing or chirruping call is quite different from that of the ordinary domestic cat, which adds to the impression the ideal Bengal gives of being a truly wild cat.

Character and Care

Self-assured and as confident as its leopard cat ancestors, the Bengal has acquired an affectionate disposition and a loving, dependable temperament.

The thick, luxuriant coat is kept in good condition with a well-balanced diet, and regular brushing and combing.

BREAKDOWN OF 100 SHOW POINTS

NB Annotated points are those set in the USA.

COAT: 45 POINTS

Texture: 10 points
Colour: 10 points
Pattern: 25 points

HEAD: 20 POINTS

Shape: 10 points
Ears: 5 points
Eye shape and colour: 5 points

BODY: 35 POINTS

Torso: 20 points
Legs and paws: 10 points
Tail: 5 points

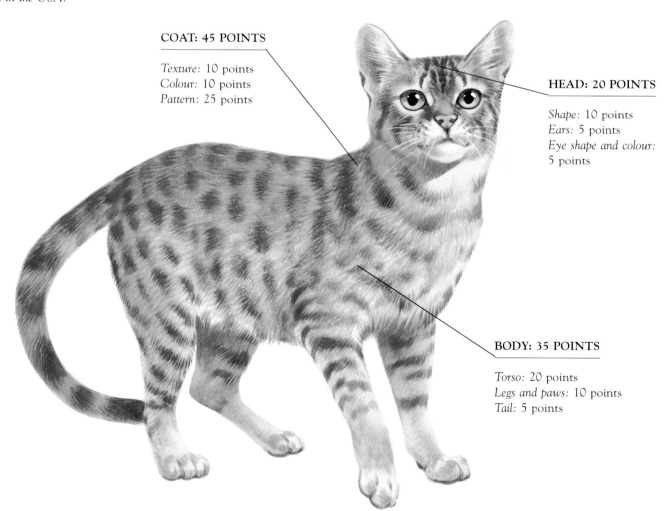

KEY CHARACTERISTICS

- **CATEGORY** Foreign Shorthair.

- **OVERALL BUILD** Large, robust and muscular.

- **COAT** Short to medium length, dense, luxuriant and unusually soft to touch.

- **HEAD** Broad, medium wedge with rounded contours, rather small in proportion to the body. Profile has a gentle curve from the forehead to the bridge of the nose; prominent brow.

- **NOSE** Large, broad nose with a puffed nose leather. Full broad muzzle and pronounced whisker pads.

- **CHIN** Strong.

- **EYES** Oval or slightly almond shaped, large but not bold, set on the slant towards base of ear.

- **EARS** Medium to small, rather short with a wide base and rounded tips; set as much on the side as the top of the head; pointing forward in profile.

- **BODY** Large and robust with a broad chest. Very muscular but long and sleek with hindquarters slightly higher than the shoulders.

- **LEGS** Medium length, strong and muscular.

- **PAWS** Large and rounded.

- **TAIL** Of medium length, thick and even with a rounded tip.

- **COLOURS** Leopard spotted or marble markings in brown tabby, blue-eyed snow or blue.

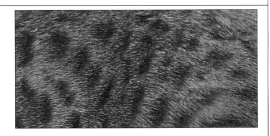

PENALTIES

The Bengal is penalized for having a long, rough or coarse coat; a ticked coat; incorrect colour of the tail tip or paw pads; a whip tail; an unspotted stomach; and white patches or spots other than the *ocelli* (light spots on the backs of the ears).

DISQUALIFICATION FEATURES

- Aggressive behaviour which threatens to harm.

BENGAL VARIETIES

IN BOTH THE Leopard Spotted and Marble Patterned the spectacles which encircle the eyes should extend into vertical streaks which may be outlined by an "M" on the forehead. Broken streaks in the Marble and streaks or spots in the Leopard run over the head on either side of a complex scarab marking, down the neck onto the shoulders. A bold "chin-strap" and "mascara" markings, unbroken or broken necklets and blotchy horizontal streaks are desirable in the Marble streaks or spots in the Leopard.

The Marble should have a distinct pattern with large swirled patches or streaks, clearly defined but not symmetrical, giving a marble-like impression, preferably with a horizontal flow. The pattern should be formed of distinct shapes and sharp outlines with sharp contrast between the base coat and the markings should bear no similarity to that of the Classic Tabby.

The Leopard Spotted should have generally large, well formed and randomly distributed spots. Extreme contrast between the ground colour and the spots, which should be arrow shaped, or rosetted in the case of larger spots. The cat's stomach must be spotted and the legs may show broken horizontal lines and/or spots along its length with a solid dark coloured tip. It is important that the spots do not run vertically into a mackerel tabby pattern.

BROWN TABBY All variations are allowed in both Leopard Spotted and Marble Bengals, but a high degree of reddish brown yielding a yellow, buff, golden or orange ground colour is preferred. The overall appearance should be of a cat dusted with gold glitter. The markings may be black or various shades of brown, and there may be *ocelli* – light-coloured spots on the backs of the ears. The whisker pads and chin must be very pale, and the chest, underbody and inner legs should be pale compared with the general ground colour. The eye rims, lips and nose leather are outlined in black; the centre of the nose leather is brick red. Paw pads and tail tip are black; eye colour is gold, green, or hazel, with deep shades preferred.

BROWN SPOTTED BENGAL

This kitten exhibits the arrow-head spots favoured in the Leopard Spotted variety of the Bengal cat.

SNOW BENGAL
This variety shows the Burmese/Tonkinese coat pattern, where the most intense colour is at the points, but the pattern is still visible on the body and has a special glittering appearance.

MARBLE BENGAL
Striking markings easily identify Bengals with the Marble pattern, with its complex whorls, distinct shapes and sharp outlines. The pattern bears little or no resemblance to the Classic Tabby.

BLUE-EYED SNOW This variety is of the Himalayan type, with the pattern restricted to the points. The ground colour is ivory to cream, with the overall appearance being that of a cat dusted with pearl glitter. The pattern varies in colour from charcoal to dark or light brown; there are light-coloured spectacles, whisker pads and chin; and *ocelli* are preferred on each ear. The eye rims, lips and nose leather are outlined in black; the centre of the nose leather is brick red. The paw pads are rosy-toned brown; the tail tip is charcoal or dark brown; the eye colour is blue.

BROWN SNOW This variety shows the Burmese/Tonkinese restriction of coat pattern. The ground colour is cream to light brown, with the overall appearance being that of a cat dusted with pearl glitter. The clearly visible pattern varies in colour from charcoal to light brown; there are light-coloured spectacles, whisker pads and chin; and *ocelli* are preferred on each ear. The eye rims, lips and nose leather are outlined in black; the centre of the nose leather is brick red. The paw pads are rosy-toned brown; the tail tip is charcoal or dark brown; the eye colour is gold, green or blue-green.

BLUE The ground colour is pinkish mushroom to warm oatmeal, with the overall appearance being that of a cat dusted with pearl glitter. The clearly visible pattern is pale blue to blue-grey; there are light-coloured spectacles, whisker pads and chin; and *ocelli* are preferred on each ear. The eye rims, lips and nose leather are outlined in slate grey; the centre of the nose leather is dark pink. The paw pads are mauvish pink; the tail tip is dark blue. The eye colour is gold, green or blue-green.

CORNISH REX

IN 1950 A CURLY-COATED kitten was born in an otherwise normal litter at a farm in Cornwall, south-west England. Microscopic examination by a geneticist of the kitten's hair samples showed they were similar to those of the Rex rabbit. When the kitten, named Kallibunker, matured, he was mated with his mother, and two of the resulting three kittens had Rex coats. The male, Poldhu, eventually sired a stunning Rex female called Lamorna Cove, which was exported to the United States to found the Cornish Rex breed on the other side of the Atlantic. British Shorthairs and Burmese cats were used as foundation stock in the early days of Cornish Rex breeding, and eventually there were sufficient curly-coated cats to establish an acceptable breed which could be registered. In Britain, the Cornish Rex achieved full breed status in 1967; in the United States, in 1979.

Character and Care

The Cornish Rex cat is intelligent, affectionate and rather extrovert by nature. Playful and mischievous, it makes a wonderful pet.

The unique curled coat does not shed hair, making it extremely easy to groom with hand stroking and the occasional use of a comb.

BREAKDOWN OF 100 SHOW POINTS

NB Annotated points (right) are those set in the UK; those below are set in the USA.

HEAD: 25 POINTS
Size and shape: 5 points
Muzzle and nose: 5 points
Eyes: 5 points
Ears: 5 points
Profile: 5 points

BODY: 30 POINTS
Size: 3 points
Torso: 10 points
Legs and paws: 5 points
Tail: 5 points
Bone: 5 points
Neck: 2 points

COAT: 40 POINTS
Texture: 10 points
Length: 5 points
Wave, extent of wave: 20 points
Close lying: 5 points

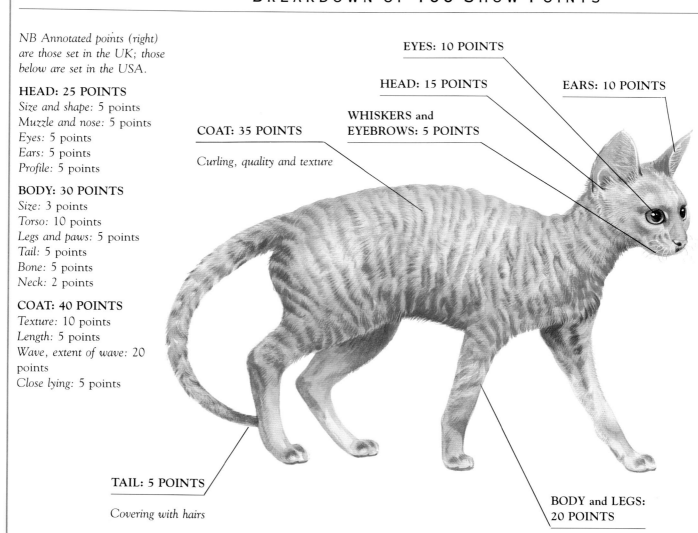

EYES: 10 POINTS

HEAD: 15 POINTS

EARS: 10 POINTS

WHISKERS and EYEBROWS: 5 POINTS

COAT: 35 POINTS
Curling, quality and texture

TAIL: 5 POINTS
Covering with hairs

BODY and LEGS: 20 POINTS

KEY CHARACTERISTICS

- **CATEGORY** Foreign Shorthair, curled.

- **OVERALL BUILD** Medium sized, slender build.

- **COAT** Short plush coat without guard hairs. Curls waves or ripples over the body particularly on the back and tail. Whiskers and eyebrows crinkled.

- **HEAD** Medium size, wedge shaped. About one third longer than it is wide.

- **NOSE** Rounded muzzle. In profile, a straight line is seen from the centre of the forehead to the end of the nose.

- **CHIN** Strong.

- **EYES** Medium to large, oval shaped.

- **EARS** Large, set high on the head.

- **BODY** Medium height. Slender, hard and muscular.

- **LEGS** Long and straight.

- **PAWS**

- **TAIL** Long, slender and tapering.

- **COLOURS** Most associations accept virtually all colours and patterns except white markings on Siamese patterned cats.

CORNISH REX VARIETIES

IN ORDER TO widen the gene pool and to ensure stamina in the Cornish Rex as a breed, it was necessary for the pioneer breeders to outcross to other breeds having the desired conformation. Foreign breeds were selected in the main, including Havana and Oriental lilac, and Burmese as well as Siamese of various colours. All the offspring of Cornish Rex to non-rexed cats resulted in cats with normal coats, all carrying the recessive gene for the Cornish curly coat, and when such cats matured, and were mated with similar cats, or back to Cornish Rex, curly-coated kittens were produced. The various colours and coat patterns of the cats selected for the original outcrosses resulted in a wide range of colour varieties in the Cornish Rex breed, and breeders soon began to show their preferences for certain colours and combinations of colours.

BLACK SMOKE & WHITE CORNISH
The tail of the Cornish Rex is long, fine and tapered and must be well covered with waved fur.

BLACK SMOKE VAN PATTERN
Virtually all the feline coat colours and patterns are found in the Cornish Rex. Perhaps one of the most unusual is the Van pattern, in which the cat's coat is basically white, with colour restricted to the head and tail.

RED CORNISH REX
The Cornish Rex is medium sized, lithe and muscular with long slender legs and small oval paws.

CHOCOLATE SMOKE CORNISH REX
The short plushy coat is dense and has uniform narrow waves extending from the top of the head across the back, sides and hips and continues to the tip of the tail.

WHITE CORNISH REX
The head should be narrow with a flat skull. A straight line can be seen from the centre of the forehead to the end of the nose.

CHOCOLATE TORTIE CORNISH REX
The eyes of the Cornish Rex are medium sized and oval, with a full eyes-width between them.

TORTIE SMOKE AND WHITE
The Cornish Rex stands tall, appearing to walk on tip toe.

191

DEVON REX

TEN YEARS AFTER the discovery of the first Cornish Rex kitten, another curly-coated kitten was discovered in the neighbouring English county of Devon. The kitten, named Kirlee, was eventually mated with some Cornish Rex queens. To everyone's surprise, all the resulting kittens were flat coated, and it was concluded that Kirlee's curls were caused by a different gene. More breeding tests confirmed this. The gene for the Cornish coat was labelled Rex gene [i]; the gene for the Devon coat Rex gene [ii]. The two rex-coated varieties were developed quite separately, and are quite distinct breeds. The Devon Rex would look rather unusual even without its wavy coat, having a quizzical, pixie-like expression and huge bat-like ears.

In Britain, a popular sub-variety of Devon Rex is known unofficially as the Si-Rex. It combines all of the characteristics of the typical Devon Rex with the Siamese coat pattern and colours.

Character and Care
The Devon is said to be the cat for the connoisseur. It is demanding as a pet, constantly craving human attention, loving, playful and intelligent.

The cat is very easy to groom with hand stroking and occasional combing. It often shows sparse areas on the body, and when it does, the cat needs extra warmth. The large ears need regular cleaning.

BREAKDOWN OF 100 SHOW POINTS

NB Annotated points (right) are those set in the UK; those below are set in the USA.

HEAD: 35 POINTS
Size and shape: 10 points
Muzzle and chin: 5 points
Profile: 5 points
Eyes: 5 points
Ears: 10 points

BODY: 30 POINTS
Torso: 10 points
Legs and paws: 10 points
Tail: 5 points
Neck: 5 points

COAT: 30 POINTS
Density: 10 points
Texture and length: 10 points
Waviness: 10 points

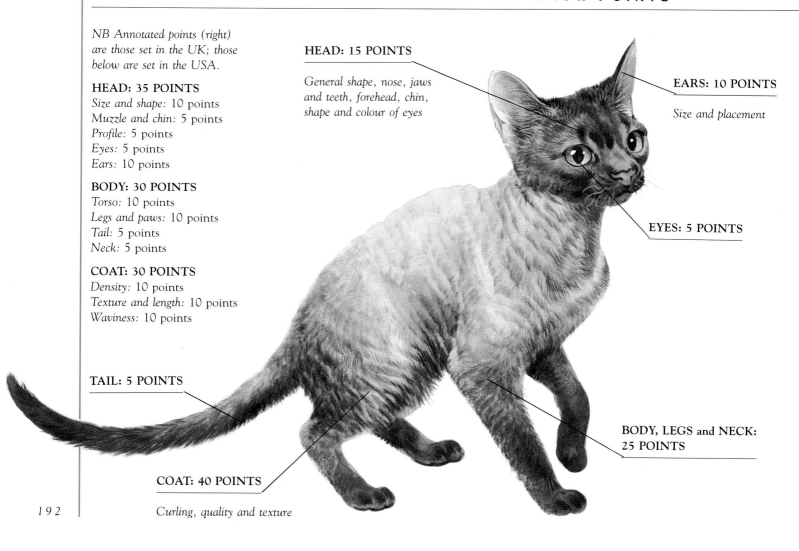

HEAD: 15 POINTS

General shape, nose, jaws and teeth, forehead, chin, shape and colour of eyes

EARS: 10 POINTS

Size and placement

EYES: 5 POINTS

BODY, LEGS and NECK: 25 POINTS

TAIL: 5 POINTS

COAT: 40 POINTS

Curling, quality and texture

KEY CHARACTERISTICS

- **CATEGORY** Foreign Shorthair, curled.

- **OVERALL BUILD** Medium size, hard and muscular, slender but with a broad chest.

- **COAT** Very short, soft, fine coat without guard hairs; curly or wavy particularly on the body and tail.

- **HEAD** Small, modified wedge shaped with short muzzle and prominent cheekbones.

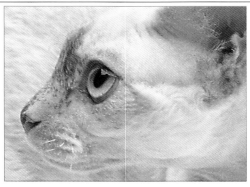

- **NOSE** No standards set.

- **CHIN** No standards set.

- **EYES** Large, oval and set wide apart, giving a unique "elfin" look.

- **EARS** Large, set low down.

- **BODY** Long and straight with a broad chest.

- **LEGS** Long and slim.

- **PAWS** Small and oval

- **TAIL** Long, fine and tapered.

- **COLOURS** All recognized colours or patterns except white markings on Siamese patterned cats.

PENALTIES

Devon Rex cats are penalized in the show ring for having incorrect head type; a short, bare or bushy tail; a straight or shaggy coat; a cobby body; small ears or ears set high and upright on the head; slack muscles or bare patches (a fault in kittens and a serious fault in cats).

DISQUALIFICATION FEATURES
- baldness
- a kinked or abnormal tail
- a squint
- weak hind legs

DEVON REX VARIETIES

WHATEVER THEIR COLOUR or coat pattern, all Devon Rex must conform to the same stringent show standard of points. The coat of the Devon Rex is quite different from that of the Cornish, and in some cats the fur may be sparse and downy on the underparts, often causing the coat colour to look indistinct. Like the Cornish Rex, the first Devons were outcrossed to cats of other Foreign breeds in order to widen the gene pool of available breeding stock. Siamese cats were extensively used and the resulting curled cats were called Si-Rex in the beginning. Si-rex is not now an accepted as correct terminology for the Siamese-patterned Devon Rex, and white markings are not permitted in cats with the Himalayan or Siamese coat pattern, where the colour is restricted to the cat's points.

Apart from this requirement, all colours and patterns accepted in the feline standards are recognized in the Devon Rex, with or without white areas.

ODD-EYED WHITE
White Devon Rex cats are accepted with blue eyes, golden eyes, or odd eyes.

CHOCOLATE TORTIE POINT
The Devon Rex appears in a range of Siamese-patterned colours. At one time these cats were called Si-rex.

BLACK SMOKE DEVON REX
The Devon Rex is totally different from the Cornish. It is of similar size, but has a unique head type and unusual bodily conformation.

**TORTIE TABBY &
WHITE**
*Tortoiseshells of all
colours may have white
markings and can be
very bright and
attractive, like this
alert young cat.*

**LILAC POINT
DEVON REX**
*Siamese patterns are
quite usual, but the
eye colour is generally
paler in the Rex breeds
than in the true
Siamese.*

TORTIE TABBY
*All feline colours are
accepted in this breed
though some
associations disallow
any white markings
except in tortoiseshell
varieties.*

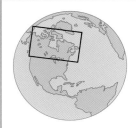

SPHYNX

ALTHOUGH IT APPEARS SO, the Sphynx is not truly hairless. The skin has the texture of soft leather and may be covered with a fine down which is almost imperceptible to the eye. A fine covering of hair is sometimes apparent on the ears, muzzle feet, tail and scrotum.

The first Sphynx appeared as a spontaneous mutation in a litter born to a black and white domestic cat in Ontario, Canada, in 1966. A breeder of Siamese cats took the hairless kitten, and with other breeders worked on the development of a new breed. The CFA gave the Sphynx provisional status, then revoked it. The CCFF recognized the breed for champion-ship status in 1971, and the first champion was chosen in 1972. Today the Sphynx is accepted only by a few feline associations, and it remains a rare and unique breed.

Character and Care

People-orientated and not fond of other cats, the Sphynx does not like being held or strongly petted. It often stands with one foreleg raised, and resists lying with its body touching the ground, preferring a warm surface.

It never needs brushing, but the suede-like body must be kept in good condition by hand grooming and rubbing down with a soft cloth.

BREAKDOWN OF 100 SHOW POINTS

NB Annotated points are those set in the UK.

HEAD: 35 POINTS

Shape, size, front and side views: 20 points
Ears: 10 points
Eyes: 5 points

BODY: 35 POINTS

Torso: 20 points
Neck: 5 points
Legs and paws: 5 points
Tail: 5 points

COAT and SKIN: 25 POINTS

COLOUR: 5 POINTS

PENALTIES

The Sphynx is penalized for being overall a small cat, for a body that is too thin or frail in appearance; for being too fine boned, too cobby, or foreign in type; for lack of wrinkles on the head; a straight profile; a narrow head; a non-amenable disposition; a significant amount of hair anywhere above the ankle; and for any indication of removal of hair.

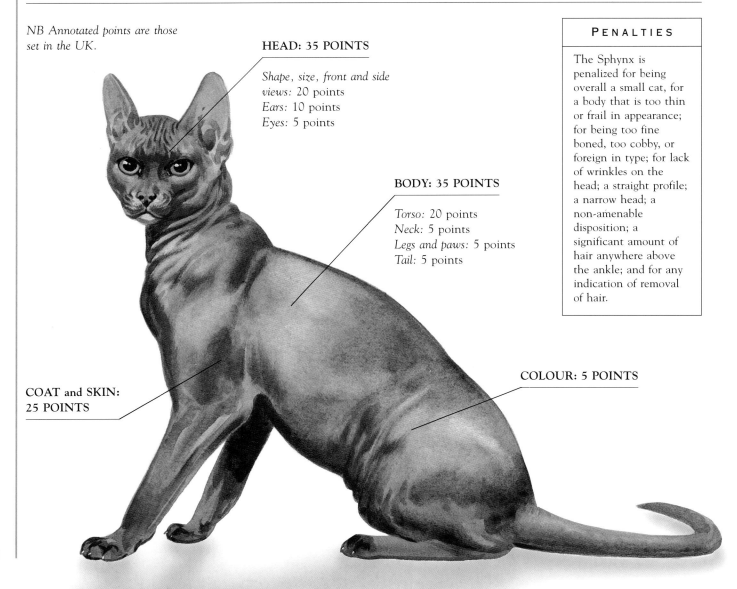

KEY CHARACTERISTICS

- **CATEGORY** Foreign.

- **OVERALL BUILD** Medium size, hard and muscular.

- **COAT** Appears hairless; may be covered with short fine down. Kittens have wrinkled skin; adults should retain some wrinkles.

- **COLOURS** All colours and patterns are acceptable; white lockets and buttons are also accepted.

- **OTHER FEATURES** Medium sized head is a modified wedge with rounded contours, skull is slightly rounded, forehead is flat, cheekbones are prominent. There is a slight stop at the bridge of the nose and the muzzle is rounded, with a distinct whisker break. Chin is firm; eyes are large and almost round, slanting towards the outer corner of the ear; ears are broad based and very open, set upright on the head, hairless inside and slightly haired on the back. The medium long body has a broad chest and well-rounded abdomen; it is hard and muscular with medium bone. Legs are in proportion to the body and of medium bone; hind legs longer than forelegs, which are widely set and muscular. Paws are medium sized, oval, with long, slender toes and thick paw pads; tail is whip-like, tapering from the body to the tip. A lion tail (with a tuft of hair on the tip) is acceptable.

The head of the Sphynx is a modified wedge with rounded contours.

BLACK & WHITE SPHYNX
The Sphynx may appear to be hairless but is usually covered with a very short, fine down.

197

JAPANESE BOBTAIL

A NATURAL BREED, WHICH has existed in its native Japan for centuries, the Japanese Bobtail is considered to be a symbol of good luck in the home, and the tri-coloured variety, known as the *mi-ke* (meaning tri-coloured), is particularly favoured.

The Bobtail first came to the attention of cat fanciers in the Western world when an American cat show judge visiting Japan became captivated by the breed. Five years later, in 1968, three Bobtails were exported from Japan to the United States. More were to follow, and Bobtails were accepted for provisional status by the CFA in May 1971.

After five years of careful breeding, the Japanese Bobtail became well established in the United States, and gained full recognition and Championship Status in the CFA in May 1976. It is also recognized in Britain by the Cat Association.

Character and Care

The Japanese Bobtail has an endearing personality and loves human company. It is a vocal cat, and has a soft melodious voice with a range of sounds. As a house cat, the Bobtail is well-behaved, intelligent and playful, and as a show cat, it is easy to handle.

The silky coat is easy to maintain in perfect condition with gentle brushing and combing, finishing with the hands or a silk scarf. The pom-pom on the tail is combed into shape, and the wide ears kept in pristine condition by wiping daily with a cotton bud.

BREAKDOWN OF 100 SHOW POINTS

NB *Annotated points are those set in the USA.*

HEAD: 20 POINTS

COLOUR and MARKINGS: 20 POINTS

TYPE: 30 POINTS

TAIL: 20 POINTS

COAT: 10 POINTS

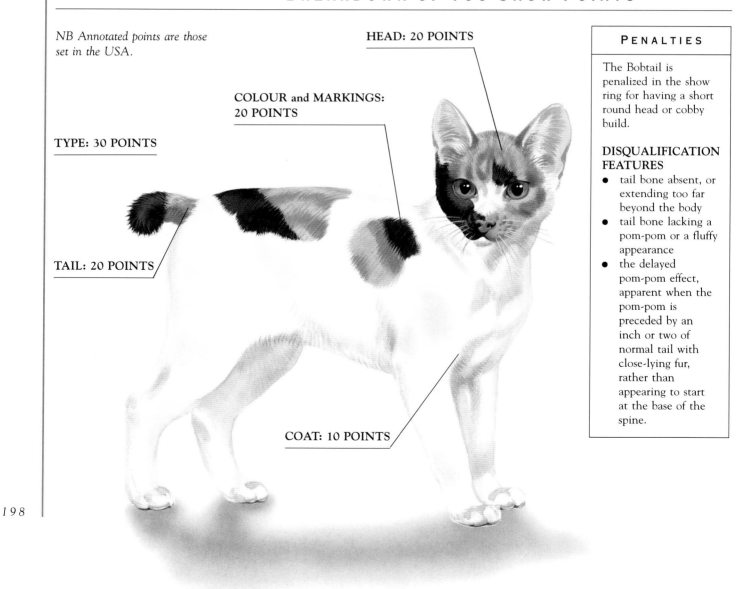

PENALTIES

The Bobtail is penalized in the show ring for having a short round head or cobby build.

DISQUALIFICATION FEATURES

- tail bone absent, or extending too far beyond the body
- tail bone lacking a pom-pom or a fluffy appearance
- the delayed pom-pom effect, apparent when the pom-pom is preceded by an inch or two of normal tail with close-lying fur, rather than appearing to start at the base of the spine.

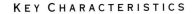

**BROWN TABBY &
WHITE BOBTAIL**
*The Japanese Bobtail is
loving and talkative,
and so makes a
perfect pet.*

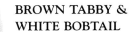

BLUE-EYED VAN
*The silky coat is very
easy to groom by
regular brushing, and
polishing with a silk
scarf.*

KEY CHARACTERISTICS

- **CATEGORY** Shorthair.

- **OVERALL BUILD** Medium size, lean and well-muscled.

- **COAT** Soft and silky, medium length; no noticeable undercoat and relatively little shedding of hair.

- **COLOURS** White, black, red, black and white, red and white, *mi-ke* (tri-colour – black, red and white), tortoiseshell. Other colours include any other colour or pattern or combination of colours and patterns except colouring that is restricted to the points, such as Himalayan, or unpatterned agouti, such as Abyssinian ticking. Patterned categories include any variety of tabby with or without areas of solid unmarked colour, preference being given to bold dramatic markings and rich vivid colouring.

- **OTHER FEATURES** Long fine head forming a perfect equilateral triangle with gentle curving lines, high cheek bones and a noticeable whisker break. The muzzle is fairly broad, rounding into the whisker break. The ears are large and upright, set wide apart and at right angles to the head and the eyes are large and oval, wide and alert. The medium-sized body is lean but well-muscled, and the legs are long and slender with neat oval paws. The short tail is said to resemble a bunny tail with the hair fanning out to create a pom-pom effect. If straightened the tail bone could be four or five inches in length. It is usually jointed only at the base and may be either straight or composed of one or more curves and angles.

**BLACK & WHITE
VAN PATTERN**
*The unique tail of the
Bobtail is short and
may be straight or bent
into one or more
curves, with the hair
fanning out to create a
pom-pom effect.*

BURMESE

ALL MODERN BURMESE cats can trace their ancestry back to a Siamese hybrid female named Wong Mau, who was taken from Rangoon to the United States in 1930. Wong Mau was almost certainly a cat of the type known as Tonkinese today. At first she was mated with Siamese males, then her offspring were inter-mated, and some back-crossed to Wong Mau herself. From these matings three distinct types of kittens emerged – some identical to Wong Mau, some Siamese, and some much darker than Wong Mau. These cats were the foundation of the Burmese breed, which was officially recognized in 1936 by the Cat Fanciers' Association, and was the first breed of pedigree cats to be developed completely in the United States.

Due to the lack of suitable Burmese cats, outcrosses to Siamese were made from time to time. Because of this, registration was suspended by the CFA from 1947 to 1953, but the breed soon became stabilized, with a strict standard of points ensuring that it maintained its unique physique and character.

Burmese cats were exported to Britain and accepted at shows during the 1950s. Since then the breed has developed to slightly different standards on opposite sides of the Atlantic.

Character and Care

The Burmese is a highly intelligent, active cat which can be strong willed, but repays firm, kind handling with affection.

Its short, glossy coat needs very little grooming to keep it in top condition.

BREAKDOWN OF 100 SHOW POINTS

NB Annotated points (right) are those set in the UK. Those listed below are for the US.

HEAD, EARS, and EYES: 30 POINTS
Roundness of head: 7 points
Breadth between eyes and full face: 6 points
Proper profile (includes chin): 6 points
Ear set, placement, and size: 6 points
Eye placement and shape: 5 points

BODY, LEGS, FEET, and TAIL: 30 POINTS
Torso: 15 points
Muscle tone: 5 points
Legs and feet: 5 points
Tail: 5 points

COAT: 10 POINTS
Short: 4 points
Texture: 4 points
Close lying: 2 points

COLOUR: 30 POINTS
Body colour: 25 points
Eye colour: 5 points

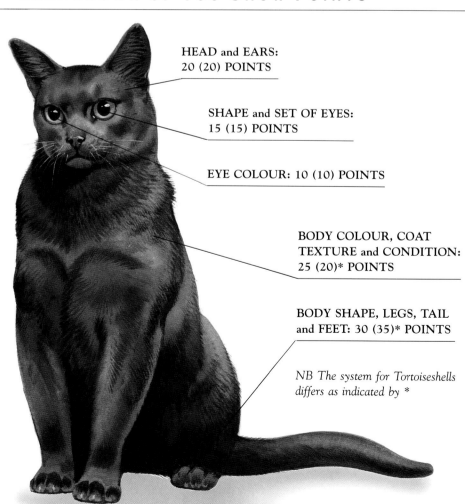

HEAD and EARS: 20 (20) POINTS

SHAPE and SET OF EYES: 15 (15) POINTS

EYE COLOUR: 10 (10) POINTS

BODY COLOUR, COAT TEXTURE and CONDITION: 25 (20)* POINTS

BODY SHAPE, LEGS, TAIL and FEET: 30 (35)* POINTS

NB The system for Tortoiseshells differs as indicated by *

KEY CHARACTERISTICS

- **CATEGORY** Foreign Shorthair.

- **OVERALL BUILD** Medium size with substantial bone structure and good muscular development. The cat is surprisingly heavy for its size.

- **COAT** Very short and close lying, fine and glossy with a satin-like texture.

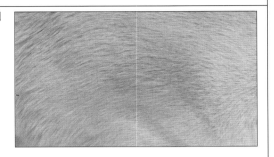

- **HEAD** Pleasingly rounded, with no flat planes whether viewed from the front or in profile. The face is full with a broad, short muzzle.

- **NOSE** In profile there is a definite nose break.

- **CHIN** Firm and rounded.

- **EYES** Large, set wide apart, with a rounded aperture.

- **EARS** Medium size, set well apart and tilted slightly forward, giving an alert expression.

- **BODY** Muscular, compact, with strong shoulders and hips.

- **LEGS** Well proportioned.

- **PAWS** Round.

- **TAIL** Medium length and straight.

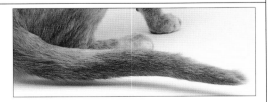

- **COLOURS** *USA* In some US associations only the sable or brown varieties are classed as Burmese. The blue, champagne or chocolate, platinum or lilac are classed as dilute division Burmese in some associations, and as Malayan in others. *UK* All accepted colours in Burmese and Malayan compete as Burmese.

PENALTIES

The Burmese is penalized in the show ring for having green eyes.

DISQUALIFICATION FEATURES
- blue eyes
- a kinked or abnormal tail
- a white locket or button

SOLID VARIETIES

STANDARDS FOR THE ideal Burmese cat differ on either side of the Atlantic Ocean. The American Burmese has a rounder head and a slightly heavier body than its British counterpart. America's Burmese also tend to have better eye-colour, but as this breed was originally developed in the United States, this is probably to be expected. Eye colour is very difficult to assess under the artificial light of a show hall, and judges often take Burmese entrants to a window with natural light if the eye colour is at all suspect.

RED The coat is actually a light tangerine, colour as even as possible though very slight tabby markings are allowed on the face. Ears are darker than the body. Nose leather and paw pads are pink; eye colour is yellow to gold, with deeper shades preferred.

CREAM The coat is pastel cream, with ears slightly darker than the body. Nose leather and paw pads are pink; eye colour is yellow to gold, with deeper shapes preferred.

SABLE or BROWN The rich, warm, sable brown coat shades almost imperceptibly to a lighter tone on the underparts, otherwise without any shading, barring or markings of any kind. Kittens may be ligher in colour. The nose leather and paw pads are brown; the eye colour ranges from yellow to gold, with the deeper shades preferred.

BLUE The coat is soft silver grey, very slightly darker on the back and tail. There should be a distinct silver sheen on the ears, face and feet. Nose leather and paw pads are blue-grey; eye colour is yellow to gold.

CHOCOLATE or CHAMPAGNE The warm milk chocolate coat should be as even as possible though the mask and ears may be very slightly deeper in colour. Nose leather is chocolate brown; paw pads are cinnamon to chocolate brown; eye colour is yellow to gold.

LILAC or PLATINUM The pale delicate dove-grey coat has a pinkish tone, as even as possible though the mask and ears may be very slightly deeper in colour. Nose leather and paw pads are lavender pink; eye colour is yellow to gold, with deeper shades preferred.

RED BURMESE
Tangerine in colour rather than red, this variety is bright and very attractive, particularly when it has the desired golden eyes.

SABLE BURMESE

It is interesting to compare this American cat with those raised in Britain, when the slight differences encouraged by the slightly differing show standards become apparent.

BROWN BURMESE

Known as the Sable Burmese in the USA where the breed was first developed, this variety has a rich dark brown coat and gold eye colour.

CREAM BURMESE

The paler colours in the Burmese often show a very slight Himalayan effect with darker colour on the points – the face, ears, legs, paws and tail.

LILAC BURMESE

Lilac Burmese appeared in litters when cats which carried both the chocolate and blue colour genes were mated together. At first they were considered to be "poor Blues", but were later accepted as a new variety.

CHOCOLATE BURMESE

With its warm chocolate coat and slightly darker points, this variety is very attractive.

BLUE BURMESE

A simple dilute of the usual brown colour, the Blue Burmese was the first additional variety to be recognized and accepted.

TORTOISESHELL VARIETIES

THE ORANGE (RED) gene was first introduced into the Burmese in Britain from three sources, a shorthaired ginger tabby, a red-pointed Siamese and a tortoiseshell-and-white domestic cat. From these beginnings a breeding programme was set up and by the mid-1970s, clear coated red Burmese, cream Burmese, and the invariably female tortoiseshells had been produced in considerable numbers, most of which were of very good Burmese type.

SEAL TORTIE Seal brown, red and/or light red, patched and/or mottled. Nose leather and paw pads are plain or mottled, seal brown and/or pink. The eye colour is yellow to gold, with deeper shades preferred.

BLUE-CREAM or BLUE TORTIE Pale tones of blue and cream, patched and/or mottled. Nose leather and paw pads are plain or mottled, pink and/or blue-grey. The eye colour is yellow to gold, with deeper shades preferred.

CHOCOLATE TORTIE Milk chocolate, red and/or light red, patched and/or mottled. Nose leather and paw pads are plain or mottled, milk chocolate and/or light red or pink. The eye colour is yellow to gold, with the deeper shades preferred.

LILAC-CREAM or LILAC TORTIE Lilac and pale cream, patched and/or mottled. Nose leather and paw pads are plain or mottled, pale pink and/or lavender pink. The eye colour is yellow to gold, with deeper shades preferred.

Painted Varieties

The 'points' are the mask (face), ears, legs and paws, and the tail. The colour of the points is the same as the body colour, and show little contrast, but should be as equal in colour density as possible.

BLUE TORTIE OR BLUE-CREAM

Tortoiseshells have mixed colours in their coats, the Blue Tortie being blue and cream. There are four colours of Tortie Burmese — brown, blue, chocolate and lilac.

In all varieties, the body colour will be paler on the underparts than on the back and legs.

The eye colour is in the yellow/gold range with deeper shades preferred. In non-tabby varieties, allowance is made in kittens and adolescent cats for an overall paler body colour, and for faint tabby barring or ghost tabby markings. Tabby markings in adult cats of non-tabby varieties and white hairs are faults.

CHOCOLATE TORTIE BURMESE

After the introduction of the red or orange gene into the breed, a range of tortoiseshell Burmese soon began to appear.

TIFFANIE

TIFFANIE

The Tiffanie is a long-coated cat of Burmese type and is accepted in all colours found in the Burmese and Malayan range.

THIS BREED COMBINES the conformation and colouring of the typical Burmese with an attractive coat of long silky hair. First developed in the United States from long-coated kittens which appeared from time to time in otherwise normal litters of pedigree Burmese, the Tiffanie was later developed as a breed in its own right. The American breeders concentrated on the sable Tiffanie, born a pale *café au lait* colour, and gradually developing the long sable coat with maturity. In Britain, long-coated cats of good Burmese conformation came from the Burmilla breeding programmes and were refined by back-crosses to Burmese, which resulted in Tiffanie kittens of all colours found in the Burmese and Malayan ranges. At the time of writing (1995) no association officially accepts this breed, and no standard of points is available, including penalties.

Character and Care

Just like its Burmese ancestors, the Tiffanie is playful and affectionate with an extrovert nature, making it a good pet.

The long coat is quite easy to care for with regular grooming.

BROWN SMOKE

In Britain, the Tiffanie is a product of the Burmilla breeding plan and is found in a range of Smoke colours.

KEY CHARACTERISTICS

- **CATEGORY** Semi-longhair.

- **OVERALL BUILD** Medium size with substantial bone; it is surprisingly heavy for its size.

- **COAT** Of medium length, fine and silky, longer at the frill (ruff) and with a flowing plume-like tail.

- **COLOURS** USA Sable UK All colours found in the Burmese and Malayan range.

- **OTHER FEATURES** Head is pleasingly rounded with no flat planes; face is full with a broad, short muzzle; nose is short with a break in profile. Chin is strong; eyes large, set wide apart, the top line showing a straight, Oriental slant towards the nose, the lower line rounded. Ears are medium size, broad based with rounded tips, set wide apart with a slight forward tilt. Body is medium length, hard, compact and muscular, with a strong, rounded chest and straight back. Legs are slender, and in proportion to the body; paws small and oval; tail medium length, not thick at the base and tapering only slightly to a rounded tip, well covered with flowing silky hair.

SINGAPURA

A N AMERICAN CAT breeder, Tommy Meadows, developed the Singapura from cats she discovered in Singapore. She decided to import some into the United States, and drew up a careful programme for the development of the breed. Her work has been rewarded by the production of an attractive, viable feline breed with considerable aesthetic appeal. The Singapura has a ticked coat, similar to that of the Abyssinian, and is of moderate Foreign Shorthair bone structure and conformation.

Character and Care

The Singapura is a happy, friendly cat with a playful nature.

The short, fine coat is extremely easy to keep in good condition with very little grooming. A light combing removes dead hairs, and occasional brushing tones the skin. Hand grooming or stroking with a silk scarf imparts a healthy looking sheen to the coat.

Note No standards are available (1995).

KEY CHARACTERISTICS
● **CATEGORY** Foreign Shorthair.
● **OVERALL BUILD** Small to medium in size, moderately stocky and muscular.
● **COAT** Very short and fine; each hair should have at least two bands of dark ticking separated by light bands of colour. Each individual hair is light next to the skin and dark at the tip.
● **COLOURS** Sepia Agouti. The ground colour is warm ivory; the ticking is dark brown. The muzzle, chin, chest and stomach are the colour of unbleached muslin; the ears and bridge of the nose are salmon toned. The nose leather is pale to dark salmon pink, outlined with dark brown; the paw pads are rosy brown; the eye rims are dark brown; the eye colour is hazel, green or yellow.
● **OTHER FEATURES** Head is rounded, with a definite whisker break; nose short and blunt; chin well developed; eyes large and almond shaped; ears large and slightly pointed, set fairly wide apart, giving an alert expression. Body is stocky and muscular; legs are heavy; paws small and oval; tail of medium length with a blunt tip.

BROWN TICKED SINGAPURA

With its short, fine ticked coat and happy, friendly nature, this rare breed makes a perfect pet.

TONKINESE

A HYBRID OF Burmese and Siamese cats, the Tonkinese has physical features of both these breeds. A mating between a Burmese and a Siamese gives all Tonkinese kittens, whereas the mating of two Tonkinese cats produces, on average, two Tonkinese kittens to one Burmese and one Siamese.

Tonkinese cats have dark points which merge gradually into the body colour, which is intermediate between the typical pale Siamese and the dark Burmese colouring. Tonkinese eye colour is blue-green or turquoise, never Siamese blue or Burmese gold.

Character and Care

The Tonkinese is a friendly and affectionate cat, with a strong sense of mischief. Extrovert and intelligent, it is generally good with other cats, as well as with dogs and children. It is less vocal than the Siamese.

The coat is very easy to keep in good condition with very little grooming. Regular combing to remove dead hair, and buffing with a silk scarf or grooming mitten imparts a healthy sheen.

BREAKDOWN OF 100 SHOW POINTS

NB Annotated points are those set in the UK.

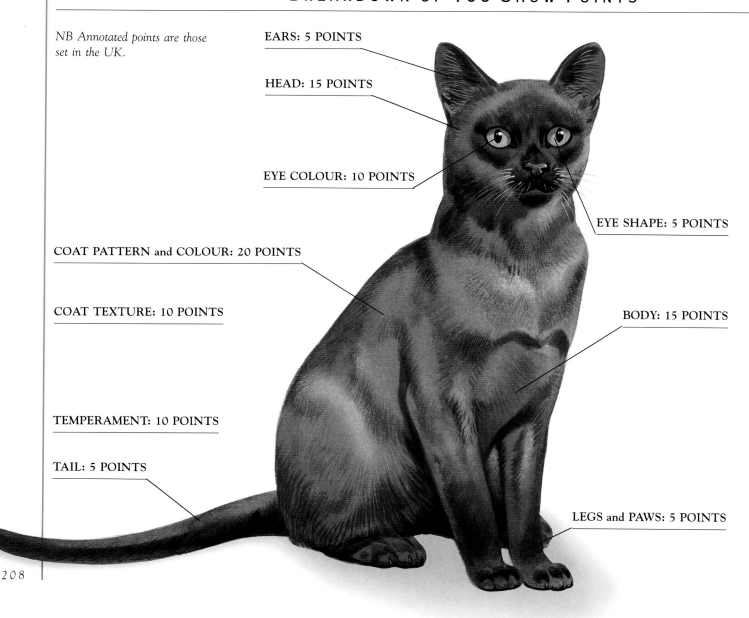

EARS: 5 POINTS

HEAD: 15 POINTS

EYE COLOUR: 10 POINTS

EYE SHAPE: 5 POINTS

COAT PATTERN and COLOUR: 20 POINTS

COAT TEXTURE: 10 POINTS

BODY: 15 POINTS

TEMPERAMENT: 10 POINTS

TAIL: 5 POINTS

LEGS and PAWS: 5 POINTS

KEY CHARACTERISTICS

- **CATEGORY** Foreign Shorthair.

- **OVERALL BUILD** Medium size, muscular and surprisingly heavy for its size.

- **COAT** Short, fine and close-lying with a soft, fur-like texture.

- **HEAD** Modified wedge shape, longer than it is wide, with high, gently planed cheekbones and strong contours to the brow, cheek and profile. In profile there should be a slight stop at eye level; a definite break is undesirable. The muzzle is blunt, with a definite whisker break.

- **NOSE** No standards available.

- **CHIN** Firm but not massive.

- **EYES** Almond shaped, slanted along cheekbone towards outer edge of ear.

- **EARS** Medium size with oval tips, set wide apart and tilted slightly forwards. The hair on the ears is very short.

- **BODY** Medium length, muscular but not coarse, with tight abdomen.

- **LEGS** Slim.

- **PAWS** More oval than round.

- **TAIL** Medium to long, tapering.

- **COLOURS** Btown, blue, chocolate, lilac, red, cream, brown tortie, blue tortie, chocolate tortie, lilac tortie.

MINK VARIETIES

THE TONKINESE IS bred from Burmese and Siamese, and as would be expected, is intermediate to those breeds in both conformation and colouring. As a pet it suits those people who find the show-type Siamese to be too extreme, but do not favour the typical chunkiness and almost uniform colouration of the Burmese. Indeed a typical Tonkinese is very similar to the 'old-fashioned' type of Siamese cat that many people today desire as pets.

BROWN A medium brown coat shades to a lighter tone on the underparts. The points and nose leather are dark brown; the paw pads are medium to dark brown; the eye colour is blue-green.

BLUE A soft grey-blue colour shades to a lighter tone on the underparts. The points are slate blue (distinctly darker than the body colour). Nose leather and paw pads are blue-grey; eye colour is blue-green.

CHOCOLATE The buff-cream body has medium brown points. Nose leather is cinnamon-brown; paw pads are cinnamon-pink to cinnamon-brown; eye colour is blue-green.

RED The golden cream coat has apricot underparts. The points are light to medium ruddy brown; the nose leather and paw pads are caramel-pink; the eye colour is blue-green.

LILAC The pale silvery grey coat has warm overtones (not white or cream). The points are pewter grey – distinctly darker than the body colour; nose leather is lavender pink to lavender grey; paw pads are lavender pink; eye colour is blue-green.

Pointed Varieties

The "points" are the mask (face) ears, legs and paws, and the tail. The points are densely marked but gradually merge into the body colour. The colour of the points is the same as the body colour but denser and darker.

The body colour in the adult cat should be rich and even and shade almost imperceptibly into a slightly lighter colour on the underparts. There is a distinct contrast between the points and body colour whatever the colour variety. The eye colour is blue-green (aquamarine), with depth clarity and brilliance.

N.B. Allowance is made for lighter body colour in kittens and adolescent cats, and for slight barring in the coat; colours darken with maturity – full colouration may take up to 16 months to develop, particularly in the dilute colour varieties.

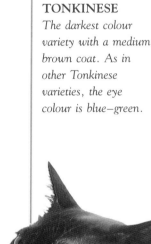

BROWN TONKINESE

The darkest colour variety with a medium brown coat. As in other Tonkinese varieties, the eye colour is blue–green.

CHOCOLATE TONKINESE
The product of Siamese and Burmese, the Tonkinese has colouring between the two breeds.

LILAC TONKINESE
Equivalent to the Lilac Burmese and Lilac Point Siamese, this cat has a pale silvery grey coat with warm overtones.

NEW VARIETIES

MEMBERS OF THE Cat Association of Britain, working with new colours in Burmese and Siamese cats, decided to introduce these into the Tonkinese, and the breeding programmes were provisionally accepted by CA prior to its becoming the British member of FIFe in 1990. The Cat Association of Britain therefore offers special awards for Tonkinese in the following colour varieties: seal, blue, chocolate, cinnamon, lilac, fawn, caramel, beige, red, cream, apricot, indigo, and all these colours as tortoiseshell, tabby and torbie.

CREAM TONKINESE

This cat should be a rich warm cream with slightly darker points, except for the legs which may be paler than in other colours.

RED TONKINESE

Red and Cream Tonkinese are often quite similar and can be difficult to tell apart as kittens.

BLUE TORTIE
Bluish silver-grey either patched or mingled with shades of cream produce this pretty variety.

CHOCOLATE TORTIE
The introduction of the red or orange gene into Tonkinese breeding soon gave rise to an entire range of tortoiseshells.

LILAC TORTIE TONKINESE
A paler version of the Blue Tortie with pale dove grey patched or mingled with pale cream. Like its darker cousin, the Lilac Tortie has blue-green eyes.

BOMBAY

BECAUSE OF ITS looks, the Bombay cat has been referred to as the "patent-leather kid with new-penny eyes", an apt description for this shining jet black feline. Developed from outstanding specimens of black American Shorthair and sable Burmese, the desired type was quickly achieved, and Bombays were found to breed true. Full recognition and championship status was granted by the CFA in 1976.

Although the cat looks like a black American-style Burmese, the early pioneers of the breed thought it looked like a miniature version of the Indian (Asian) black panther and so, after much deliberation, chose Bombay as the breed name.

Character and Care

The Bombay has a very even temperament. It is generally strong and healthy, affectionate and playful, making it a good pet.

The coat is easy to maintain with a balanced diet and minimal grooming. Buffing with a silk scarf or velvet grooming mitt enhances the typical patent-leather gloss.

BREAKDOWN OF 100 SHOW POINTS

NB *Annotated points are those set in the USA.*

HEAD and EARS: 25 POINTS

Roundness of head: 7 points
Full face and proper profile: 7 points
Ears: 7 points
Chin: 4 points

EYES: 5 POINTS

Placement and shape: 5 points

COAT: 20 POINTS

Shortness: 10 points
Texture: 5 points
Close lying: 5 points

BODY: 20 POINTS

Body: 15 points
Tail: 5 points

COLOUR: 30 POINTS

Body colour: 20 points
Eye colour: 10 points

PENALTIES

Bombay cats are penalized in the show ring for excessive cobbiness or ranginess.

DISQUALIFICATION FEATURES
- incorrect colour of nose leather, paw pads or eyes
- incorrect dentition
- kinked or abnormal tail
- a white locket or spots
- an extreme nose break interfering with normal breathing or tear production

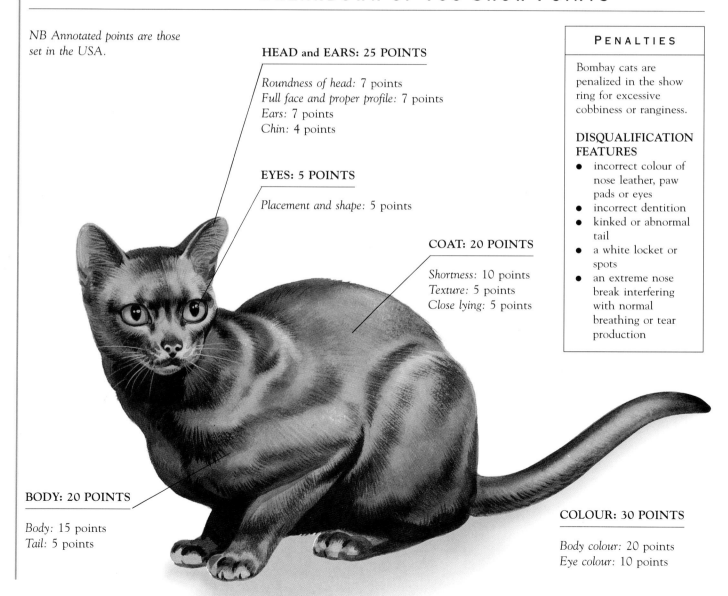

BOMBAY

The true Bombay from the United States was produced from Sable Burmese and American Shorthairs and is a unique, jet black and shiny cat with large golden eyes.

KEY CHARACTERISTICS

- **CATEGORY** Foreign Shorthair.

- **OVERALL BUILD** Medium size, muscular, surprisingly heavy for size.

- **COAT** Fine and short with satin-like texture, close lying and with a sheen like patent leather.

- **COLOUR** Black only. Coat-jet black to the roots with a patent-leather sheen. Nose leather and paw pads, black. Eye colour, gold to copper; deeper shades preferred.

- **OTHER FEATURES** Pleasingly round head with no sharp angles, full face with good width between the eyes, tapering to a short, strong muzzle. In profile there is a visible nose break. Medium sized ears with slightly rounded tips set wide apart and tilting slightly forward giving an alert expression. Muscular, medium sized body with legs in proportion, round paws and a straight, medium length tail.

BOMBAY (ASIAN BLACK)

In Britain, the black Asian, a product of Burmese and Shorthair, is known as the Bombay.

215

BURMILLA

AN ACCIDENTAL MATING between a lilac Burmese female and a Chinchilla Silver male in 1981 resulted in the birth of four black shaded silver female kittens. All were of foreign conformation, and had short dense coats. They looked so spectacular and caused so much interest that similar matings were carried out. In 1983, the Cat Association of Britain accepted breeding programmes and a standard of points for the breed to be known as Burmilla, to be developed as a shorthaired silver cat of medium foreign type, showing a striking contrast between the pure silver undercoat and the shaded or tipped markings. FIFe granted international breed status to the Burmilla in 1994.

This elegant cat is of medium foreign type with a muscular body, long sturdy legs and a moderately thick, long tail. The head is a medium wedge, with large ears, a short nose and large expressive eyes. Its most impressive feature, however, is the sparkling shaded or tipped ("shell") coat. The ground colour is pure silver white, with shading or tipping in any of the recognized solid or tortoiseshell colours,

BREAKDOWN OF 100 SHOW POINTS

NB Annotated points are those set in Europe.

HEAD: 50 POINTS

Shape, nose and chin:
20 points
Ear placement and shape:
10 points
Eye placement, shape and colour: 20 points

BODY: 25 POINTS

Shape and structure; legs and paws; tail shape and length

COAT: 20 POINTS

Length and texture: 10 points
Evenness of shading/tipping:
10 points

CONDITION: 5 POINTS

which must be uniformly distributed. The eyelids, lips and nose leather are rimmed with the basic colour, and delicate tracings of tabby markings are present on the points, which are more clearly defined on the shaded Burmilla.

Character and Care

The Burmilla is easy going and relaxed, has a playful nature and is very affectionate.

The dense coat is best groomed with a rubber brush to loosen dead hairs before being given a thorough combing.

KEY CHARACTERISTICS

- **CATEGORY** Foreign Shorthair.

- **OVERALL BUILD** Medium size and build.

- **COAT** Short and dense with a silky texture; with sufficient undercoat to give a slight lift to the coat.

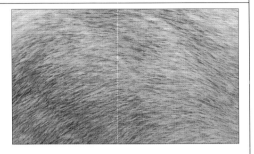

- **HEAD** Gently rounded at the top with medium width between the ears; wide at eye level and tapering to a short, blunt wedge.

- **NOSE** The profile shows a gentle nose break.

- **CHIN** Firm, level with the tip of the nose.

- **EYES** Large, set well apart and slightly oblique, luminous and expressive.

- **EARS** Medium to large, broad based and with rounded tips. Set with a slightly forward tilt.

- **BODY** Medium length, with a straight back and rounded chest.

- **LEGS** Slender, with strong bone; the hind legs are slightly longer than forelegs.

- **PAWS** Neat and oval.

- **TAIL** Medium to long, fairly thick at the base and tapering slightly to a rounded tip.

- **COLOURS** Shaded or tipped in the following colours: black, blue, brown, chocolate, lilac, red, cream, red tortoiseshell, blue tortoiseshell, brown tortoiseshell, chocolate tortoiseshell, lilac tortoiseshell.

BURMILLA VARIETIES

ELEGANT CATS OF medium foreign conformation, the Burmilla male is larger and more stocky than the dainty female. Any tendency to the fine bone of the Siamese, or the cobby type of the Shorthair, is regarded as a fault.

BLACK SHADED or TIPPED The coat is pure silver white, shaded or tipped with black. The nose leather is brick red; the paw pads and soles are black; the eye colour is green.

BLUE SHADED or TIPPED The coat is pure silver white, shaded or tipped with blue-grey. The nose leather is brick red; the paw pads and soles are blue-grey; the eye colour is green.

BROWN SHADED or TIPPED The coat is pure silver white, shaded or tipped with dark brown. The nose leather is brick red; the paw pads and soles are dark brown; the eye colour is green.

CHOCOLATE SHADED or TIPPED The coat is pure silver white, shaded or tipped with milk chocolate. The nose leather is brick red; the paw pads are chocolate tinged with pink; the soles are chocolate; the eye colour is green.

BLACK TIPPED
The pure silver white coat of the Burmilla is lightly tipped with black in this variety.

CHOCOLATE TIPPED BURMILLA
In the Chocolate Tipped the pure silver undercoat is tipped with milk chocolate at the ends of each hair.

BROWN SHADED BURMILLA

The shaded varieties are more heavily tipped than the tipped varieties, producing a stronger colour. In the Brown Shaded the shading is in dark brown on the silver base coat.

BROWN TIPPED BURMILLA

This Brown Tipped Burmilla is typical of the breed, playful and affectionate.

LILAC SHADED or TIPPED The coat is pure silver white, shaded or tipped with lilac (light grey with a pinkish tinge). The nose leather is brick red; the paw pads are lavender pink; the soles are grey tinged with pink; and the eye colour is green.

RED SHADED or TIPPED The coat is pure silver white, shaded or tipped with red. The nose leather and paw pads are pink; the soles are red; the eye colour is green or amber.

CREAM SHADED or TIPPED The coat is pure silver white, shaded or tipped with pale cream. The nose leather and paw pads are pink; the soles are cream; the eye colour is either green or amber.

RED TORTOISESHELL SHADED or TIPPED The coat is pure white, shaded or tipped with a patchwork of black and red. The nose leather and paw pads are black, pink, or mottled black and pink; the soles are black and/or red; the eye colour is green or amber.

BLUE TORTOISESHELL SHADED or TIPPED The coat is pure white, shaded or tipped with a patchwork of blue-grey and cream. The nose leather and paw pads are blue-grey, pink, or mottled blue-grey and pink; the soles are blue-grey and/or cream; the eye colour is either green or amber.

BLUE SHADED BURMILLA

A silver white coat shaded with blue-grey, set off by a brick red nose and large luminous green eyes.

BROWN TORTOISESHELL SHADED or TIPPED The coat is pure white, shaded or tipped with a patchwork of dark brown and red or light red. The nose leather and paw pads are dark brown, pink, or mottled dark brown and pink; the soles are dark brown and/or red; the eye colour is green or amber.

CHOCOLATE TORTOISESHELL SHADED or TIPPED The coat is pure white, shaded or tipped with a patchwork of milk chocolate and light red. The nose leather and paw pads are chocolate, pink, or mottled chocolate and pink; the soles are chocolate and/or light red; the eye colour is green or amber.

LILAC TORTOISESHELL SHADED or TIPPED The coat is pure white, shaded or tipped with a patchwork of lilac (light grey with a pinkish tinge) and cream. The nose leather and paw pads are lavender pink, pink, or mottled lavender pink and pink; the soles are grey tinged with pink; the eye colour is either green or amber.

Note In all colours, the Tipped Burmilla is lighter overall than the Shaded Burmilla.

BLACK SHADED BURMILLA

As in all Burmilla cats, the paw pads and soles (the area from the paw to the hock) match the colour of the shading or tipping on the silver coat.

ASIAN

THE BURMILLA IS just one variety in a larger family of cats known as the Asian Group. All of the variants are of Burmese type and basic conformation, but do not have the Burmese coat colour or slight restriction of colour to the "points" area as found in the usual Burmese cat.

TICKED TABBY

Each hair of the coat is ticked with two or three bands of colour which produces the effect commonly seen in a wild rabbit. All ticked tabby Asian cats should have clear tabby bars marking the legs and tail.

Rather the cats of the Asian Group bear the same relationship to Burmese as the Orientals do to Siamese. Within the Asian Group are found a range of cats with unusual and very attractive coats, for colour pattern and texture. It includes the Burmilla, Asian Smoke, Asian Tabby, Bombay and Tiffanie. The Burmilla is by far the most successful in terms of numbers and popularity, and, in fact, most of the other Asians have arisen as off-shoots of the carefully controlled programmes designed to breed the Burmilla in a wide range of colours, and with the creation of a broad and viable base from which to select second and third generation crosses.

ASIAN EYES

All varieties of Asian cats have characteristically large, full and expressive eyes which are set well apart. They are slightly Oriental in setting, but are neither Oriental nor round in shape.

224   Siamese
230   Colorpoint
234   Balinese
238   Oriental
249   Seychellois
250   Javanese

ORIENTAL BREEDS

SIAMESE

PROBABLY THE BEST KNOWN of all pedigree breeds, the Siamese cat of today is quite different from that seen in the early 1900s, though it still retains its points, caused by the Himalayan factor, the gene which restricts the true colouring to the animal's face, ears, legs, paws and tail.

Seal-pointed cats were presented by the Royal Court of Siam to British and American diplomats towards the end of the nineteenth century, and the breed gained public interest which has continued to grow.

Although the original Royal Cats of Siam were seal pointed some had lighter brown points, and were eventually recognized as being a separate colour variety which was called Chocolate Point. A naturally occurring dilute factor also became apparent when the almost black coloration of the seal point gave rise to

cats with slate-grey extremities. These were eventually accepted as the colour variety Blue Point.

With increasing knowledge of feline colour genetics, breeders of Siamese cats realized that they could increase the range of colour varieties by first making judicious out-crosses, then back-breeding the offspring to Siamese of excellent type. The red series of points colours was added by out-crossing to red, red tabby and tortoiseshell cats, and a range of colours in tabby-pointed cats was developed from out-crosses with tabbies.

Britain's GCCF and the CA recognize all short-coated pointed cats of Oriental type as Siamese, as do some foreign associations, in particular FIFe. Others such as America's CFA accept only the four original, naturally occurring colours as Siamese, and register the red

BREAKDOWN OF 100 SHOW POINTS

NB Annotated points (right) are those set in the UK (some varieties have differing points in the GCCF); those below are for Europe.

HEAD: 25 POINTS
General shape, nose, profile, jaws, teeth, forehead and shape of eyes

EYE COLOUR: 15 POINTS

BODY: 25 POINTS
Shape, size, bone structure, length of legs, shape of paws, length and shape of tail

COAT: 30 POINTS
Body colour: 10 points
Points: 10 points
Quality and texture: 10 points

CONDITION: 5 POINTS

LEGS and FEET: 5 POINTS

BODY: 15 POINTS

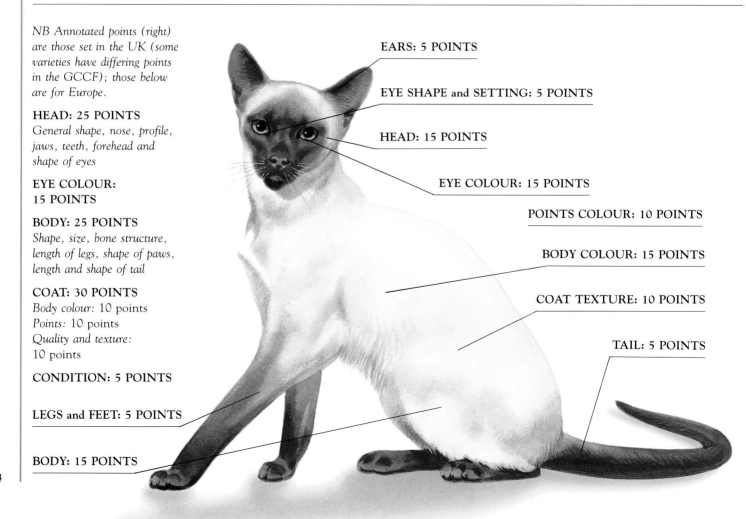

EARS: 5 POINTS

EYE SHAPE and SETTING: 5 POINTS

HEAD: 15 POINTS

EYE COLOUR: 15 POINTS

POINTS COLOUR: 10 POINTS

BODY COLOUR: 15 POINTS

COAT TEXTURE: 10 POINTS

TAIL: 5 POINTS

series and the tabby (or lynx point) series as Colourpoint Shorthairs.

Character and Care

The typical Siamese cat has an extrovert personality. It is very affectionate with people and pets that it likes, is lively and intelligent, and can be very vocal. Siamese cats do not like being left alone for long periods, and do better as pets when kept in pairs or small groups. They are naturally fastidiously clean, and make perfect house pets.

The short fine coat is kept in good condition by stroking with clean hands or buffing with a silk scarf. The large ears need regular cleaning, and Siamese should be provided with a scratching post and lots of toys.

PENALTIES

The Siamese is penalized for having belly spots or spots on the flanks; white or lighter coloured hairs, or ticked hairs in the points; bars and stripes in the points, except in Tabby-pointed varieties; insufficient contrast in colour between the body colour and the points; white patches or white toes; any eye colour other than blue; a kinked tail; and mal-occlusion resulting in either an undershot or overshot jaw.

KEY CHARACTERISTICS

- **CATEGORY** Foreign Shorthair.

- **OVERALL BUILD** Medium size, long and svelte.

- **COAT** Very short and fine, glossy, silky and close-lying.

- **HEAD** Medium sized in proportion to the body; wedge-shaped with straight lines, the wedge starting at the nose and gradually increasing in width in straight lines on each side to the ears. No whisker break.

- **NOSE** Long and straight without any break.

- **CHIN** Medium size, the tip forming a vertical line with the tip of the nose.

- **EYES** Medium size and almond shaped, set slightly slanting towards the nose in harmony with the lines of the wedge.

- **EARS** Large and pointed, wide at the base, placed to continue the line of the wedge.

- **BODY** Long and svelte, well muscled but still dainty and elegant. The shoulders should not be wider than the hips.

- **LEGS** Long and fine, in proportion to the body.

- **PAWS** Small and oval.

- **TAIL** Very long, thin at the base and tapering to a fine point.

- **COLOURS** Seal point, blue point, chocolate point, lilac point, red point, cream point, seal tortie point, blue tortie point, chocolate tortie point, lilac tortie point, seal tabby point, blue tabby point, chocolate tabby point, lilac tabby point, red tabby point, cream tabby point, seal tortie tabby point, blue tortie tabby point, chocolate tortie tabby point, lilac tortie tabby point.

SIAMESE VARIETIES

THE BODY MUST be even in colour with subtle shading when allowed in the colour variety. The points – mask, ears, legs, feet and tail – must be all of the same shade and clearly defined. The mask should cover the entire face including the whisker pads, and be connected to the ears by traced markings. There should be no ticking or white hairs in the points. The eye colour of all the following varieties is deep, vivid blue.

SEAL POINT The body colour is beige to cream or pale fawn; the points colour dark seal brown. The nose leather and paw pads are dark seal brown; the eye colour is deep, vivid blue.

RED POINT The body colour is creamy white; the points colour bright, warm orange. Nose leather pink; paw pads pink and/or red.

BLUE POINT The body colour is bluish white of a glacial tone; the points colour blue-grey. The nose leather and paw pads are blue-grey.

RED POINT SIAMESE
This is a cat of extreme show type with its large flared ears following the lines of the wedge-shaped head. The body is creamy white and the matching points are a warm orange.

SEAL POINT SIAMESE
The original colour, once known as the Royal Cat of Siam. This cat has a pale fawn body and dark seal-brown points which may appear to be black.

BLUE POINT SIAMESE

Blue Point Siamese often show more shading on the body than cats of other points' colour.

CHOCOLATE POINT The body colour is ivory; the points colour milk chocolate. The nose leather is milk chocolate; the paw pads are cinnamon to milk chocolate.

LILAC POINT (FROST POINT) The body colour is glacial white (magnolia); the points colour frosty grey with a slight pinkish tone. The nose leather and paw pads are lavender pink.

CREAM POINT The body colour is creamy white; the points colour pastel cream. The nose leather and paw pads are pink.

SEAL TORTIE POINT The body colour is beige shading to fawn; the points colour seal, patched or mingled with red and/or light red.

CHOCOLATE POINT SIAMESE

The Chocolate Point has an ivory body and points of a warm milk chocolate.

The nose leather and paw pads are seal brown and/or pink.

BLUE TORTIE POINT The body colour is bluish white; the points colour blue-grey patched or mingled with pastel cream. The nose leather and paw pads are blue-grey and/or pink.

CHOCOLATE TORTIE POINT The body colour is ivory; the points colour milk chocolate patched or mingled with red and/or light red. The nose leather is milk chocolate and/or pink; paw pads are cinnamon to milk chocolate and/or pink.

FROST TORTIE POINT The body colour is glacial white (magnolia); the points colour frosty grey with a pinkish tone patched or mingled with pale cream. Nose leather and paw pads lavender pink and/or pale pink.

SEAL TABBY POINT The body colour is beige; the points colour dark seal tabby; the rims around the eyes and nose are seal brown. The nose leather is brick red, pink or seal brown; the paw pads are seal brown.

BLUE TABBY POINT The body colour is bluish white; the points colour blue-grey tabby; the rims around the eyes and nose are blue-grey. The nose leather is old rose or blue-grey; the paw pads are blue-grey.

CHOCOLATE TABBY POINT The body colour is ivory; the points colour milk chocolate tabby; the rims around the eyes and nose are milk chocolate. The nose leather is light red, pink or milk chocolate; the paw pads are cinnamon to milk chocolate.

FROST TABBY POINT The body colour is glacial white (magnolia); the points colour lilac tabby – frosty grey with slightly pinkish toned tabby markings – the rims around the eyes and nose are lavender pink. The nose leather is lavender pink or pink; the paw pads are lavender pink.

LILAC POINT SIAMESE

This is the palest of the Siamese with a magnolia coloured coat and points of a pink toned frosty grey. It is known as the Frost Point in some of the cat associations.

CREAM POINT SIAMESE

The creamy white body of this variety is accented by points of a delicate pastel cream.

RED TABBY POINT The body colour is off white with a slight red tinge; the points colour warm orange tabby; the rims around the eyes and nose are dark pink. The nose leather is brick red or pink; the paw pads are pink.

CREAM TABBY POINT The body colour is creamy white; the points colour cream tabby with a cold tone; the rims around the eyes and nose are dark pink. The nose leather and paw pads are pink.

SEAL TORBIE POINT The body colour is beige; the points colour has seal tabby markings patched or mingled with red or light red tortie markings. The nose rims are seal; the nose leather and paw pads are seal, brick red or pink, or seal mottled with brick red and/or pink.

BLUE TORBIE POINT The body colour is bluish white; the points colour has blue tabby markings, patched or mingled with cream tortie markings. The nose rims are blue-grey; the nose leather is blue-grey, old rose or pink, or blue-grey mottled with old rose and/or pink; the paw pads are blue-grey and/or pink.

CHOCOLATE TORBIE POINT The body colour is ivory; the points colour has milk chocolate tabby markings, patched or mingled with red or light red tortie markings. The nose rims are chocolate; the nose leather milk chocolate, pale red or pink, or milk chocolate mottled with pale red or pink; the paw pads are cinnamon to milk chocolate and/or pink.

FROST TORBIE POINT The body colour is glacial white (magnolia); the points colour has lilac tabby – frosty grey with slightly pinkish toned tabby markings – patched or mingled with pale cream tortie markings. The nose rims are lavender pink; the nose leather and paw pads are lavender pink, pale pink, or lavender pink mottled with pale pink.

BLUE TABBY POINT SIAMESE
Originally called Lynx Points, Tabby Point Siamese were produced by breeders entranced by a litter of kittens which resulted from a mis-mating.

RED TABBY POINT SIAMESE
In this variety the off-white body has a slightly red tinge, and the points are a warm orange tabby.

COLORPOINT SHORTHAIR

WHEN SIAMESE CATS were mated with cats of other varieties, such as the tabby shorthair, in order to achieve new colours and patterns the Colorpoint Shorthair was the result. As the gene which restricts the colour to the points in Siamese is recessive, the resulting kittens were coloured all over.

When these cross-bred cats were mated back to high quality Siamese, however, Siamese patterned offspring were produced, and successive back-crossing to Siamese upgraded the "new" Siamese to conform to the rigorous standards set by various associations. In Britain, the new colours were gradually accepted as additions to the Siamese varieties, but in the United States, some associations decided to accept such cats as Colorpoint Shorthairs.

Character and Care

Siamese in everything but name, the Colorpoint Shorthair is a delightfully intelligent, agile and affectionate pet.

It is very easy to maintain in top condition by feeding a good diet, and needs minimal grooming, just combing through to remove any dead hair, and buffing the fine coat either with the hands or a silk scarf.

BREAKDOWN OF 100 SHOW POINTS

NB Annotated points are those set in the USA.

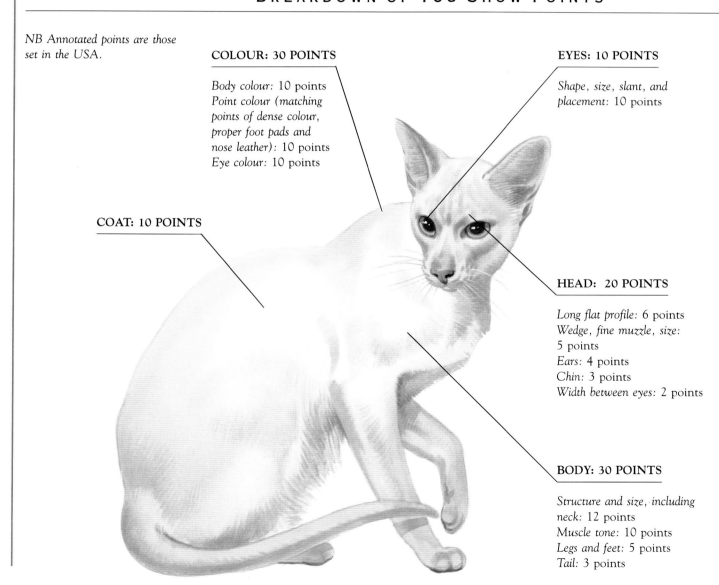

COLOUR: 30 POINTS

Body colour: 10 points
Point colour (matching points of dense colour, proper foot pads and nose leather): 10 points
Eye colour: 10 points

EYES: 10 POINTS

Shape, size, slant, and placement: 10 points

COAT: 10 POINTS

HEAD: 20 POINTS

Long flat profile: 6 points
Wedge, fine muzzle, size: 5 points
Ears: 4 points
Chin: 3 points
Width between eyes: 2 points

BODY: 30 POINTS

Structure and size, including neck: 12 points
Muscle tone: 10 points
Legs and feet: 5 points
Tail: 3 points

KEY CHARACTERISTICS

- **CATEGORY** Foreign Shorthair.

- **OVERALL BUILD** Medium size, svelte and dainty.

- **COAT** Short, fine textured, glossy and close lying.

- **HEAD** Long, tapering and wedge shaped, with a fine muzzle.

- **NOSE** Long and straight.

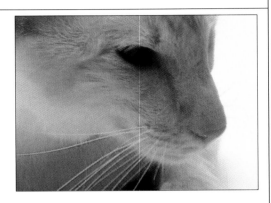

- **CHIN** Tip of chin lines up with tip of nose.

- **EYES** Medium sized and almond shaped, slanting towards the nose.

- **EARS** Strikingly large and pointed, continuing the line of the wedge-shaped head.

- **BODY** Long and slender, with fine bones, firm muscles and a tight abdomen. Slim shoulders and hips.

- **LEGS** Long and slim.

- **PAWS** Small and oval.

- **TAIL** Long and thin, tapering to a fine point.

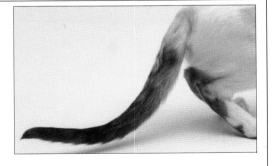

- **COLOURS** Red point, cream point, seal lynx point, blue lynx point, chocolate lynx point, lilac lynx point, red lynx point, seal tortie point, chocolate tortie point, blue-cream point, lilac-cream point.

PENALTIES

The Colorpoint Shorthair is penalized for lack of pigment in the nose leather.

DISQUALIFICATION FEATURES
- any evidence of poor health
- weak hind legs
- a visible tail kink
- incorrect eye colour
- white toes

COLOURPOINT VARIETIES

SIAMESE CATS UNDER a different title in some American associations, the Colorpoint Short-hair group embraces all the Siamese varieties produced by outcrossing to others breeds to introduce the orange (red) and tabby genes.

RED POINT The body is clear white, with any shading toning with the points, which should be bright apricot to deep red. Deeper shades are preferred, with no barring. Nose leather and paw pads are flesh or coral pink; and the eye colour a deep, vivid blue.

CREAM POINT The body is clear white, with any shading toning with the points, which should be pale buff to light, pinkish cream with no barring. Nose leather and paw pads are flesh or coral pink; eye colour a deep vivid blue.

SEAL LYNX POINT The body is cream or pale fawn, shading to a lighter colour on the stomach and chest. Ghost striping is allowed as body shading. The points are distinct seal brown bars, separated by the lighter background colour. Ears are seal brown with a paler thumb-print in the centre. Nose leather is seal brown, or pink edged in seal brown; paw pads are seal brown; eye colour a deep, vivid blue.

BLUE LYNX POINT The body is bluish white to platinum grey, cold in tone, shading to a lighter colour on the stomach and chest. Ghost striping is allowed as body shading. The points

are distinct deep blue-grey bars, separated by the lighter background colour. Ears are deep blue-grey with a paler thumb-print in the centre. Nose leather is slate-coloured or pink-edged in slate; paw pads are slate; eye colour a deep, vivid blue.

CHOCOLATE LYNX POINT The body is ivory. Ghost striping is allowed as body shading. The points are distinct warm milk chocolate bars, separated by the lighter background colour. Ears are warm milk chocolate with a paler thumb-print in the centre. Nose leather is cinnamon, or pink edged in cinnamon; paw pads are cinnamon; eye colour is deep blue.

LILAC LYNX POINT The body is glacial white. Ghost striping is allowed as body shading. The points are frosty grey with distinct pinkish-toned bars, separated by the lighter background colour. Ears are frosty grey with a paler thumb-print in the centre. Nose leather is lavender pink or grey edged with lavender pink; paw pads are lavender pink; eye colour is a deep, vivid blue.

RED LYNX POINT The body is white. Ghost striping is allowed as body shading. The points are distinct deep red bars, separated by the lighter background colour. Ears are deep red with a paler thumb-print in the centre. Nose leather and paw pads are flesh or coral pink; eye colour is a deep, vivid blue.

SEAL TORTIE POINT The body is pale fawn to cream, shading to a lighter colour on the stomach and chest. It may be mottled with cream in older cats. The points are seal brown uniformly mottled with red and light red. A blaze is desirable. Nose leather is seal brown; flesh or coral pink mottling is permitted where there is a facial blaze. Paw pads are seal brown; flesh or coral mottling is permitted where the points' colour mottling extends into the paw pads. Eye colour is a deep, vivid blue.

CHOCOLATE TORTIE POINT The body is ivory and may be mottled in older cats. The points are warm milk chocolate uniformly mottled with red and/or light red. A blaze is desirable. Nose leather is cinnamon; flesh or coral mottling is permitted where there is a facial blaze. Paw pads are cinnamon; flesh or coral mottling is permitted where the points' colour mottling extends into the paw pads. Eye colour is a deep, vivid blue.

BLUE-CREAM POINT The body is bluish white to platinum grey, cold in tone, shading to a lighter colour on the stomach and chest. The body colour is mottled in older cats. The points are deep blue-grey uniformly mottled with cream. A blaze is desirable. Nose leather is

CHOCOLATE TORTIE POINT SIAMESE

The Tortie Point Siamese are found in a full range of colours, and appeal to those who like to have a completely unique cat – no two tortie points have the same markings.

SEAL TABBY POINT SIAMESE

The body is often shaded with ghost tabby markings. The points are patterned with tabby bars and stripes of the main colour. In the Seal Tabby, the markings are in deep seal brown.

slate; flesh or coral pink mottling is permitted where there is a facial blaze. Paw pads are slate; flesh or coral mottling is permitted where the points' colour mottling extends into the paw pads. Eye colour is a deep, vivid blue.

LILAC-CREAM POINT The body is glacial white, and may be mottled in older cats. The points are frosty grey with a pinkish tone uniformly mottled with pale cream. A blaze is desirable. Nose leather is lavender pink; flesh or coral pink mottling is permitted where there is a facial blaze. Paw pads are lavender pink; flesh or coral mottling is permitted where the points' colour mottling extends into the paw pads. Eye colour is a deep, vivid blue.

SEAL TORTIE POINT

In the Seal Tortie Point the points are patterned in a mixture of black and red or light red, and the cat, like this one, may have a red or light red blaze down the face.

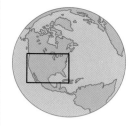

BALINESE

THE LONG-COATED kittens that appeared from time to time in otherwise normal litters of Siamese cats were developed into the Balinese. At first such kittens were quickly discarded and sold as pets, but in the 1940s two breeders in New York and California began to work towards the development of a separate breed. The name was chosen because of the cats' gracefulness and svelte lines, reminiscent of the dancers on the island of Bali. The breed soon gained a lot of admirers, but it was not until 1970 that the CFA first recognized it and granted it championship status. The long coat is nothing like that of the Persian. It has no woolly undercoat, and lies flat to the body.

Character and Care

As might be expected from their ancestry, Balinese are very similar to Siamese in character – affectionate, demanding of attention, extremely active and inquisitive.

The coat is relatively easy to care for with regular gentle combing, and brushing of the frill (ruff) and plumed tail.

BREAKDOWN OF 100 SHOW POINTS

NB Annotated points are those set in the UK; those below are for Europe.

HEAD: 25 POINTS

EYE COLOUR: 15 POINTS

BODY: 25 POINTS

COAT: 30 POINTS
Body and points colour:
10 points
Quality and texture:
10 points
Length: 10 points

CONDITION: 5 POINTS

COLOUR and COAT: 50 POINTS

Eye colour: 15 points
Points colour: 10 points
Body colour: 10 points
Coat Texture and Length:
15 points

TYPE: 50 POINTS

Head: 15 points
Ears: 5 points
Eye shape: 5 points

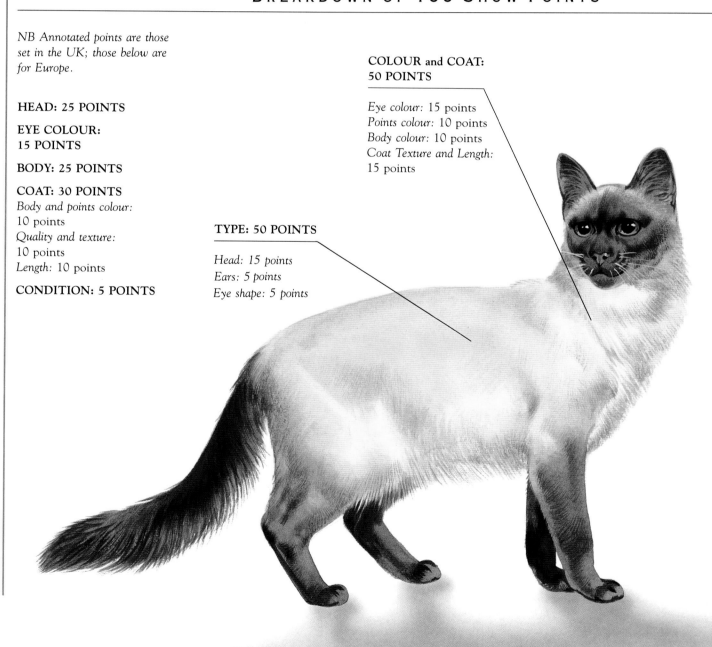

KEY CHARACTERISTICS

- **CATEGORY** Longhair.

- **OVERALL BUILD** Medium size, svelte and elegant.

- **COAT** Fine and silky.

- **HEAD** Medium size, a long tapering wedge shape which starts at the nose and gradually increases in width in straight lines on each side, as far as the ears. No whisker break.

- **NOSE** Long and straight, continuing the line from the forehead without any break.

- **CHIN** Medium size, the tip forming a vertical line with the tip of the nose.

- **EYES** Medium size and almond shaped, set slightly slanted towards the nose.

- **EARS** Large and pointed, wide-based, placed to continue the lines of the wedge.

- **BODY** Long, svelte, well-muscled but dainty. The shoulders should be no wider than the hips.

- **LEGS** Long and fine, in proportion to the body.

- **PAWS** Small, dainty and oval.

- **TAIL** Very long and thin, tapering to a fine point; the tail hair spreads out like a plume.

- **COLOURS** All the colours found in the Siamese (and Colourpoints): Seal point, blue point, chocolate point, lilac (frost) point, red point, cream point, seal tortie point, blue tortie point, chocolate tortie point, lilac (frost) tortie point, seal tabby point, blue tabby point, chocolate tabby point, lilac (frost) tabby point, red tabby point, cream tabby point, seal tortie tabby point (seal torbie point), blue tortie tabby point (blue torbie point), chocolate tortie tabby point (chocolate torbie point), lilac (frost) tortie tabby point (lilac (frost) torbie point). Some associations accept only seal point, blue point, chocolate point and lilac (frost) point.

PENALTIES

The Balinese is penalized for lack of pigment in the nose leather or paw pads; and for having a squint.

DISQUALIFICATION FEATURES
- any evidence of poor health
- weak hind legs
- mouth breathing due to nasal obstruction
- kinked tail
- eye colour other than blue
- white toes and/or feet
- downy undercoat

BALINESE VARIETIES

CHOCOLATE POINT The body colour is ivory; the points colour milk chocolate. The nose leather is milk chocolate; the paw pads are cinnamon to milk chocolate.

LILAC POINT The body colour is glacial white (magnolia); the points colour frosty grey with a slight pinkish tone. The nose leather and paw pads are pink.

RED POINT The body colour is creamy white; the points colour bright, warm orange. The nose leather is pink; the paw pads pink or red.

CREAM POINT The body colour is creamy white; the points colour pastel cream. The nose leather and paw pads are pink.

SEAL TORTIE POINT The body colour is beige shading to fawn; the points colour seal, patched or mingled with red and/or light red. The nose leather and paw pads are seal brown and/or pink.

BLUE TORTIE POINT The body colour is bluish white; the points colour blue-grey patched or mingled with pastel cream. The nose leather and paw pads are blue-grey and/or pink.

CHOCOLATE TORTIE POINT The body colour is ivory; the points colour milk chocolate patched or mingled with red and/or light red. The nose leather is milk chocolate and/or pink; the paw pads are cinnamon to milk chocolate and/or pink.

LILAC TORTIE POINT The body colour is glacial white; the points colour frosty grey with a slight pinkish tone patched or mingled with pale cream. The nose leather and paw pads are lavender pink and/or pale pink.

SEAL TABBY POINT The body colour is beige; the points colour dark seal tabby; the rims around the eyes and nose are seal brown. The

CREAM BALINESE

The Balinese is a long-coated version of the Siamese. It is accepted in the same range of points' colours.

THE BODY MUST be even in colour with subtle shading when allowed in the colour variety. The points – mask, ears, legs, feet and tail – must be all the same shade and clearly defined. The mask should cover the entire face, including the whisker pads, and be connected to the ears by traced markings. There should be no ticking or white hairs in the points. Eye colour for all varieties is deep, vivid blue.

SEAL POINT The body colour is beige to cream or pale fawn; the points colour dark seal brown. The nose leather and paw pads are dark seal brown.

BLUE POINT The body colour is bluish white of a glacial tone; the points colour blue-grey. The nose leather and paw pads are blue-grey.

BLUE POINT BALINESE

As only top quality Siamese cats were used in the breeding programmes for Balinese, most of today's Balinese cats are of outstanding type.

nose leather is brick red, pink or seal brown; the paw pads are seal brown.

BLUE TABBY POINT The body colour is bluish white; the points colour blue-grey tabby; the rims around the eyes and nose are blue-grey. The nose leather is old rose or blue-grey; the paw pads are blue-grey.

CHOCOLATE TABBY POINT Body colour is ivory; the points colour milk chocolate tabby; the rims around the eyes and nose are milk chocolate. The nose leather is light red, pink or milk chocolate; the paw pads are cinnamon to milk chocolate.

LILAC TABBY POINT The body colour is glacial white; the points colour lilac tabby – frosty grey with slightly pinkish toned tabby markings – the rims around the eyes and nose are lavender pink. The nose leather is lavender pink or pink; the paw pads are lavender pink.

RED TABBY POINT The body colour is off white with a slight red tinge; the points colour warm orange tabby; the rims around the eyes and nose are dark pink. The nose leather is brick red or pink; the paw pads are pink.

CREAM TABBY POINT The body colour is creamy white; the points colour cream tabby with a cold tone; the rims around the eyes and nose are dark pink. The nose leather and paw pads are pink.

SEAL TORTIE TABBY POINT The body colour is beige; the points colour has seal tabby markings patched or mingled with red or light red tortie markings. The nose rims are seal; the nose leather and paw pads are seal, brick red or pink, or seal mottled with brick red and/or pink.

BLUE TORTIE TABBY POINT The body colour is bluish white; the points colour has blue tabby markings, patched or mingled with cream tortie markings. The nose rims are blue-grey; the nose leather is blue-grey, old rose or pink, or blue-grey mottled with old rose and/or pink; the paw pads are blue-grey and/or pink.

CHOCOLATE TORTIE TABBY POINT The body colour is ivory; the points colour has milk chocolate tabby markings, patched or mingled with red or light red tortie markings. The nose rims are chocolate; the nose leather milk chocolate, pale red or pink, or milk chocolate mottled with pale red or pink; the paw pads are cinnamon to milk chocolate and/or pink.

CHOCOLATE TORTIE POINT BALINESE

Patched or mingled points of milk chocolate and light red allied with an ivory coat make this an unusual and attractive variety.

SEAL TABBY POINT BALINESE

This cat epitomizes the Balinese breed, conforming almost exactly to the standard of points.

ORIENTAL

Cats of the distinctive Siamese body conformation, but without having the true colour restricted to the points, are recognized by some associations as Orientals.

In the main, the Oriental is identical to the Siamese in all respects except for not having its colour restricted to the points, and not having blue eyes. It has a slightly quieter voice than the Siamese, but is equally talkative. Oriental cats have been known for many years, but first became popular in the early 1960s when a small number of fanciers began to breed them in a wide range of colours, some individuals specializing in just one or two colours or patterns, but each taking extreme care with the selection of their foundation stock to ensure strength, stamina and good temperament in their cats, as well as beauty. Some Orientals were produced as off-shoots to the breeding programmes for the red-, tortie- and tabby- or lynx-pointed Siamese, and others were developed after much genetic research.

A light-brown gene was recognized, and gave rise to a whole new series of attractive feline colours, and a pure white Oriental, in fact a Siamese with white masking its points, entranced show visitors with its sapphire eyes. Britain's GCCF designate the self-coloured cats of Siamese type "Foreign", and so they are known as the Foreign White, Foreign Black, Foreign Blue, Foreign Lilac and so on, yet the "Foreign Chocolate" is called the Havana, the name having been changed from Chestnut Brown Foreign in the 1950s. Europe's FIFe and its British member, the Cat Association of Britain, recognize the entire group as Oriental, as does the largest of the American associations, the CFA.

Colour terminology varies too, black being called ebony, chocolate chestnut, lilac lavender, and there is some controversy over the cinnamon, caramel and fawn colours. The showing system in the CFA proved the most helpful to breeders of Orientals, dividing the

BREAKDOWN OF 100 SHOW POINTS

NB Annotated points (right) are those set in the UK (for the Foreign White see p. 240); those below are for Europe.

HEAD: 25 POINTS

EYE COLOUR: 15 POINTS

BODY: 25 POINTS

COAT: 30 POINTS
Body colour: 20 points
Quality and texture: 10 points

CONDITION: 5 POINTS

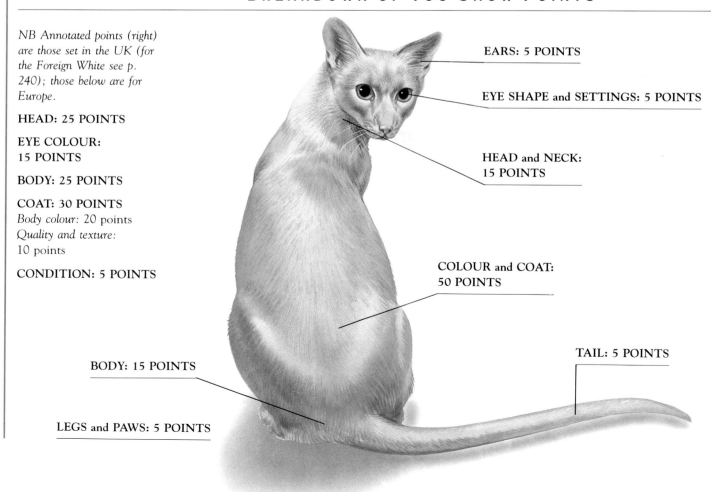

EARS: 5 POINTS

EYE SHAPE and SETTINGS: 5 POINTS

HEAD and NECK: 15 POINTS

COLOUR and COAT: 50 POINTS

TAIL: 5 POINTS

BODY: 15 POINTS

LEGS and PAWS: 5 POINTS

breed into five groups: solid colours; shaded; smokes; tabbies and parti-colours. In this way the Orientals reached championship status level in 1977, and the following year a number of Orientals featured among the CFA's top twenty. In Britain, each colour variety had to work separately towards a breed number and in 1995 their status as a group is still in confusion in the GCCF.

Character and Care

The Oriental is extroverted, intelligent and very affectionate with its own family and friends. It is active and playful and hates being left alone for long periods.

They are naturally very clean cats and the very short, fine coat can be kept in good condition with daily hand grooming and buffing with a silk scarf. The large ears need regular cleaning, and Orientals should be provided with a scratching post and plenty of toys to play with.

KEY CHARACTERISTICS

- **CATEGORY** Foreign Shorthair.

- **OVERALL BUILD** Medium size, long and svelte.

- **COAT** Very short and fine, glossy, silky and close-lying.

- **HEAD** Medium sized in proportion to the body; wedge-shaped with straight lines, the wedge starting at the nose and gradually increasing in width in straight lines on each side to the ears. No whisker break.

- **NOSE** Long and straight without any break.

- **CHIN** Medium size, the tip forming a vertical line with the tip of the nose.

- **EYES** Medium size and almond shaped, set slightly slanting towards the nose in harmony with the lines of the wedge.

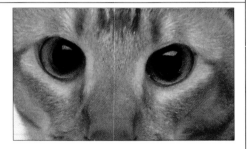

- **EARS** Large and pointed, wide at the base, placed to continue the line of the wedge.

- **BODY** Long and svelte, well muscled but still dainty and elegant. The shoulders should not be wider than the hips.

- **LEGS** Long and fine, in proportion to the body.

- **PAWS** Small and oval.

- **TAIL** Very long and thin, thin at the base, and tapering to a fine point.

- **COLOURS** Black, white, blue, havana chocolate, lilac , cinnamon, caramel, fawn, red self, cream, black tortie, blue tortie, chocolate tortie, lilac tortie, cinnamon tortie, caramel tortie, fawn tortie, black smoke, blue smoke, chocolate smoke, lilac smoke, cinnamon smoke, caramel smoke, fawn smoke, red smoke, black tortie smoke, blue tortie smoke, chocolate tortie smoke, lilac tortie smoke, cinamon tortie smoke, caramel tortie smoke, black shaded, blue shaded, chocolate shaded, lilac shaded, cameo, black tabby, blue tabby, chocolate tabby, lilac tabby, red tabby, cream tabby, cinnamon tabby, fawn tabby,, silver tabby. Tipped: all recognized colours.

SOLID VARIETIES

UK STANDARDS

Oriental white

HEAD and EARS:
20 POINTS

**EYES SHAPE and
SETTING:**
5 POINTS

BODY: 15 POINTS

LEGS and PAWS:
10 POINTS

TAIL: 10 POINTS

EYE COLOUR:
15 POINTS

BODY COLOUR:
15 POINTS

**COAT TEXTURE
and LENGTH:**
10 POINTS

AS SIAMESE CATS without the gene which restricts the colour to the points; the first Orientals to appear in half-Siamese litters were blacks and blues. Later, the elusive chocolate gene produced the Chestnut Brown Foreign, a self chocolate-coloured cat, which is now known as the Havana in the UK, and the Oriental Chestnut elsewhere. Some of the early Chestnut Browns were exported to the US where they formed the nucleus of a totally different breed, with its own characteristic features, known as the Havana Brown. When the gene for dilution was also present in the cats used for breeding chocolate, lilac or lavender kittens began to appear.

ORIENTAL WHITE, FOREIGN WHITE, SIAMESE WHITE The coat colour is pure white without markings or shadings of any kind. The nose leather and paw pads are pink; the eye colour is deep, vivid blue.
Note: In the CFA the Oriental White should have green eyes. Blue eye colour is also accepted, but odd-eyed cats are not.
BLACK The coat colour is dense coal black, sound from the roots to the tips of the hair, free from any rusty tinge, and without any white hairs or other markings. There should be no grey undercoat. The nose leather is black; the paw pads are black or seal brown; the eye colour is vivid, intense green.
BLUE The coat colour is any shade of blue-grey, but lighter shades are preferred. The colour must be sound and even throughout, without any white hairs, shadings or other markings. Nose leather and paw pads are blue-grey; eye colour is vivid, intense green.

ORIENTAL BLUE
*Any shade of blue is
permitted in this
variety, but lighter
shades are preferred.*

CHOCOLATE (CHESTNUT) The coat colour is any shade of warm chocolate (chestnut) brown, sound and even throughout without any white hairs, shadings or other markings. There should be no grey undercoat. The nose leather is milk chocolate; the paw pads are cinnamon to milk chocolate; the eye colour is vivid, intense green.

LILAC The coat colour is faded lilac with a slight pinkish tinge, sound and even throughout without any white hairs, shadings or other markings. The nose leather and paw pads are lavender pink or faded lilac; the eye colour is vivid, intense green.

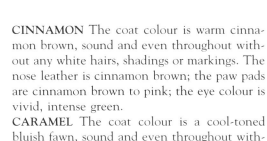

CINNAMON The coat colour is warm cinnamon brown, sound and even throughout without any white hairs, shadings or markings. The nose leather is cinnamon brown; the paw pads are cinnamon brown to pink; the eye colour is vivid, intense green.

CARAMEL The coat colour is a cool-toned bluish fawn, sound and even throughout without any white hairs, shadings or markings. Nose leather and paw pads are bluish fawn; the eye colour is vivid, intense green.

ORIENTAL CINNAMON

This beautiful, unusual colour variety excited geneticists when it first appeared in recent years.

HAVANA BROWN

The name Havana was originally chosen to describe the rich tobacco-brown colour of this breed's coat, likened to that used for making the best of the Havana cigars. It is far more descriptive than other names used for the warm brown coat.

ORIENTAL LILAC

The Lilac or Lavender was one of the first Oriental or Foreign Shorthair varieties to be developed and was bred from Havana or Oriental Chocolates.

FAWN The coat colour is a warm beige fawn (buff), sound and even throughout without any white hairs, shadings or markings. The nose leather is pinkish fawn; paw pads are pink or pinkish fawn; eye colour is vivid, intense green.

RED SELF The coat colour is deep, rich, clear and brilliant red, sound and even throughout, without any white hairs, lighter shadings or markings. The nose leather and paw pads are brick red or pink; the eye colour is vivid, intense green.

Note: Slight shading is allowed on the face and legs, and dark whiskers are permitted.

CREAM The coat colour is pale, pure pastel cream, with no warm tone, sound and even throughout without any white hairs, shadings or markings. There must be no light or white undercoat. The nose leather and paw pads are pink; the preferred eye colour is vivid, intense green.

Note: Slight shading is allowed on the face and legs, and dark whiskers are permitted.

ORIENTAL RED

The type of the Oriental is exactly the same as the Siamese; in fact Oriental cats are merely Siamese, without the factor restricting the colour to the points of the body. With the loss of the Himalayan factor comes the change of eye colour from blue to green.

ORIENTAL CREAM

Tabby markings may be evident in the coat of the cream Oriental, and an otherwise good cat will not be penalized for this excusable fault.

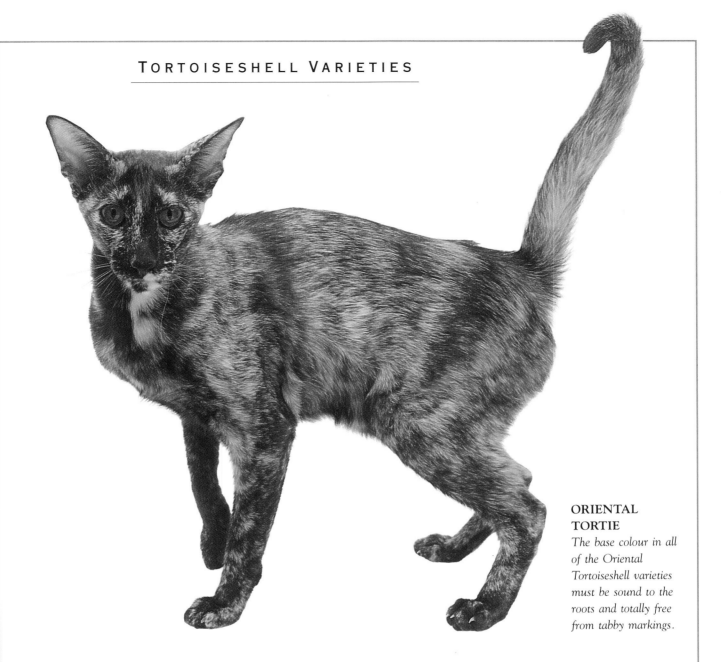

ORIENTAL TORTIE
The base colour in all of the Oriental Tortoiseshell varieties must be sound to the roots and totally free from tabby markings.

WITH THE INTRODUCTION of the sex-linked gene which produced the red and the cream, litters included female kittens of various combinations of colours in the pattern called tortoiseshell.

BLACK TORTIE The coat colour is black, patched or mingled with red and/or light red. The nose leather and the paw pads are black, brick red or pink, or black mottled with brick red and/or pink.

BLUE TORTIE The coat colour is light blue-grey patched or mingled with pale cream. The nose leather and paw pads are blue-grey or pink, or blue-grey with pink.

CHOCOLATE TORTIE The coat colour is milk chocolate patched or mingled with red or light red. The nose leather is milk chocolate, pale red or pink, or milk chocolate mottled with pale red and/or pink; the paw pads are cinna-mon to milk chocolate, pale red or pink, or cinnamon to milk chocolate mottled with pale red and/or pink.

LILAC TORTIE (LAVENDER-CREAM) The coat colour is faded lilac with a slight pinkish tinge, patched or mingled with pale cream. The nose leather and paw pads are lavender pale pink, or lavender pink mottled with pale pink.

CINNAMON TORTIE The coat colour is warm cinnamon brown patched or mingled with red or light red. The nose leather and paw pads are cinnamon brown, pinkish red or pink, or cinnamon brown mottled with pinkish red and/or pink.

CARAMEL TORTIE The coat colour is cool-toned bluish fawn patched or mingled with rich beige and/or cream. The nose leather and paw pads are bluish fawn or pink; or bluish fawn mottled with pink.

TABBY

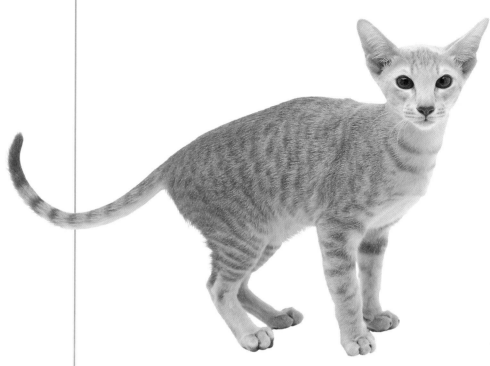

CARAMEL SPOTTED TABBY

A young Oriental tabby with a nicely spotted coat pattern, good overall type and a lovely colour.

ORIENTAL TABBY CATS may have any of the following four tabby patterns – Classic, Mackerel, Spotted or Ticked. In the Classic, there should be dense and clearly defined broad markings; the legs should be evenly barred with bracelets coming up to join the body markings. The tail should be evenly ringed; and there should be several unbroken necklaces on the neck and upper chest. Frown marks on the forehead form a letter "M". In Mackerel tabbies, there should be dense and clearly defined stripes like narrow pencil marks; the legs should be evenly barred with narrow bracelets coming up to join the body markings. The tail should be barred; and there should be distinct chain-like necklaces on the neck and

chest. The head should be barred, with an "M" on the forehead. For the Spotted, the spots on the body may vary in size and shape but those that are round and evenly distributed are preferred. They must not run together to form a broken mackerel pattern. A dorsal stripe runs the length of the body to the tip of the tail and is ideally composed of spots.

The body hairs are clearly ticked and there are no other spots, bars or stripes on the body. Typical tabby markings including the forehead "M" are found on the face, and thumb prints on the backs of the ears.

BLACK TABBY (EBONY TABBY) The base coat is brilliant coppery brown; the markings are dense black. The lips and chin should be the same colour as the rings round the eyes. The backs of the legs from paw to heel are black; the nose leather is black or brick red rimmed with black; the paw pads are black or seal brown; the eyes are green.

BLUE TABBY The base coat, including the lips and chin, is pale bluish ivory, or warm grey in the ticked tabby, with markings any shade of blue-grey affording a good contrast with the base colour. The backs of the legs from paw to heel are a darker shade of blue-grey; the nose leather is blue or old rose rimmed with blue; the paw pads are blue-grey or rose; the eyes are green.

CHOCOLATE TABBY (CHESTNUT TABBY) The base coat, including the lips and chin, is warm fawn, or sandy beige in the ticked tabby, with markings a rich chocolate brown. The

CHOCOLATE CLASSIC TABBY

The classic tabby pattern is shown to perfection by this superbly marked Oriental cat.

**CHOCOLATE
SPOTTED TABBY**
*Although all the tabby
markings are correct
on the head, legs and
tail, this cat needs to
develop better spotting
on the body.*

backs of the legs from paw to heel are chocolate brown; the nose leather is chocolate or pale red rimmed with chocolate; the paw pads are cinnamon to chocolate; the eyes are green.

LILAC TABBY (LAVENDER TABBY) The base coat is off white to palest lilac, with markings rich lilac (lilac grey with a pinkish tinge) or lavender, affording a good contrast with the base colour. The backs of the legs from paw to heel are a darker shade of lilac; the nose leather is lavender or pink rimmed with lavender; the paw pads are lavender pink; the eyes are green.

RED TABBY The base coat is red, with markings a deep rich red. The backs of the legs from paw to heel are dark red; the nose leather is brick red or pink; the paw pads are pink (Europe); brick red (USA), the eyes are any shade of copper to green, green preferred.

CREAM TABBY The base coat, including the lips and chin, is very pale cream, with markings buff or cream, affording a good contrast with the base colour. The backs of the legs from paw to heel are dark cream; the nose leather and paw pads are pink, the eyes are any shade of copper to green, green preferred.

**CHOCOLATE
TICKED
ORIENTAL**
*The ticked Orientals
have two or three
bands of ticking on
each hair. The basic
colour also shows at
the heels of the hind
legs and at the tip of
the tail.*

CINNAMON TICKED ORIENTAL

A superb specimen with a perfectly ticked cinnamon coat which is similar to that of a sorrel Abyssinian.

CINNAMON TABBY The base coat is deep apricot, with markings clear, warm, cinnamon brown. The backs of the legs from paw to heel are cinnamon brown; the nose leather is pale pink; the paw pads are cinnamon brown to pinkish brown.

CARAMEL TABBY The base coat is cool-toned beige; cool-toned bluish fawn markings; back of leg from paw to heel is a darker bluish fawn; the nose leather is bluish fawn, or pink rimmed with bluish fawn; the paw pads are pink to bluish fawn.

FAWN TABBY The base coat is dull beige, with markings any shade of beige-brown, affording a good contrast with the base colour. The backs of the legs from paw to heel are a darker beige-fawn; the nose leather is pink; the paw pads are pinkish fawn.

SILVER TABBY The base coat, including the lips and chin, is pure pale silver, with dense black markings. The backs of the legs from paw to heel are black; the nose leather is black or brick red with black rims; paw pads are black.

Note There are other colours in the Silver Tabby series – Blue Silver Tabby, Chocolate Silver Tabby, Lilac Silver Tabby, Red Silver Tabby, Cream Silver Tabby, Cinnamon Silver Tabby, Caramel Silver Tabby, Fawn Silver Tabby. In these varieties the colour of the markings is as for the non-silver varieties, but on a base coat of pale silver.

CINNAMON SPOTTED ORIENTAL

The effect of the tabby pattern, whether it is spotted or ticked, is to brighten the normal base colour.

TORTIE TABBY (PATCHED TABBY) Any colour recognized in the Oriental group; the coat patched or mingled with areas of red or light red in the non-dilute colours; rich beige or cream in the Caramel and the Fawn. The nose leather is the solid basic colour, pink-rimmed with the basic colour, or basic colour mottled with pink; the paw pads are basic colour mottled with pink. The eyes are any shade of copper to green, green preferred.

BLACK SILVER SPOTTED

Ideally this cat should have more clearly marked spots, though the rest of its tabby markings are excellent. Spotting often improves with maturity.

CHOCOLATE TORTIE SILVER TICKED

An amazing combination of colour and pattern combined in a typical Oriental.

SMOKE, SHADED AND TIPPED VARIETIES

CHOCOLATE SILVER SHADED ORIENTAL
This variety has chocolate markings on a paler, silvery chocolate ground.

BLACK SMOKE ORIENTAL
Looking like a black in repose, the smoke undercoat becomes apparent as the cat moves.

THE INTRODUCTION OF silver to the Oriental breeding programmes excited many Oriental fanciers, and before long, cats with short, fine silvery-white coats were bred with various amounts of coloured tipping. The most heavily tipped are the smokes, the lightest tipped are just called "tipped" and the intermediates are known as "shaded."

In the Smoke, the hairs are tipped with the appropriate colour and have a narrow silver-white band at the roots which can only be seen when the hair is parted. The undercoat is silver-white. In repose the cat appears to be of solid colour, but in motion the silver-white undercoat is clearly visible. In the Shaded, the hair is tipped to about one-third of its length and the undercoat is white, producing the characteristic sparkling appearance of this colour group. The face and legs may be shaded with tipping. In the Tipped, the hair is tipped just at its extremity, and the tipping is evenly distributed over the cat's body. The face and legs may be shaded, but in adults, ghost tabby markings are considered a serious fault. The tipped cat is considerably lighter in overall colour than the shaded.

SEYCHELLOIS

FOLLOWING A BREEDING programme approved by the Cat Association of Britain, the Seychellois was developed by a small group of breeders interested in Oriental cats. It is of medium size and typical Oriental conformation, with a long svelte body, slim legs and dainty paws. The head is wedge-shaped with very large pointed ears and almond-shaped eyes. It is unusual in having a predominantly white coat, with splashes of colour on the head, legs and body, and a coloured tail. Seychellois markings are classified into three groups. The Seychellois Longhair is identical in every respect to the Shorthair except in its coat, which is of medium length, soft and silky in texture and longer on the frill or ruff. It has ear tufts and a full, plume-like tail.

SEYCHELLOIS NEUVIÈME Almost entirely white with a coloured tail and a few tiny coloured markings on the head.

SEYCHELLOIS HUITIÈME Mainly white with a coloured tail and splashes of colour on the head and legs.

SEYCHELLOIS SEPTIÈME White with a coloured tail and splashes of colour on the head, legs and body.

KEY CHARACTERISTICS

- **CATEGORY** Foreign Shorthair (Oriental).

- **OVERALL BUILD** Medium size, long and svelte.

- **COAT** *Shorthair* Very short and fine, glossy, silky and close-lying. *Longhair* Of medium length, fine, silky and longer on the frill (ruff) and tail.

- **COLOURS** Any colour or combination of colours is allowed.

- **OTHER FEATURES** Head medium sized, in proportion to body, wedge shaped with straight lines starting at nose and gradually increasing in width to ears, no whisker break. Nose is long and straight; chin medium sized, the tip forming a vertical line with tip of nose; eyes are medium sized, almond shaped and set slightly slanting towards nose to follow lines of wedge; ears are large and pointed, wide at base and placed to continue lines of wedge. Body is long and svelte, well muscled but dainty and elegant; shoulders should not be wider than hips. Legs are long and fine boned, in proportion to body; paws small and oval; tail very long and thin, tapering to a fine point. *Longhair* Tail hair spreads out like a plume.

SEYCHELLOIS SHORTHAIR

This rare breed is of Oriental type and is a predominantly white cat with splashes of colour on the head, tail and body.

JAVANESE

THE LONGHAIRED ORIENTAL, now known as the Javanese, was selectively bred from Oriental cats and long-coated cats of exceptional Oriental type. In the CFA, the name Javanese was given to Balinese cats not conforming to the four main Siamese colours, seal point, blue point, chocolate point and lilac point. These were the red- and tabby-based colours which in the short-coated varieties are termed Colourpoints by the CFA. In New Zealand, where the red- and tabby-, or lynx-pointed cats with long coats are accepted, along with the four main Siamese colours, as Balinese, it is the spotted and self-coated varieties which are called Javanese. In the UK, the CA, as a member of FIFe, accepts all long-coated colours of Orientals as Javanese.

Medium long on the body, and without undercoat, the coat of the Javanese cat is fine, with a silky texture. It flows over the body and forms a frill round the shoulders and chest. The cat has a full, plume-like tail.

Character and Care

Active, always alert and very inquisitive, the Javanese has an extrovert personality and is intelligent and quite vocal. It is a very affectionate cat and loves human company, hating to be left alone for long periods.

Regular gentle brushing keeps the coat in good condition; the frill (ruff), underparts and tail can be gently combed with a broad-toothed comb.

BREAKDOWN OF 100 SHOW POINTS

NB Annotated points are those set in Europe.

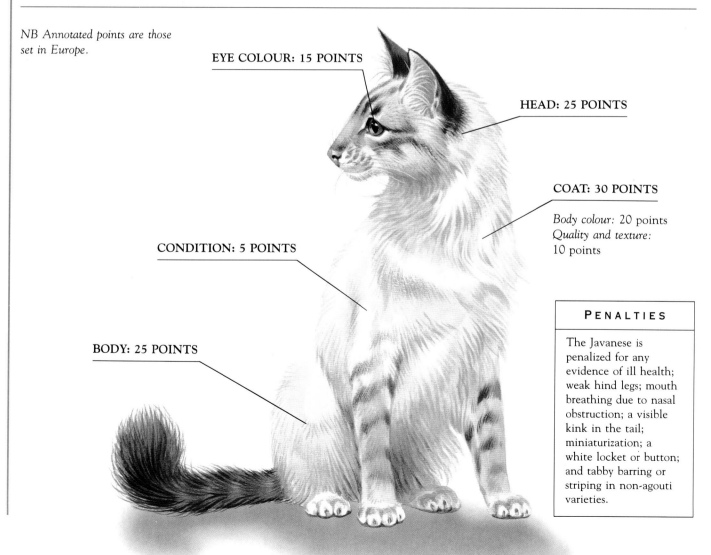

EYE COLOUR: 15 POINTS

HEAD: 25 POINTS

COAT: 30 POINTS

Body colour: 20 points
Quality and texture:
10 points

CONDITION: 5 POINTS

BODY: 25 POINTS

PENALTIES

The Javanese is penalized for any evidence of ill health; weak hind legs; mouth breathing due to nasal obstruction; a visible kink in the tail; miniaturization; a white locket or button; and tabby barring or striping in non-agouti varieties.

SEAL LYNX POINT JAVANESE

In the United States, the Javanese is the name given to the longcoated variants of the Siamese colours which they call Colorpoints.

KEY CHARACTERISTICS

- **CATEGORY** Semi-longhair (Foreign Longhair).

- **OVERALL BUILD** Medium size, svelte and elegant.

- **COAT** Fine and silky.

- **COLOURS** *(UK and Europe)* As for the Oriental Shorthair – black, blue, chocolate, lilac, red, cream, cinnamon, fawn, tortoiseshell (all colours), smoke (all colours), tabby (all colours), tabby-tortoiseshell or torbie (all colours). The eye colour for all colour varieties is vivid, intense green.

- **OTHER FEATURES** Medium-sized head, a long, tapering wedge which starts at the nose and gradually increases in width in straight lines on each side to the ears, with no whisker break in these lines. Long, straight nose, continuing the line from the forehead without a break; medium-sized chin, its tip lining up with the nose in the same vertical plane; medium-sized eyes, almond shaped, and set slightly slanted towards the nose; ears are wide based, large and pointed, placed to continue the lines of the wedge; body is long, svelte, well muscled but dainty, with the shoulders no wider than the hips. Legs are long and fine, in proportion to the body, ending in small, dainty, oval paws; tail is very long and thin, tapering to a fine point, with the hair spreading out like a plume.

BLUE LYNX POINT JAVANESE

The Javanese has the same type and conformation as Siamese and Orientals and is long and svelte with fine bones. The coat is fine and silky, and very easy to care for.

251

INDEX

Page numbers in *Italic* refer to illustrations and captions

A

Abyssinian, 8, 14, *15*, *24*, 164–7, *164*
  Beige-Fawn, 167, *167*
  Black SIlver, 167
  Blue, 166, *167*
  Blue Silver, 167
  Sorrel (Red), 166, *167*
  Usual (Ruddy), 166, *166*
ACA *see* American Cat Association
ACC *see* American Cat Council
ACFA *see* American Cat Fanciers' Association
American Cat Association (ACA), 44
American Cat Council (ACC), 44
American Cat Fanciers' Association (ACFA), 45
American Curl, 40
American Shorthair, 146–7, *146*
American Wirehair, *22*, *31*, 154–5, *154*
Angora, 58, 60, 63, 94, 112–15, *112*
  Bi-colour, 114–15
  Black, 114, *115*
  Black Smoke, 115
  Blue, 114
  Blue Smoke, 115
  Blue Tabby, 115
  Blue-cream, 114
  Brown Tabby, 115
  Calico, 114
  Cream, 114
  Odd-eyed White, *114*
  Red, 114
  Red Tabby, 115
  Silver Tabby, 115
  Tortoiseshell, 114
  Turkish, 88, 112
  White, 114, *114*
anthelmintics, 46
anus, *49*
Asian Black, *215*
Asian Group, *221*
  Ticked Tabby, *221*
Asian Smoke, 221
Asian Tabby, 221

B

Balinese, 234–48, *234*
  Blue Point, 236, *236*
  Blue Tabby Point, 237
  Blue Tortie Point, 236
  Blue Tortie Tabby Point, 237

Chocolate Point, 236
Chocolate Tabby Point, 237
Chocolate Tortie Point, 236, *237*
Chocolate Tortie Tabby Point, 237
Cream Point, 236, *237*
Cream Tabby Point, 237
Lilac Point, 236
Lilac Tabby Point, 237
Lilac Tortie Point, 236
Red Point, 236
Red Tabby Point, 237
Seal Point, 236
Seal Tabby Point, 236–7, *237*
Seal Tortie Point, 236
Seal Tortie Tabby Point, 237
Bast (cat goddess), 10, 11, *11*, 13
beckoning cat, 13, *13*
behaviour, 8, 26–31
  communication, 30–31, *30*, *31*
  hunting, 8, 26–7
  sexual, 32–4, *32*, *33*, *34*
  sleeping, 28, *28*
  washing, 29, *29*
Bengal, 184–7, *184*
  blue-eyed Snow, 187
  Brown Snow, 187
  Brown Spotted, *186*
  Brown Tabby, 186
  Leopard Spotted, 186
  Marble-Patterned, 186, *187*
  Snow, *187*
Birman, *15*, 88–93, *88*
  Blue Point, 90, *90*, 92
  Blue Tabby Point, 92, *92*
  Blue Tortie Point, 93
  Blue Tortie Tabby Point, 93
  Chocolate Point, 90, *91*, 92
  Chocolate Tabby Point, 92
  Chocolate Tortie Point, 93
  Chcolate Tortie Tabby Point, 93
  Cream Point, 91
  Cream Tabby Point, 92
  Lilac Point, 91, *91*, 92
  Lilac Tabby Point, 92
  Lilac Tortie Point, 93
  Lilac Tortie Tabby Point, 93
  Red Point, 91
  Red Tabby Point, 92, 93
  Seal Point, 90, *90*, 92
  Seal Tabby Point, 92, 93
  Seal Tortie Point, 92, *92*
  Seal Tortie Tabby Point, 92
Blue Persian Society, 64
body language, *30*
body shape, 16–25
Bombay, 214–15, *214*, *215*, 221
breeding, 38–41
  gestation chart, 39
  selective, 11, *11*, 40, *40*
  starting out, 38, 40
  symbolizing genes, 41, *41*
Burmese, *15*, *25*, *30*, 88, 200–205, *200*
  Blue, 202, *204*
  Blue-cream (Blue Tortie), 205, *205*

Chocolate (Champagne), 202, *204*
Chocolate Tortie, 205, *205*
Cream, 202, *203*
Lilac (Platinum), 202, *204*
Lilac-cream (Lilac Tortie), 205
Pointed varieties, 205
Red, 202, *203*
Sable (Brown), 202, *203*
Seal Tortie, 205
Burmilla, *27*, 216–20, *216*
  Black Shaded (or Tipped), 218, *218*, 220
  Blue Shaded (or Tipped), 218, *420*
  Blue Tortoiseshell Shaded (or Tipped), 219
  Brown Shaded (or Tipped), 218, *219*
  Brown Tortoiseshell Shaded (or Tipped), 220
  Chocolate Shaded (or Tipped), 218, *219*
  Chocolate Tortoiseshell Shaded (or Tipped), 220
  Cream Shaded (or Tipped), 219
  Lilac Shaded (or Tipped), 219
  Lilac Tortoiseshell Shaded (or Tipped), 220
  Red Shaded (or Tipped), 219
  Red Tortoiseshell Shaded (or Tipped), 219

C

CA *see* Cat Association of Britain
calicivirus, 46
Calico cat *see* Persian, Tortoisehell and White
Canadian Cat Association (CCA), 44
cat care, 46–8, *46*, *47*, *48*
carbohydrates, 53
castration, *37*
Cat Association of Britain (CA), 44, 45
Cat Fanciers' Association (CFA), 44
Cat Fanciers' Fedderation (CFF), 44
cat fights, 32–3, *33*
cat 'flu, 46
cat shows, 42–3, *42*, *43*
cats
  behaviour *see* behaviour
  breeding *see* breeding
  domestication of, 11
  feeding, 52–3, *52*, 53
  female, 32, 34, *34*
  lifespan, *47*
  male, 32–3, *32*
  stud, 40

CCA *see* Canadian Cat Association
CCFF *see* Crown Cat Fanciers' Federation
Central Maine Coon Cat Club, 94
CFA *see* Cat Fanciers' Association
CFF *see* Cat Fanciers' Federation
character, 8
Chartreux, 134–5, *134*
China, 13
Chinchilla, *15*, *42*
Chintz cat *see* Persian, Tortoiseshell and White
claws, 20, *20*, 50
coat
  colours and patterns, 23–5
    Abyssinian, *24*
    coloured tips, *24*
    Himalayan, *24*
    multiple colours, *25*
    solids, *23*
    tabby colours, *23*
    tabby markings, *23*
    Tonkinese, *25*
  types, 22, *22*
Colourpoint Longhair, 78–9, *78–81*, *78*
  Blue Point, 80, *80*
  Blue-cream Point, 81
  Chocolate Point, 80
  Cream Point, 81, *81*
  Lilac Point, 80–81
  Red Point, 81, *81*
  Seal Point, 80, *80*
  Tortie Point, 81
Colourpoint Persians, 78–9, *78*, *82*
Colourpoint Shorthair, 230–33, *230*
  Blue Lynx Point, 232
  Blue-cream Point, 232–3
  Chocolate Lynx Point, 232
  Chocolate Tortie Point, 232, *232*
  Cream Point, 232
  Lilac Lynx Point, 232
  Lilac-cream Point, 233
  Red Lynx Point, 232
  Red Point, 232
  Seal Lynx Point, 232
  Seal Tabby Point, *233*
  Seal Tortie Point, 232, *233*
communication, 30–31, *30*, *31*
Cornish Rex, 14, *22*, 188–91, *188*
  Black Smoke Van Pattern, *190*
  Black Smoke and White, *190*
  Chocolate Smoke, *191*
  Choclate Tortie, *191*
  Red, *190*
  Tortie Smoke and White, *191*
  White, *191*
Crown Cat Fanciers' Federation (CCFF), 44
Cymric, 139
  Tortoiseshell, *139*

D

deafness, 60
declawing, 20
descent of the modern cat, *12*
Devon Rex, *22*, 192–5, *192,*
194, 195
Black Smoke Devon Rex,
194
Chocolate Tortie Point, *194*
Lilac Point, *195*
Odd-eyed White, *194*
Tortie Tabby, *195*
Tortie Tabby and White, 195
diet *see* feeding
Dinictis, 10
diseases, 46

E

ears, 19, *19*, 49
Egypt, ancient, 11, 13
Egyptian Mau, 180–81, *180*
Bronze, *181*
Silver, *181*
Smoke, *181*
eyes, 18, *18, 21*, 49

F

facial expressions, *31*
falling, *17*
fats, 53
Federation Internationale Feline
(FIFe), 44, 45
feeding, 46, 52–3, *52, 53*
Felidae, 11
feline associations and
governing bodies, 44–5
feline leukaemia virus, 46
Felis catus, 41
Felis chaus, 11
Felis domesticus, 11
Felis lunensis, 11
Felis lybica, 11
FIFe *see* Federation
Internationale Feline
fleas, 46, 49
Flehmen Reaction, 18, *18*
Foreign Shorthairs, 17, 21, *21,*
164–221
Abyssinian, *8*, 164–7, *164*
Asian, 221, *221*
Bengal, 184–7, *184, 187*
Bombay, 214–15, *214, 215,*
221
Burmese, *88*, 200–205, *200,*
202, 203, 204, 205
Burmilla, 216–20, *216, 218,*
219, 220

Colourpoint, 224–5, 230–33,
230, 232, 233
Cornish Rex, 188–91, *188,*
190, 191
Deveon Rex, 192–5, *192,*
194, 195
Egyptian Mau, 180–81, *180,*
181
Havan Brown, 178–9, *178,*
179
Japanese Bobtail, 198–9, *198,*
199
Korat, 176–7, *176, 177*
Ocicat, 182–3, *182, 183*
Russian Blue, 174–5, *174,*
175
Seychellois, 249, *249*
Siamese, *88*, 174, 224–9
Singapura, 207, *207*
Somali, 168–73, *168*
Sphynx, 196–7, *196, 197*
Tiffanie, 206, *206*, 221
Tonkinese, 208–13, *208, 210,*
211, 212, 213

G

GCCF *see* Governing Council
of the Cat Fancy
genes, 41
gestation chart, 39
Governing Council of the Cat
Fancy (GCCF), *43, 44, 45*
grooming, 48, *48*

H

Havana Brown, 178–9, *178,*
179
head, 21, *21*
health, 49–54
regime of care, 54
signs of ill health, 50, *51*
watching out for problems, 49
hearing, 19, *19*
Himalayan, *24*, 88
see also Colourpoint Longhair
hunting, *8*, 26–7, *27*

I

India, 13
infectious enteritis, 46
International Society for the
Preservation of the Maine
Coon, 95

J

James, Mrs H.V., 66
Japan, 13
Japanese Bobtail, 25, 198–9,
198
Black and White Van
Pattern, *199*
Blue-eyed Van, *199*
Brown Tabby and White, *199*
Javanese 250–51, *250*
Blue Lynx Point, *251*
Seal Lynx Point, *251*
Japanese (Oriental), 114

K

Kashmir, 84, *84*
kittens
birth, 35–6, *35*
development, 36, *36, 37*
and sexual behaviour, *32, 33*
sexual differences, *32*
Korat, 176–7, *176, 177*

L

lifespan, 47
lion-cats, 13
litter tray, 36, 46, 47, 49, 50
Longhairs, 58–85, *58, 88, 89,*
112, 156
Balinese *see* Balinese
Bi-colour, 70–71
Black, 60, 61, *61*
Black Smoke, 66, *67*
Black and White Bi-colour,
70, *70*
Blue, 60, 64, *64*
Blue Point Counterpoint, 80,
80
Blue Smoke, 67, *67*
Blue Tabby, 73, *74*
Blue Tabby Point, 82–3
Blue Tortie, *65*
Blue Tortie Tabby, *74*
Blue Tortie and White, *75*
Blue and White Bi-colour,
70, *71*
Blue-cream, 65, *65, 75*
Blue-cream Cameo, *69*
Blue-cream Point
Colourpoint, 81, 83
Blue-cream Smoke, *68*
Blue-eyed White, 60, *60*
Brown, *62*
Brown Tabby, 72, 73, *73*
Brown Tortie Tabby, *74*
Cameo, 69, *69*
Cameo Tasbby, *73*
Chinchilla, *76*

Chinchilla Golden, 76, *77*
Chinchilla Silver, 76, *76*
Chocolate, 84, *84*
Chocolate Point Colourpoint,
80
Chocolate Smoke, 67, *68*
Chocolate Tabby Point, 83
Chocolate Tortie, *75*
Chocolate Tortie
Colourpoint, 83
Chocolate Tortie tabby, *74*
Colourpoint *see* Coloupoint
Longhair
Cream, *62, 63, 63*
Cream Point Colourpoint, 81,
81
Cream Smoke, *6*
Creawm Tabby, *73*
Cream and White Bi-colour,
70, *71*
Dilute Calico, *75*
grooming, *48*
Himalaya *see* Colourpont
Longhair
Javanese *see* Javanese
Llac, 84, *85*
Lilac Point Colourpoint,
80–81
Lilac Smoke, *67*
Lilac Tabby Point, 83
Lilac Tortie Smoke, *68*
Lilac-cream, *85*
Mackerel Tabby, *72*
Odd-eyed White, 60, *60*
Orange, *62*
Orange Self, *62*
Orange Tabby, *62*
Orange-eyed White, 60, *60*
Persian *see* Persian
Pewter, *77*
Red, 62, *62*
Red Chinchilla, *69*
Red Point Colourpoint, 81,
81
Red Shaded, *69*
Red Shell, *69*
Red Smoke, 67, *68*
Red Tabby, *62*, 72, 73, *73*
Red Tabby Point, *82*
Red and White Bi-colour, 70,
70
Seal Point Colourpoint, 80,
80
Seal Tabby Point, 82, *82*
Seychellois *see* Seychellois
Shaded Cameo (Red
Shaded), *69*
Shaded Golden, *77*
Shaded Silver, 76–7, *77*
Shell Cameo (Red
Chinchilla), *69*
Shell Tortoiseshell, *69*
Silver Tabby, *15*, 72, *72*
Silver Tortie Tabby, *74*
Smoke, 66–7, *69*
Smoke Cameo, *69*
Smoke Tortoiseshell, *68*
Solid Points, 80–81
Tabby, 72–74
Tabby Points, 82–3
Tortie Point Colourpoint, *81*
Tortie Tabby, *73*

Tortoiseshell, 69, 75, *75*
Tortoiseshell and White, 75, *75*
Van Bi-colour, 71, *71*
lordosis, *34*

M

Maine Coon, 22, 94–9, *94, 106*
  Bi-colour, 96
  Black, 96
  Black Smoke, 97
  Blue, 96
  Blue Smoke, 97
  Blue Tabby, 98
  Blue-cream, 96
  Blue-cream and White, 96, *96*
  Blue-cream-and-white, 96, *96*
  Brown Mackerel Tabby, 98
  Brown Tabby, 98
  Cameo Tabby, 99
  Cream, 96
  Cream Smoke, 97
  Cream Tabby, 98
  Green-eyed White, 96
  Mackerel Tabby and White, 98
  Red, 96
  Red Smoke, 97
  Red Tabby, 98
  Shaded Red, 97, *97*
  Shaded Silver, 97
  Silver Tabby, 98, *99*
  Silver Tortie Tabby and White, *99*
  Tabby, *94*
  Tabby-and-white, 99
  Tortie tabby, 99, *99*
  Tortie Tabby-and-white, 99
  Tortoiseshell, 96
  Tortoiseshell-and-White, 96
  White, 96
male cats, 32–3, *32*
Maltese Blue *see* Russian Blue
Manx, *14*, 136–9, *136*
Martelli's wildcat, *11*
maternity, 35–7, *35, 36*
mating, 34, *34*, 40
meals, *49*, 52–3, *52, 53*
Miacis, 11
minerals, 53
mouth, *49*
muscles, *17*

N

National Cat Club, 66
neutering, 37, *37*
Norsk Skaukatt see Norwegian
  Forst Cat

Norwegian Forest Cat, 106–9, *106, 112*
  Bi-colour, 110
  Black, 112
  Black Smoke, 111, *111*
  Blue, 112
  Blue Silver Tabby, *113*
  Blue Smoke, 111
  Blue Tabby, 113
  Blue-cream, 110
  Blue-cream-and-white, 110
  Brown Tabby, 113, *113*
  Brown ticked Tabby, *113*
  Chinchilla, 111
  Cream, 112
  Cream Tabby, 113
  Red, 112
  Red Shaded Cameo, 111
  Red Shell Cameo, 111
  Red Silver Tabby and White, *113*
  Red Smoke, 111
  Red Tabby, 113
  Red and White, *110*
  Shaded Silver, 111
  Silver Tabby, 113
  Tortoiseshell, 110, *110*
  Tortoiseshell-and-white, 110
  White, 112, *112*
nose, *49*
nutritional requirements, 53

O

Ocicat, 182–3, *182*
  Black Silver, *183*
  Blue Spotted, *183*
  Chocolate Silver, *183*
oestrus, 34, *34*, 40
onychectomy, 20
Orange, Cream, Fawn and
  Tortoiseshell Society, 62
Oriental, 22, 238–48, *238*
  Black, 240
  Black Silver Spotted, *247*
  Black Smoke, *248*
  Black Tabby, 244
  Black Tortie, *243*
  Blue, 240, *240*
  Blue Tabby, 244
  Blue Tortie, *243*
  Caramel, 241
  Caramel Spotted Tabby, *244*
  Caramel Tabby, *246*
  Caramel Tortie, *243*
  Chestnut, 241
  Chestnut Brown Foreign, 240
  Chestnut Tabby, 244–5
  Chocolate, 241
  Chocolate Classic Tabby, *244*
  Chocolate Silver Shaded, *248*
  Chocolate Spotted Tabby, *245*
  Chocolate Tabby, 244–5
  Chocolate Ticked, *245*
  Chocolate Tortie, *243*

Chocolate Tortie Silver
  Ticked, *247*
  Cinnamon, 241, *241*
  Cinnamon Spotted, *246*
  Cinnamon tabby, 246
  Cinnamon Ticked, *246*
  Cinnamon Tortie, 243
  Classic Tabby, 244
  Cream, 242, *242*
  Cream Tabby, 245
  Ebony Tabby, 244
  Fawn, 242
  Fawn Tabby, 246
  Foreign White, 240, *240*
  Havana Brown, 240, *241*
  Lavender Tabby, 245
  Lavender-cream, 243
  Lilac, 241, *241*
  Lilac Tabby, 245
  Lilac Tortie, 243
  Mackerel Tabby, 244
  Patched Tabby, *247*
  Red Self, 242, *242*
  Red Tabby, 245
  Shaded, 248
  Siamese White, 240
  Silver Tabby, 246
  Smoke, 248
  Spotted Tabby, 244
  Ticked Tabby, 244
  Tipped, 248
  Tortie, 243, *243*
  Tortie Tabby, 247
  White, 240, *240*
Oriental breeds, 10, *10*, 17, 20,
  21, 27, 52
  see also Balinese; Colourpoint;
    Javanese; Oriental;
    Seychellois; Siamese
Oriental (Javanese), 114
origins, 11–15

P

panleukopaenia, 46
parasites, 46
Persian, 11, *11*, 14, 17, 20, 21,
  21, 22, 27
  see also Longhairs, Persian
points system, 43
proteins, 53
Pseudaelurus, 11

R

Ragdoll, 100–104, *100*
  Blue Bi-colour, 103
  Blue Colourpoint, 104, *104*
  Blue Mitted, 102, *102*
  Chocolate Bi-colour, 103, *103*
  Chocolate Mitted, 102

Lilac Colourpoint, 104, *104*
  Lilac Mitted, 102
  Seal Bi-colour, 103, *103*
  Seal Colourpoint, 104, *104*
  Seal Mitted, 102, *102*
Rex cats, 17
  see also Cornish Rex; Devon
    Rex
rhinotracheitis, 46
Ross, Charles H., 58, 63
Russian Blue, *15*, 174–5, *174,
  175*

S

scent marking, 27
Scottish Fold, *40*, 140–41, *140*
scratching post, 47, 50
self-righting reflex, 17
Semi Longhaired *see* Angora;
  Birman; Javanese; Maine
  Coon; Norwegian Forest Cat;
  Ragdoll; Snowshoe; Turkish
sexual behaviour, 32–4, *32, 33,
  34*
sexual differences, *32*
Seychellois, 249, *249*
  Huitieme, 249
  Neuvieme, 249
  Septieme, 249
Shorthairs, 14, 20, 21, *21*, 22
  Colourpoint *see* Colourpoint
    Shorthair
  grooming, 48
Shorthairs, American, 17,
  146–53, *146*
  Blue Patched tabby, 153
  Blue Tabby, 149, *149*
  Brown Patched Tabby, 153,
    153
  Brown Tabby, 151
  Brown Torbie, *152*
  Cameo Tabby, 151, *151*
  Classic Tabby, 148, 149, *150*
  Cream Tabby, 151
  Mackerel Tabby, 149, *150*
  Marbled Tabby, 148
  Patched Tabby or Torbie, 153
  Red Tabby, 151, *151*
  Silver Patched Tabby, 153
  Silver Tabby, 148, *152, 153*
  Spotted Tabby, 148
Shorthairs, American
  Wirehair, 154–5, *154*
  Black and White, *155*
Shorthairs, British, 17, 120–33,
  120, 148
  Bi-colour, 124–5
  Black, 122, *122*
  Black SMoke, 132
  Black Tipped, *133*
  Blue, 122, 123, *123*
  Blue Cream Coloupoint, *133*
  Blue Smoke, *30*, 132
  Blue Spotted, *129*
  Blue Tabby, 131, *131*

Blue Tortie and White, *127*
Blue and White Bi-colour, *125*
Blue-cream, 124, *124*
Blue-eyed White, 122, *122*
Brown Classic Tabby, *128*
Brown Spotted, *128*
Brown Tabby, 130
Chocolate Tortie, *126*
Classic Tabby, 128–9
Colour Pointed, *132*
Cream, 123, *123*
Cream Colourpoint, *132*
Cream Tabby, 131
Cream and White Bi-colour, *125*
Lilac, *124*
Lilac Cream Colourpoint, *133*
Lilac Tortie, *126*
Mackerel Tabby, 128, 129
Orange-eyed White, 122
Red Colourpoint, *132*
Red Mackerel Tabby, *128*
Red Silver Tabby, *131*
Red Tabby, 130, *130*
Silver Spotted, *129*
Silver Tabby, 130, *130*
Spotted Tabby, 128, 129
Tabby, 128–31
Tortie Tabby, *131*
Tortoiseshell, 126, *126*
Tortoiseshell-and-white, 127, *127*
White, 122
Shorthairs, chartreux, 134–5, *134*
Shorthairs, European, 17, 142–5, *142*
Bi-colour, 145
Classic tabby, 145
Mackerel Tabby, 145
Smoke, 144
Solid, 144
Tabby Van, 145
Tabby varieties, 144
Tortie, 144, 145
White, 144
Shorthairs, Exotic, 17, 156–61, *156*
Bi-colour, 159
Black, 158
Blue, 158, *158*
Blue Tabby Colourpoint, 159
Blue Tortie and White, *160*
Blue and White, 159
Blue-cream, 160
Blue-cream Smoke, 161
Blue-cream and White, 160
Brown Tabby, 160
Chinchilla, 160
Chinchilla Golden, 160
Chocolate, 158
Classic Tabby, 159
Colour Pointed, 161
Cream, 158, *158*
Lilac, 158
Mackerel Tabby, 159
Red, 158
Shaded Golden, 160
Shaded Silver, 160, *161*
Shaded Tortoiseshell, 161

Shell Tortoiseshell, 161
Silver Tabby, *161*
Smoke, 161
Spotted Tabby, 159
Tipped, 161
Tortie Tabby, 159
Tortie-and-white, 160
Tortoiseshell, 160
Van Bi-colour, 159
Van Blue-cream and White, 159
Van Tri-colour, 159
White, 158
Shorthairs, Foreign *see* Foreign Shorthairs
Shorthairs, Manx, 136–9, *136*
Blue Tortie and White, *139*
Cymric, 139
Red Spotted, *138*
Tortie Tabby and White, *138*
Tortoiseshell Cymric, *139*
Shorthairs, Oriental, 238–48
Shorthairs, Scottish Fold, 140, *140*
Black and White, *141*
Calico Fold, *141*
Longhaired variety, *141*
Patched Silver Tabby and White, *141*
showing, 42–3, *42, 43*
Siamese, *15, 17, 38,* 88, 174, 224–9, *224*
Blue Point, 224, 226, *437*
Blue Tabby Point, 228, *229*
Blue Torbie Point, 229
Blue Tortie Point, 228
Chocolate Point, 224, 227, *227*
Chocolate Tabby Point, 228
Chocolate Torbie Point, 229
Chocolate Tortie Point, 228
Cream Point, 227, *228*
Cream Tabby Point, 229
Frost Tabby Point, 228
Frost Torbie Point, 229
Frost Tortie Point, 228
Lilac Point (Frost Point), 227, *228*
Red Point, 226, *226*
Red Tabby Point, 229, *229*
Seal Point, 224, 226, *226*
Seal Tabby Point, 228
Seal Torbie Point, 229
Seal Tortie Point, 227–8
sight, 18, *18*
Simpson, Frances, 63
Singapura, 207
Brown Ticked, *207*
skeleton, *17*
skin, *49*
sleeping, 28, *28*
smell, 18, *18*
Snowshoe, 105, *105*
solids
coat colour, 23
Somali, 168–73, *168*
Blue, 170, *170*
Blue Silver, 172, *173*
Chocolate, 170–71, *171*
Chocolate Silver, 173
Fawn, 170, 171, *171*
Fawn Silver, 173

Lilac, 171
Lilac Silver, 173
Lilac Usual, 170, *170*
Red Silver, *172*
Silver, 170
Sorrel, 170, 171
Sorrel Silver, 173
Usual Silver, 172, *172*
spaying, *37*
Sphynx, *22, 40,* 196–7, *196, 197*
Black and White, *197*
stud cats, 40

T

Tabbies
colours, *23*
markings, *23*
taste, 18
territorial marking, 27
The International Cat Association (TICA), 45
TICA *see* The International Cat Association
Tiffanie, 206, *206,* 221
Brown Smoke, *206*
tipping, *22, 24*
toilet training, 36, 37
Tonkinese, *25,* 208–13, *208*
Blue, 210, *212*
Blue Tortie, *213*
Brown, 210, *210*
Chocolate, 210, *211*
Chocolate Tortie (?), *213*
Cream, *212*
Lilac, 210, *211*
Lilac Tortie, *213*
Pointed varieties, 210
Red, 210, *212*
Tortoiseshell colours, *25*
Turkish Van, 116–17, *116*
Auburn, *117*
Cream, *117*

U

UCF *see* United Cat Federation
United Cat Federation (UCF), 44

V

vaccination, 46, *49,* 50, *51*
veterinarian, 50, *51*
vitamins, 53

W

washing, 29, *29*
weaning, 36, 37
witches, 14, *14*

ACKNOWLEDGEMENTS

Quarto Publishing would like to thank all the owners who kindly allowed us to photograph their cats for inclusion in this book and Rose Forrester for her invaluable help in researching breed lists and approaching cat owners.

Additional photographs were supplied by: **Page 8** Nick Nicolson and Harry Rinker Jnr; **9** Solitaire Photographic; **11 l, c, t** archive; **11 r** Mansell Collection; **12** Ardea; **13 a** CM Dixon; **14 l** CM Dixon; **18 cl** Marc Henrie, Asc.; **21 b & 26 r** Solitaire Photographic; **27 cr** Marc Henrie, Asc.; **27 bl & 26 br** Solitaire Photographic; **28 al** Image Bank; **34 ar** Solitaire Photographic; **35 bl & 37** Marc Henrie, Asc.; **38, 42, 43** Solitaire Photographic; **50–51** Marc Henrie, Asc.; **53 ar** Bradley Viner; **54 ar** Solitaire Photographic; **148** TFH Publications, Inc.

Key: **a** above, **b** bottom, **c** centre, **l** left, **r** right, **t** top

All other photographs are the copyright of Quarto Publishing.